Postmodernism Is Not What You Think

Twentieth-Century Social Theory

Series Editor: Charles Lemert

Twentieth-Century Social Theory invites authors respected for their contributions in the prominent traditions of social theory to reflect on past and present in order to propose what comes next. Books in the series will consider critical theory, race, symbolic interactionism, functionalism, feminism, world systems theory, psychoanalysis, and Weberian social theory, among current topics. Each will be plain to read, yet provocative to ponder. Each will gather up what has come to pass in the twentieth century in order to define the terms of social theoretical imagination in the twenty-first.

Titles in the series include:

Postmodernism Is Not What You Think

Charles Lemert

BLACKWELL
Publishers

First published 1997

2 4 6 8 10 9 7 5 3 1

Blackwell Publishers Inc.
350 Main Street
Malden, MA 02148
USA

Blackwell Publishers Ltd
108 Cowley Road
Oxford OX4 1JF
UK

Library of Congress Cataloging in Publication Data

Lemert, Charles C., 1937–
    Postmodernism is not what you think / Charles Lemert.
      p. cm. — (Twentieth-century social theory)
    Includes bibliographical references and index.
    ISBN 1–55786–082-3. – ISBN 1–55786–286–9
    1. Postmodernism – Social aspects.   2. Sociology – Philosophy.
  I. Title. II. Series.
  HM73.L45   1997   96-45360
  301'.01 — dc21   CIP

British Library Cataloguing in Publication Data

A CIP catalogue record for this book is available from the British Library.

Typeset in 10 on 12pt Sabon by
Grahame & Grahame Editorial, Brighton
Printed in Great Britain by Hartnolls Limited, Bodmin, Cornwall

This book is printed on acid-free paper

To Matthew and Noah,
and their generation,
who must live in the world mine has made.

Contents

Series Editor's Preface

I am not one on whom the name "postmodernist" sits comfortably. The name is too often a moniker — a nickname attributed to characters of shadowy reputation. When postmodernists are thought of as reputationally unreliable specific reference is usually made to their alleged desire to pervert the normal course of human conduct. Many postmodernists, aware of the low esteem in which they are held, tidy up their presentation by describing this penchant as irony — a way of seeing and speaking required by the duplicitous nature of the present world. Yet, the self-consciously normal are seldom impressed by this move. They believe that even irony is too perverse by far, notwithstanding the delight it often inspires when used by comedians and other poets of the human condition.

In the end, irony is not too much more than a clever way of bringing to public attention the many deviations from the normal which add spice to the course of daily life. Robert Merton somewhere remarked upon Calvin Coolidge's famously parsimonious comment that his preacher was "unexceptionably against sin." Having been a preacher in my youth, I can say with confidence what every parishioner knows but will not say. A preacher's official duties provide weak immunity to a thoroughly exceptional acquaintance with sin. Thus, this particular irony offends by calling attention to a near universal fact of human behavior. Those under professional obligation to police the normal do their duty well not because they are pure but because they so finely appreciate the intricacies of human misbehavior. The Book of Psalms, to say nothing of the writings of Erving Goffman, provide ample evidence to the point.

Therefore, if there are persons who may comfortably think of themselves as postmodernists, the very self-consideration entails the normal expectation that they will also be ironists. But this does not mean that such characters will be ironists pure and simple, any more than a preacher's official attitude toward sin renders him incapable of enjoying it. When, for immediate example, an author, by virtue of being the editor of a series in which his book appears, writes a series editor's preface to his own book, the very act may or may not be ironic or otherwise perverse. In this instance, if my opinion counts for anything, I think it is not.

I preface my own book, at the risk of overplaying the hand dealt me, because, as author of the book prefaced, were I not to do myself this favor, the book would be left without the account a series editor alone can give as to the place it ought to hold in the company it is meant to keep. It has been my pleasure, and duty, to do this for the distinguished books that have preceded this one in the series. Were I to deny myself this pleasure I would also fail in my duty to have someone say in advance just why, in this case, a book on postmodernism and social theory is worth the reader's attentions.

Postmodernism Is Not What You Think is a book I have avoided writing because too much already has been said about the subject. I do not believe that postmodernism, whatever it turns out to be, can be reliably understood by examining what people think it is, and certainly not from what they say about it. I mean no irony in the qualification "whatever it turns out it be." Postmodernism, if it is anything real, is an actual historical process the facts of which, being arguable like the facts of any account of the near present, cannot be determined by reference to theory alone. I am not among those who could be accused of hating theory. I think theory is a good thing. Like poetry, it can bestow pleasure even where it is incapable of sufficient explanation of some set of hard-won facts. Yet, holding this belief does not, in and of itself, require me or anyone else to trust all theories stupidly.

It is true that there is stupid theory done in the name of postmodernism just as there is stupidity done in the name of social psychology or cultural studies or economics. Opponents of postmodernism, of which there are very many, seize upon the unexceptional stupidity of *some* things post-modern in order to mock the thing itself. This amounts to the same as judging the Russian people by the failures of the Soviet regime or, for that matter, judging the merits of sin by the unexceptional fact that preachers commit it in spite of their theories. Postmodernism, the Russian people, and sin are among those human inventions which, while being all vulnerable to theories, have their own enduring and local places in the wider scheme of things. But it is unlikely that an understanding of them can ever be derived from the better known theories of them. I am one of the few people I know who believes that theories of all three subjects can be very interesting and valuable. The Soviets, for example, had some excellent ideas about how a large agrarian-based society might to be run. The problem was that they could not find a way to get the Russian people to obey their ideas without killing a large number of them. Much the same could be said of the theories of sin with which I am familiar, as it could be, within severe limits, of some possible postmodernisms.

This is not to say that it is impossible to find in the world objects or phenomena susceptible of being rendered coherent by a good theory, and not much else. So far as I am qualified to tell, the prevailing theory for what causes the boundaries between time and space to collapse in the far regions of the cosmos is very nearly a pure theory by virtue of the condition that direct observation of these interstellar events is impossible. Similarly, the axiom I learned in economics that the prices of valuable commodities fluctuate in tune with the music of the something called the marketplace is an excellent theoretical principle entirely sufficient to satisfy those willing to speak intelligibly about the subject in public. The grandeur of the axiom is unqualified by the inconvenience that the marketplace in question is at best a mathematical guess. Theories can be useful, even beautiful, quite apart from the data by which they might ideally be sustained.

Postmodernism, thereby, like sin and Russia, is something that tends to excite the development of theories inversely to the availability of the thing itself to be satisfactorily described by any known theory of it. I am not here proposing an analytic category into which various social things might be characterologically thrown, as though all Russians were sinners and postmodernists. It is true that one precursor line of postmodernism did come from Russia as it is probable that some Russians are sinners. The category I propose yields very little analytic pay-off of the expected kind.

I mean by postmodernism, simply, a species of naturally occurring events which are somehow like the velocities of stellar bodies and prices in that theories of them may be interesting but only accidentally urgent to their reality. I will not here attempt further definition of postmodernism, since the whole of chapter 2 and much of chapter 3 are lengthily devoted to that end. What I can say, by way of preface, is that a book on the subject belongs in a series of books on the state of social theory near the end of the twentieth century because it is the job of social theory to discuss what is going on in the world where real people live.

Whether "postmodern" is the best name for what is going on in this world may be reasonably doubted. *That* something powerful, deep, and potentially far-reaching is going on seems to me beyond doubt. Yet, I am aware that many, perhaps most, do indeed doubt it. Not long ago I had the experience of spending several days in an international colloquium of psychologists, philosophers, and sociologists held at Oxford University, surely one of England's, and the world's, most refined and elegant institutions. Though I understood why we were called to the meeting, I never fully understood the philosophical theme we were called to dispute. I was not alone in this confusion. Nonetheless, we held forth wordily for two long days on this subject, whatever it was. Academics, you may know, are people who compare themselves to each other according to three discrete and exhaustive categories: "brilliant," "smart" (or "very smart"), and "interesting." One hopes to be in the first category, and to avoid at all costs the third, but being simply "smart" will do. The people at the Oxford meeting were, with rare exception, at least very smart, and several were brilliant. Yet, when the subject of postmodernism raised its ugly head, as it always does at academic meetings these days, the greater number of people in that company were predictably repulsed by the very mention of it. At a certain point, two of us foolishly took up the defense of the postmodern thesis, thus causing the level of ambient hostility to rise apace.

When collective agitation approached its point of maximum silliness, I made reference to the possibility that, when measured in real demographic terms, we then gathered at Oxford were among the world's most privileged people, well provisioned at no cost to ourselves in one of the world's most privileged places. Perhaps, I reckoned, these social qualifications might affect our ability to suffer with the millions who are poor and hungry far outside the city walls. I had in mind the millions in Sub-Saharan Africa and many parts of Asia, to say nothing of the American inner cities, suffering from the threat of AIDS and the reality of food scarcity and civil violence or the utter lack of healthcare and decent shelter. Whereupon one member of our little group, a person I would classify as "very interesting," took insult at the idea that there was anything seriously wrong with where the world was headed. I was quick to meet his insult with one of my own. And there the matter rested. I tell the story because we alleged postmodernists are exposed to this sort of thing all the time.

Postmodernism, if it is about anything, is about the prospect that the promises of the modern age are no longer believable because there is evidence that for the vast majority of people worldwide there is no realistic reason to vest hope in any version of the idea that the world is good and getting better. The modern age is (some would say, was) about the inevitability of human progress. I am myself a modernist before all else in that I like the idea of human progress and would like very much to believe in it. I am old-enough, male-enough, and white-enough to have been brought up in a time and place (the 1950s, in petty-bourgeois Cincinnati, Ohio) when and where all us white boys believed the world was getting better; as indeed it did for most of us. I do not consider myself politically virtuous when I say that there is now good reason to doubt that the faith of our fathers makes sense to us today as it did then to them. I see the difference not just in empirical evidence that so many of the statistical curves are turned against the likelihood of short-term improvement for those who suffer without much hope. But, closer to home, I see it also in the prospects facing my two, young-adult sons. They are both educated in elite schools and both at least as smart as I am, but neither can confidently embrace the world of his youth as even the least interesting of my classmates could and did in the 1950s.

Postmodernism, therefore, is about a question. What is to be made of the world-concern that preoccupies people outside the cloisters of privilege who believe the world is not what it used to be? There are good theories of postmodernism and some bad ones, but they all, one way or another, have something to do with this question. Hence, the justification for still another book on the subject — a book written not to celebrate or proclaim the postmodern, but more to describe how much of what is called by this name is properly joined to so much of what is said in the wider world of human suffering about how things may have changed.

This book has come into being, partly out of earlier work, as I have been forced, or forced myself, to study less the theories that led to postmodernism than the terrible prospects so many of the world's children face. By world standards my children, and the students I teach, may have less than we had, but they are still among the world's better provided-for. Thus, though the chapters following contain some earlier work, nearly everything has been recently chastened by the feelings aroused when persons of my type are confronted at long last by the global realities modern culture hides behind its false, if well-meant, dreams.

Part I is my best attempt both to describe the lay of the land with respect to postmodernism (chapter 1), then to describe the thing itself as clearly as I think possible (chapters 2 and 3). Some readers will find parts of Part II a little technical, especially the last third or so of chapter 5. This section, even the whole of Part II, could well be passed over by those who might be less amused by an account of the prior political and intellectual events that have made postmodern social theory what it is today. The final section of the book, Part III, covers three of the most urgent topics brought forward by postmodern social theorists and, I should say, left largely unresolved by academic social sciences, including sociology: identities, the science question, and the unconscious. I should add that I am a professional sociologist, but when I speak of sociology in chapter 8 I have in mind the importance of the practical sociologies upon which the professional field depends. This connection is made explicit in the concluding chapter, in which I return to the themes hinted at in this preface, simply summarized as follows.

The world has changed; not for the good. People may want to call it postmodern. Whatever they call it, sociologies of all kinds, the practical ones most urgently, must learn anew how to speak of a world in which, at the least, the promises of progress and social hope are so often pious vanities or, worse, testimony to the desire of the well-settled to hold on to the familiar at all costs. Measured against the nasty cynicism abroad in the world, actual existing postmodernisms must be given their due as among the reasonable social theories of the present situation.

Charles Lemert

Part I

Disturbances

1

Beasts, Frogs, Freaks, and Other Postmodern Things

Not long ago my youngest son graduated from college, whereupon he entered the world such as it is. He leaves tonight on his first independent voyage to the new world — for San Francisco where, he says, he will find work "for a while." Well-trained bourgeois parent that I am, I have struggled with some success to suppress the obvious questions. What work? How long a while? How much will this cost me? When will you be back home? These are the questions asked today by those of a class rank formerly sufficient to assure their children safe, life-affirming, and parent-pleasing answers. But now parents of even my relatively secure social position join the thousands upon thousands of other-than-white-or-middle-class people who reasonably doubt that the world is safe or welcoming for their children.

What work can one do? For how long? To what effect? Where? If there is any truth to the rumors that the world is postmodern, these are the questions the currency and poignancy of which lend them weight. It is not just work but human worth that is at issue. Whatever postmodernism is about, it must be about one question above all others: Does the modern world still realistically offer what for so long it had promised? When posed as a point of theory, the question stirs the blood of controversy. When posed as a matter of fact, the same question dampens the spirits. However much we may retreat into controversy, as if the fire of political battle can truly rekindle moral hope, the somber realities of the modern world at the end of the current millennium are hard to get around.[1]

- Personal income, worldwide, is declining nearly at the same perverse rate as economic productivity and cumulative wealth are growing.
- Continuous working employments, that is: jobs productive of personal

income and benefits sufficient to support family life, are disappearing for the majority.

- Meanwhile, social and economic inequalities are growing worse, not better — most dramatically in the United States up to which the modern world had always looked as the land of opportunity.
- Food supplies are declining to their lowest levels in decades with world grain reserves dropping to just 48 days worth at current consumption levels.
- Social conflict — ranging from violence against women and children to ethnic, class, and racial conflict — is epidemic.

The modern world promised economic progress, social equality, freedom from want, and peace. In the lack of which, people today rightly wonder whey they face so much poverty, inequality, hunger and disease, civil strife.

Modernism — that is, roughly: the culture of the modern world — had always extended the ethical promise that if people worked hard at legitimate enterprises things would get better, for their children, if not themselves. But now people ask: Is the modern world still a place in which children can find work as a means to worth — or, even, if not by work, is it a place that assures them some other means to a decent life?

Postmodernism — that is, roughly: the culture of a purportedly postmodern world — is mostly about questions of this sort. The questions themselves are perfectly reasonable. Good women and men, whether of middling or lesser status, but especially those who are parents of recent school graduates, are right to ask them. Their worries are realistic, thus reasonable. If reasonable, then why so much fuss about the various postmodernish theories of the failures or endings of the modern? It is hardly unreasonable for parents to worry about their kids, or to entertain the idea that the world is fundamentally different from the one they inherited. So, why then do many parents and others with an ardent interest in the state of world affairs exhibit so much hostility to postmodernism? Or, differently, it is often asked: Why are these postmodernist theories of the modern world so terribly provocative such that reasonable people asking reasonable questions are disinclined to take them seriously? Hence one of the more interesting incongruities of the day. Given that the modern world is not what it used to be (who disagrees on this?), why then the impression that theories of the after-modern world are unreasonable monsters?

During one of the several family celebrations of the graduation of my youngest son, the gathered clan of mother, father's brother, step-mother, father, and cousin chattered nervously of the early days when the youngest was a child in fact. One topic of shared recollection was the books his mother and I had read to him and his brother (who, it turns out, was not there because he, also a recent college grad, was finding work in Alaska). One of the most eerie of those stories was one that, it seems to me now, may be an allegory, even a parable, of the feelings many have toward postmodernism's disturbing intrusion on their troubled worlds. The story went like this:

> One fine morning the residents of a small village awoke to find a very big but not unfriendly beast well settled in the center of their small town and mundane lives. Being by nature trusting and kind, the people repressed fear and welcomed the beast. In spite of its enormous height and girth, and the mass of its settled flesh, the beast posed no threats. All he did, in the most matter of fact way, was to say: "Feed me." The villagers complied. Upon devouring what he had been fed, he simply repeated his demand, without inflection, "Feed me." Eventually, without vote or complaint, feeding the beast came to be what the village was about.

I do not remember the ending of the story. Somehow the point of it was in the beast's ability to get his way without ever menacing, not once. It may well have been a moralistic lesson about how children take over their worlds by their demands. (My dear little niece — age five on the occasion of her last invasion — is perfectly capable of controlling the waking attentions of as many as four adults from earliest light to late at night.) But, whatever the story was supposed to mean to kids, it comes to me now as apt to the situation many find themselves in today.

Every now and then, monsters of a kind, even tame ones, present themselves in the midst of a public. Such beasts, whatever their true purposes, have the capacity to become what some villages, and perhaps a few worlds, are about. For many people, postmodernism is just such a beast. Postmodernism demands to be fed, and so it is. Kind people ply it with fodder. Before long it grows to become that which preoccupies, even defines, the villages.

In any one of the villages that constitute the world of daily life illustrations of the phenomenon are generously available. Referring for the moment to members of one with which I am directly familiar, academic sociologists spend a fair percentage of their collective energy in the feeding of this postmodern beast. Though the number of professional sociologists who claim actually to be postmodernists is small in ratio to the whole, the number of occasions upon which the subject is mentioned, often oddly out of context, is great. It is not uncommon for solicited reviews of scholarly articles or books, even of tenure and promotion cases, to contain unsolicited evaluations judging the merits of a case by the degree of its perceived proximity to (bad!) or from (good!) postmodernism. I have heard a story in which an esteemed senior member of one of the field's more respected departments is said to so hate postmodernism as to have told untenured junior colleagues they stood no chance of promotion should they be seen in its company. One would suppose this story to be apocryphal were it not that scrutiny of this department's roster of surviving members, when compared to departed ones, suggests otherwise. True or not, there is ample public evidence elsewhere of members of the profession, including at least one former president of its official association in America, going out of their ways to feed the beast by writing of the supposed bad effects of this thing upon the field. On more than a few occasions these feedings take place in public — at symposia entertaining the gathered at meetings of learned societies, in published reviews of books, and, even, under the guise of contributions to the field's scholarly journals. On one occasion of which I was a participant, one of the field's most honored scholars rose from the audience to address a panel of colleagues who had just said relatively nice things about postmodernism. Her purpose was to counter their heresies with, *inter alia*, the following slip of tongue: "Why is it that you people are all so egocentric when the rest of us are . . . well, what is the word?" She faltered on the oppositive that must have come uneasily to mind, "eccentric."

Postmodernism does indeed have the ability to drive people crazy, even to distraction, as measured by the word's utility as a viable invective. One of the field's most eloquent and famous spokesmen, meaning to comment on the word which had hitherto served to express the worst that could possibly be said of a sociologist, observed:

> A dictionary of modern culture recently gave this tongue-in-cheek definition of postmodernism: "Postmodernism: This word is meaningless. Use it often." Much the same could be said of "positivism," save that it has become more of an epithet than a word used in an approving way.[2]

Save for a very few provincial outposts, mostly in the barren Middle West of the United States, and California of course, "postmodernism" is seldom used by sociologists in an approving way. All in all, the state of collective feeling that can be supposed to motivate this feeding frenzy is well summarized by the random observations one author has made under the title "Postmortemism For Postmodernism":

> A postmodern hypothesis subject to postmodern testing is the scholarly equivalent of Godzilla meeting Frankenstein. The earth trembles, but in the

end the fantasy plays out, and we leave the theatre to resume our humdrum lives.[3]

The frenzy is in fact a fetish arising, as it is supposed all fetishes do, from the very death-wish this author refers to in his title. The fear is vastly out of proportion to the reality of postmodernisms's effects either within a field like sociology (by contrast to the English departments wherein there is better cause for alarm), or in the wider world. Wild disproportions of feeling to fact are symptoms of what Steven Seidman has called post-modern anxiety and some others call "PoMo Phobia."[4] Godzilla versus Frankenstein, indeed.

I have not been able to measure the exact extent to which this monster-fetish has infested precincts of the sociological village. Apparently, though, my experience of the dread is confirmed by others whose feelings about the beastly presence are different from my own. Some years ago, Todd Gitlin, a sociologist of recently respectable standing, said:

> Journals, conferences, galleries and coffee houses are spilling over with talk about postmodernism. What is this thing, where does it come from, and what is at stake?[5]

It is well known to social scientists that anxiety with respect to "things" is code for the more autochthonal fear that the truly human might slip back into the muck from which, before human memory, we are thought to have evolved. Gitlin signals his symptomatic use of the code by making refer-ence to the primeval fecal ooze in the title of his essay: "Hip Deep in Postmodernism." Frankenstein monsters . . . now, things arising from the muck!

Like those in the village of a child's story, many — and not by any means just sociologists — are at risk of becoming a people who organize their wide-awake lives with respect to a subject they wish would go away.

One Saturday morning in May, 1996, readers of *The New York Times* awoke to a front-page story, captioned: "Postmodern Gravity Deconstructed." The subject of the story soon became the buzz among participants in, and observers of, American university culture. Though perhaps pleased that the topic with which they are identified should make the front page, various alleged postmodernists were embarrassed to learn that a bad joke had been played on them.

A teacher of physics at New York University, Alan Sokal, had hood-winked the editors of *Social Text*, a magazine widely known for its interest in subjects like cultural studies, poststructuralism, and, to be sure, post-modernism. Sokal's ruse eventuated in the publication of a pseudo-article, "Transgressing the Boundaries: Toward a Transformative Hermeneutics of Quantum Gravity" which he concocted out of quotations from what he considered the most obscure jargon current in the academic circles in which one would find readers of *Social Text*. By Sokal's standards of truth even the title of his false copy of a true article was manifest nonsense. The cleverly composed pretense of academic sense was well marked as nonsense, perhaps most glaringly by the 12 pages of footnotes and the additional 10 pages of bibliography which together dwarfed the 14 pages of articular text. The joke was in the dispersion of quotations from incommensurable literatures in the humanities and the sciences to create sufficient verisimilitude as to deceive the editors of *Social Text*. One editor, Andrew Ross, declared, after the fact of publication, what he had believed upon accepting the false copy as though it were the real thing: "We read it as the earnest attempt of a professional scientist to seek some sort of philosophical justification for his work."[6] There is no *prima facie* reason to doubt the authenticity of the editor's representation of his good faith in the authenticity of an unknown author's motives than there is to question Sokal's, which were to produce the false copy that would unmask the true falsity which, Sokal believed, lies behind the postmodern-like enterprises.

There followed a flurry of comments and responses, to say nothing of faxes and e-mails, among those delighted or offended by the hoax. Those delighted by Sokal's hoax shared his belief that activities variously associated with the term "postmodernism" are themselves a hoax unmasked by the apparent inability of the supposedly postmodernish editors of *Social Text* to distinguish a seemingly real thing from a deceptively false one. For example:

> The comedy of the Sokal incident is that it suggests that even the postmodernists don't really understand one another's writing and make their way through the text by moving from one familiar name or notion to the next like a frog jumping across a murky pond by way of lily pads. Lacan . . . performativity . . . Judith Butler . . . scandal . . . (en)gendering (w)holeness . . . Lunch![7]

You will notice that the monsters here take the form of frogs which, like locusts and other pests, are known to have been occasionally sent by the gods to punish the wicked. Monsters . . . aboriginal things . . . now, frogs in murky waters.

The Sokal scam was beautifully orchestrated such that simultaneous with the publication of the phoney article in *Social Text*, counterfeiter Sokal separately published a self-exposé in which he avowed the well-meant fraud by which the evil fraud of the alleged postmodernists was supposedly revealed. (In one of the few truly verifiable statements to be found amid the claims and counterclaims, Stanley Fish remarked that Sokal had at least "successfully pretended to be himself."[8]) Sokal's true revelation of his false deed appeared in *Linguafranca*, a magazine devoted to high-minded muckraking among the muddy cultures of academe. Its muckraking style is at least evident in the fact that *Linguafranca* did not initially invite the editors of *Social Text* to respond even though *Linguafranca*'s exposé of Sokal's self-exposure was printed in a section called "Research File."[9]

In one of the more curious outcomes of the affair, it appears that at least one authentic member of the cultural (if not political) Right, Roger Kimball, who for years had been writing about the monstrosities he finds on the cultural Left (that is, postmodernism and its fellow travelers) was taken in by Sokal (a self-professed member of the political, but not the cultural, Left). In *The New Criterion*, a magazine of the cultural Right, Kimball wrote a serious review of the unserious copy of the seriously foolish (and presumed dangerous) postmodernist article in *Social Text*. In all seriousness, Kimball, thinking it the real thing, called the Sokal piece "pure drivel"! It is reported that he also referred to such writing as the piece he *thought* he was reading (but was not) as an "intellectual freak show.[10] The preternatural beast rears its truly ugly head again. Monsters . . . primeval things . . . frogs . . . now, freaks.

One of the true advantages of having Sokal's declaration of the good faith intentions behind the bad faith of his false copy is that a comparison of the two (that is: the true text in *Linguafranca* with the false one in *Social Text*) provides data on the basis of which one can at least determine where in the matter Sokal locates his most earnest moral principles. Being a physicist of unannounced accomplishment, it is not surprising that the idea he finds most ridiculous in the postmodernist scheme of things has to do with *reality*. In this respect he is exactly right, postmodernism has something to do with reality and how it is understood. In Sokal's words:

> In the first paragraph [of "Transgressing the Boundaries"] I deride the dogma imposed by the long post-Enlightenment hegemony over the Western intellectual outlook that there exists an external world, whose properties are independent of any individual human being and indeed of humanity as a whole; that these properties are encoded in "eternal" physical laws; and that human beings can obtain reliable, albeit imperfect and tentative, knowledge of these laws by hewing to the "objective" procedures

and epistemological strictures prescribed by the (so-called) scientific method.[11]

This, remember, is Sokal quoting Sokal's invented text — that is: Sokal taking seriously his own simulation of a "real" postmodernist text in order to demonstrate that the reality of postmodernist cultural studies is patently unreal.

In other words, Sokal's false text was sufficiently real in appearance to have fooled those who doubt: that reality is a self-evidently available thing; that true science is free of its own cultural confusions; that knowledge is produced by means of immutable, if not obvious, methods. Thus, in his *Social Text* spoof, Sokal slyly mocks these postmodernist suspicions by the use of diacritical marks on and around certain terms, as in: "eternal" physical laws, "objective" procedures, and (so-called) scientific method.

Thus mocking within the simulated text, Sokal freed himself for serious business in *Linguafranca* in which he presented himself for what he truly believes, namely: that postmodernists are guilty on three counts: 1) being unserious about reality, 2) being fraudulent in method and deficient in intellectual rigor, and, 3) being untrue to the true canons of Left politics. The third of these will shock those who, being familiar with the hostility of the political Right to the cultural Left, were not hitherto aware that the political Left is nearly as upset with the "postmodern" cultural Left as is the cultural Right (to say nothing of the political Right). Thus, Sokal, having left his scientific accomplishments unannounced, proclaims his true Left political credentials in order to attack these beastly postmodernists: "Politically, I'm angered because most (though not all) of this silliness is emanating from the self-proclaimed Left."[12]

Though it quickly becomes near impossible to tell the players and their teams without a score card, one thing is clear. The controversy was about reality, method, and politics. Yet, Sokal's readiness to mix politics with the other two is a bit shocking inasmuch as proponents of the rigor of method as the true means to a sense of reality usually do not, as Sokal surprisingly does, throw in the third. On the relation of method to reality, Sokal *qua* physicist proposes an elegantly parsimonious experiment in order to demonstrate his distaste for the notorious linguistic turn of postmodern social theory:

In the second paragraph [of the *Social Text* essay] I declared, without the slightest evidence or argument, that "physical 'reality' (note the scare quotes) . . . is at bottom a social and linguistic construct." Not our *theories* of physical reality, mind you, but the reality itself. Fair enough: Anyone who believes that the laws of physics are mere social conventions is invited to try transgressing those conventions from the windows of my apartment. (I live on the twenty-first floor.)[13]

As he would say, fair enough: Some one ought to have caught that line, even if, as another physicist, Steven Weinberg, implies, it might have been passed over under certain biographical conditions by a real physicist, like Heisenberg in his later years.[14] Whether any cultural sociologist whom Sokal would direct toward the looming pavement outside his apartment would agree were the subject social, not physical, is another matter. That the uncertainty of physical reality may be less obviously contested by physicists than the indefinite reality of social constructs are by sociologists only goes to show that, when it comes to reality, there are some differences of opinion. These are the differences which allow, whether Sokal understands it or not (there is no way to tell), for the addition of the third member in his trilogy of righteous concerns, the political.

If "reality," whether external and physical or otherwise, is an uncertain proposition, then there is no method with which to know the truth in order to do the good. When all was said and done (and most would agree that little was said in what was done), there remains one fundamental principle upon which all sides might agree: *trust*. Sokal admits he violated the principle of trust essential to community life (for a higher good, of course). His victims and a number of the third-party commentators agree, of course. Trust was violated. Trust is essential to communities, even professional scientific ones. Everything depends on it, including, it turns out, truth. Whoever is right in all this cannot be determined except with reference to which, if any, of the parties or principles one trusts.

In the same week in May, 1996, when the Sokal affair awakened readers of *The New York Times*, there appeared in *The New Yorker* another story the lesson of which was also trust, truth, and the standards in science.[15] *The New Yorker* essay was but the latest instalment of a long, protracted intrigue among natural scientists. For a full decade from 1986 to 1996, the story of Nobel Prize-winning biologist David Baltimore and several of his former associates, had come to be nearly as perplexing to natural scientists as the postmodernism beast had become, over the same time period, for numerous others.

When he was not yet forty, Professor Baltimore had won the 1975 Nobel Prize in Medicine for his work at MIT on the reproductive mechanisms of viruses — work which came to have implications for research on the AIDS virus. Everything good lay ahead of him, including the presidency of Rockefeller University, one of the most prestigious graduate centers of biological research in the world. Except for the dispute that began in 1986 between two of Baltimore's junior laboratory colleagues at MIT, he would surely stand today as one of the nation's most respected and influential scientists. Instead, Baltimore was forced out of the Rockefeller presidency soon after he had ascended to it, and still today must live with a reputation tarnished by the (apparently) mere fact that he had used his prestige to defend the honor of one colleague against the charges of another. No one, so far as I know, has ever accused Baltimore himself of scientific fraud. He had not directly been involved in the contested research. The worst that was said of him was that he had trusted, then defended, a colleague too aggressively without knowing, or (possibly) wanting to know, all the facts. Yet, this error of pride and prominence was enough to bring him down a few pegs and to embroil, eventually, much of the scientific community and a good bit of the political community in a decade-long turmoil. By the summer of 1996, the story seems to have ended well for Baltimore when a federal court ruled in favor of those whom he defended, leaving them and him with the experience of a troubled ten years of life.[16]

Ten years before, in 1986, the dispute began, much as it ended, as a moral affair involving nothing less than the most fundamental question of any and all sciences: Can one scientist replicate (that is: make a true copy) of the empirical work of another? Nothing is more fundamental to sciences of all kinds than the belief that nothing is considered real and true unless results reported by one researcher are reproduced using the same procedures under similar circumstances. In the case which shook the sciences, one scientist, Margot O'Toole, became frustrated, then suspicious, when she was unable to replicate the results of another. Thereza Imanishi-Kari was one of six authors of a paper published in *Cell* — one of the most prestigious journals in all of science. Seeking advice from Imanishi-Kari, O'Toole went over the original data with her. According to *The New Yorker* article, during one of the meetings between the two, O'Toole thought she observed Imanishi-Kari overlooking, perhaps intentionally, disconfirming data. This is a serious matter in science.

As the dispute grew more and more public, it came to turn on whether a now famous Figure 1 in the 1986 *Cell* article was a true copy of real data in its entirety. Other scientists, it seems, had difficulties similar to O'Toole's in replicating the study which, in turn, lent credence to her *mistrust* of her colleague, Imanishi-Kari, whom Baltimore seemed for a while to have *overtrusted* in his defense of her. Soon former colleagues, even friends, in the Cambridge–Boston science community were no longer on speaking terms. Eventually, the National Institutes of Health, which were responsible for funding the scientific work, entered the matter; and soon after, the Energy and Commerce Committee of the House of Representatives (then chaired by John Dingell, Democrat of Michigan). Then, finally, an agency of the NIH called, if you can believe it, the Office of Scientific Integrity (OSI) entered the now politically driven controversy in response to the pressure exerted by the congressional committee. When the affair was settled legally in July, 1996 by court decision, the more embarrassed parties were the politicians and bureaucrats who had taken it upon themselves to judge the truth of the science. This was foolhardy, given that the scientists themselves were unable to convince each other. Neither politicians nor bureaucrats are known for their skill in distinguishing the foolish from the true. Their jobs are to announce or administer truths others invoke. They were, thus, nothing more than the visible public proponents of a real state of affairs that is well in evidence whenever scientists argue about the truth. If factual reality relies, as it does, on the human confidence scientists have in each other, then all science is vulnerable to political trouble. If it can happen once, or several times, it can happen all the time. In the Baltimore case, the final arbiters were the judges who, though they heard testimony by scientists, were no more competent to judge the truth of the data in the 1986 *Cell* article, than the scientific disputants were able to prove their sides of the argument. When trust is broken, the truth is beyond even scientific rigor to restore.

The parallel of this story to the Sokal affair is worth a glance. Though, in the Baltimore affair, it is far from clear that anyone knowingly falsified data, much less an entire article, as Sokal did, the central point of controversy is much the same. Which are the true data? How does anyone distinguish the real from the copy? Did the truth-seekers act in a trustworthy manner? It is plain indeed that these are the questions that must be asked of academic work of any kind. But the deeper, harder to resolve, question is: How are they related? That is, simply put: Can there be truth without trust? If there cannot be, then truth *always* relies on trust and is, accordingly, always embedded in quite unreliable, external to science, human competencies. There is no evidence whatsoever that a scientist, by virtue of being a scientist, is more trustworthy than any other person. Sokal proves this point. Apart from the politicians in the Baltimore affair, Sokal was the only avowedly untrustworthy character in either of the two stories.

Trust is the fundamental issue of the day. There is, in fact, survey evidence that two-thirds of all Americans feel they cannot trust others they meet in the world.[17] To be sure, parents of recent school graduates are every bit as unsure of the trustworthiness of the world as is any physicist, biologist, or postmodernish student of culture. Whether the subject of concern is the well-being of children or the truth of reality, everything in the world comes back to trust. Which, in turn, is why the postmodernism question is so reasonably, or unreasonably, upsetting. Creeping out from under the basic sociological question of trust in the world is the question of whether or not we are throwing our children into a world of beasts.

Doubt so overwhelms trust that parents, sociologists, and all the members of the cultural and political rights and lefts may have well forgotten that, in point of historical fact, modern science itself arose in large part over a well-regarded solution to the still prior question of the origins of the human in beastly life.

On December 7, 1831, Charles Darwin departed on the famous five-year round-the-world voyage of the Beagle. Darwin was 22, just the age of my youngest when he left for God knows where eventually. Darwin's voyage changed his life, and the history of modern science.

Over the course of those five years until his return in 1836, Darwin observed the natural world, took notes and collections, sent specimens back to England, and gradually came to define himself less as a gentleman hunter and failed candidate for the Anglican ministry, than as a naturalist. Soon after his return, Darwin presented to England's leading scientists bits and pieces of what he had observed on his voyage. Being unable to replicate his voyage exactly, they trusted him — as well they might have because of his Cambridge pedigree and good family name. Yet, it was to be nearly a quarter of a century before Darwin would dare to publish his masterwork, *On the Origin of the Species in Natural Selection*. In the intervening years he worked and fretted over the revolutionary nature of his ideas. One of the more disturbing to his vaguely declining Christian beliefs was, of course, the idea that man was descended not from God's hand but from the beasts. The prospect still has the power to disturb some people. In the mid-nineteenth century it was, needless to say, truly revolutionary. Darwin was willing and able, in the end, to pronounce it with conviction *only* because of his careful scientific work.

The voyage of the Beagle, though funded by the Crown for any number of commercial and empire-building reasons, was a replication of most colonizing voyages. Naturalists (usually the ship's surgeon) were regular members of crew on nineteenth-century exploring ships. Darwin, therefore, had the reports, drawings, and specimens of other such voyagers — each seeking to describe and comprehend the strange corners of the natural and human world. Places like the jungles of Brazil, the plains of the Tierra del Fuego, the Galápagos islands, the mountains of Chile and

Scotland were visited and revisited. What Darwin and most naturalists of his day were attempting to do was to construct a theory of the origins of worldly things — mountains, mollusks, and other diverse species of land and marine beasts. Few, even the most hard-bitten geologists, were fully prepared for Darwin's 1859 declaration that man was originally a beast.

In 1844, some fifteen years before *Origin of the Species*, a journalist by the name of Robert Chambers published *Vestiges of the Natural History of Creation*. The book became an immediate best-seller. Every one in the know talked about it. It described in reasonable facsimile what Darwin was just then beginning to believe but would not say in public for many years to come. *Vestiges* was, in short, the outline of the theory of natural selection, including the doctrine that man was sprung from the beasts, which was to change science and culture. Yet, history credits Darwin with the idea while barely remembering Chambers.

Was Chambers the Alan Sokal of his day? Well no, not exactly. Though he did fabricate without any important scientific evidence a true copy of the theory that would change the world, he did not intend to copy that which, truth be told, was not yet available for copy. Chamber's *Vestiges* was a true copy of what was, in a word, *not* — at least not yet. What Chambers did was to anticipate the theory on the basis of perfectly amateurish gleanings from journals, field reports, and narratives of more true scientific observers. One lesson we (not excluding Sokal) can learn from Chambers is that even the most revolutionary and unimaginable scientific ideas are not all that difficult to divine.

Those who hate these postmodern beasts, frogs, freaks, and other such murky things may be on occasion overwrought, but they are not wrong to worry as they do. The modern world is undergoing some kind of change. Even those who wish it were not concede this point. The cultural order that was founded in the colonizing sixteenth and seventeenth centuries, that achieved its grand political moment in the eighteenth, that revolutionized science and industry in the nineteenth, that perfected so many technologies in the twentieth is not what it once was. Whether the modern world can ever be a semblance of what it was cannot be said. What can and must be said is that the investigation of these facts is a foremost and righteous responsibility of all with a stake in the nature of what, through the years, we have so blithely called, as though its reality were never in doubt, "the world."

The worlds in which we live are what we make of them. Whether one approves of the idea or not, worlds are, thus, made-things. The world we live in, for better or worse, was definitively made in the form we live in it today more or less about the time Darwin discovered, then proved to a majority's satisfaction, that the world of human things is certifiably not truly different from the world of natural things pure and simple. The theory of natural selection which in its sociological after-life came to be used as a justification for the excellent prospects of human progress was, in *its* original form, a dark scientific theory that required the people of mid-nineteenth century England, Europe, and the Americas to rethink, hence to remake, their worlds. As Janet Browne says of Darwin's world construction:

> Darwin faced the arduous task of reorienting the way Victorians looked at nature. He had to show them that their generally received ideas about a benevolent, near perfect natural world, in which insects and seeds were designed to feed birds and birds to feed cats, and beauty was given to things for a purpose, were wrong — that the idea of a loving God who created all living things and brought men and women into existence was at the very least a fable. . . . The world steeped in moral meaning which helped mankind seek out higher goals in life was not Darwin's. Darwin's view of nature was dark — black.[18]

Indeed, and noting the racial connotations Browne (and surely Darwin) left unglossed, she (and he) got the circumstances of the modern world just right. Underneath its benefits to the few, the modern world promised the rest much that would never be without struggle. This is the terrible darkness of the modern world. Is it not, among much else, the dark of the jungles and swamps from which arise such beastly things?

Hence, Darwin — like Marx, like Weber and Durkheim, not to mention Spencer, and not excluding anyone of the day who was preoccupied with creating one or another scientific theory that could, in all true adherence to the factual reality of things, reconstruct the world. All in their ways were concerned, as many are today, with the fall of the human back into the dark, murky slime of things. During just about the same years Darwin was puzzling through to his theory of natural selection, Marx was perfecting his theory of capitalism which had begun in his famous rethinking of Hegel's concern with the reification, the thingification, of the human. Weber's iron cage was in its way a poetic refiguring of this most famous of nineteenth-century concerns. Durkheim, in much the same manner, feared that human society was man's only protection from falling back into the animal passions. Spencer and others, assuming a more robust liberal denial of these dark prospects, did little more than capture Darwin's theoretical alter-ego. Life springs from the dark things, from the beasts — but spring it does. Durkheim and many others were the more Malthusian pessimists. Their pessimism was soon forgotten generally (though not strictly) speaking, until the first murmurings of what today we fear to be postmodernly beasts. In Darwin's day, at the very time the institutional form of the science Sokal believes to be true (even when it punishes those like Baltimore who misplace their trust) was coming into its mature modern form, there was much in the world to encourage faith in the progressive ideal. But that encouragement was, in Weber's word, bought at the price of the disenchantment of the natural world. Modern society required that the mysterious monsters and murky things be killed, leaving the world open to competitive progress, if bereft of native imagination. As Browne says further of Darwin's world-constructing science:

> What most people saw as God-given design [Darwin] saw as mere adaptations to circumstance, adaptations that were meaningless except for the way in which they helped an animal or plant to survive. Much of this was perhaps familiar to a nation immersed in competitive affairs: Darwin had transformed the generalized entrepreneurial ethos of English life into a biological theory which, in turn, derived much of its support from these all-pervasive commitments.[19]

Is it then a postmodernist fad to believe, as even Sokal and his fans do, that scientific truth rests on human trust in others who share their well-made world?

Forgotten in all the postmodern anxiety is the fact that postmodernism is merely the currently fashionable name for a complicated series of cultural and theoretical inventions, each of which were adjustments to the realities of the world in the second half of the twentieth century. It is not by accident that the first postmodern voyage was conducted by Claude Lévi-Strauss just a century after Darwin's voyage of the Beagle. Like Darwin, Lévi-Strauss made his first and most important stop in the south American jungles and plains. It was in Brazil, in the 1930s, just when Hitler was beginning to demonstrate Europe's own beastly proclivities, that Lévi-Strauss furthered his theory that human history was not so pure and unique as the West had come to believe. Among the Brazilian peoples who lived in such close proximity to the beasts, Lévi-Strauss saw what Darwin had seen. Even the most advanced of human cultures could not distinguish the human from its natural origins. Both Darwin and Lévi-Strauss, in a sense, believed that the very ideas of *human* history and culture are taxonomically local conceits. Culture is culture and even culture has more to do with the struggle to survive than with the idealization of the most modern human ideals.

One of the ironies of modern culture is that the very science of which Darwin was such a pure and rigorous proponent became the very cultural emblem of the superiority of the human to the beastly, which ideal, in turn, came to represent, even to ground, the most distinctive cultural belief of those who considered themselves most truly modern: that as human things arise from the beasts, so (some) men arise before and above others such that the continuous struggle of men with each other gives rise over all to the ideal of human progress. Modernism, the cultural theory, seemed of course to draw factual support from the historical witness of the modern age. From the vantage of the most modern of men it seemed that each progressive move across the seas, into the jungles and mountains, across the plains made the world as we know it and, in the process, confirmed the most moral fact of all: that the reality of things is that things can and will get better.

It is the truth of this fact that now worries parents who send their kids off to unknown parts. It is not that prior generations were free of such worries, but that the parental obligation to worry is now oddly associated with the suspicions that the monsters, freaks, the frogs are still out there, close to home, haunting the night air. The postmodernisms and related theories are but a few of these murky things that disturb the sleep of parents of wandering kids.

2

Postmodernism Is Not What You Think

Just weeks before sitting down to write this chapter, I was in Kyongju, South Korea, a small provincial city about 250 kilometers southeast of Seoul. Kyongju was once the center of the ancient Silla Kingdom that dominated the Korean peninsula significantly from the sixth century AD until the rise of the Koryo dynasty in the tenth century. Crafts, culture, and Buddhism flourished under Silla's medieval culture. UNESCO considers ancient Kyongju one of the world's ten most important ancient cities.

Today, however, Kyongju is a tourist city served by a modern interstate expressway and ringed by newly developed ultra-modern hotels. Through the miracle of satellite television I watched the third game of the 1995 Houston–Orlando NBA championship series in my hotel room. Later that evening, I walked along a small lake with my Korean host, Hong-Woo Kim. The night was calm, a slight breeze cooled the air. We talked quietly of sociology and other common interests. In a cafe across the lake, a singer crooned American popular love songs in perfect English. I tried to tell Professor Kim of the many other times I had strolled on summer evenings by the lakes and seasides of my youth listening to songs like these. But I was not quite able to convey the exact sense of summers in Maine and American teen-age romance. Cultures are just too different on the fine points of feelings and memories.

Early the next day, I prayed somewhat self-consciously in a Buddhist temple high in the mountains above Kyongju. The main temple at Kirim-sa was already packed with monks and other devotees sitting, bowing, and joining in the ancient chants that were broadcast, in highest fidelity sound, across the monastery grounds. Buddhist monks like those chanting that morning had chanted similarly in that same place since the temples were first built in AD 643. Save for electricity and plumbing nothing was different, though I did notice one of those TV satellite dishes discreetly mounted just off the perimeter of the monastery compound. On the way out, I bought a compact disk recording of the monks chanting. The ancient lives on with, and through, modern technology!

The world is like this today, and has been for some time now. Postmodernism has something to do with experiences of this kind. But, in saying this, I refer not as much as you might suppose to the miracles of technology and transport that put different people in surprisingly close contact with each other and their different cultures. This is only part of what makes the world today peculiar and a bit shocking. At a deeper level, experiences such as the one I had in Kyongju are an increasingly normal feature of daily life among people of widely different social positions and geographic places. It is not just that technology *allows* people closer communication with each other, creating a global village (as Marshall McLuhan once put it[1]), but that the globalizing processes are of such a nature as to have fundamentally changed the way the world is experienced. Human contact today is not just intensified, it is also reorganized, strangely — and not always for the better.

In the simplest of terms, some say that postmodernism is about this odd fact that historical aspects of the world that do not belong together are, today, jumbled up with each other. Postmodernism, though it is a very complicated thing to understand, has mostly to do with such an idea. Accordingly, postmodernists are those who believe the world has changed in some hard-to-describe, but unmistakable, way in which things are out of kilter, though meaningfully so. The reasonable kilters of modern life are somehow rearranged in odd, incongruent ways that, nonetheless, seem normal in spite of their abnormality.

Just how odd these new arrangements are will become apparent, a little later on, when I explain that it is impossible to talk about postmodernism and its social theories without also talking about modernism. So strongly do I believe this to be so that when I turn to a direct exposition of the three main groups of postmodern theories, I include a discussion of *radical modernism* along with two different kinds of postmodernisms — one that considers modernism done with (*radical postmodernism*) and another that considers modernity at least in need of a thorough remaking (*strategic postmodernism*). When I come to these three groups of theories I will provide the definitions and explanations the reader no doubt seeks. But I mention them here merely to establish the idea that postmodernism, including the theories it has spawned, is no simple matter, and certainly not one that can be treated as though any one theory of it could render others, even the strongest theories of the modernism, somehow defunct.

I realize this is not the easiest way to begin a discussion of post-modernism. But, in fact, there is no easy way to begin a discussion of it. I believe, for example, that such a discussion must include an attempt to dispel the most common misconceptions about postmodernism. This I do in the section below where I turn directly to the book's title theme, "Postmodernism Is Not What You Think." Postmodernism being a hard to understand thing, it is easily misunderstood. But this does not mean that one should not attempt, from the first, to say as clearly as possible where in the world those interested in it might look for it.

Postmodernism — Where Does One Look For It?

It hardly need be said that postmodernism has something to do with what is allegedly happening to modernism. So, if *modernism* is the culture of the modern age (or, simply, of *modernity*), then *postmodernism* has something to do with the breaking apart of modernism. Thus, if one wants to find postmodernism, it is necessary first of all to look at culture — not because culture is the only important thing in the world, but because culture is a particularly sensitive aspect of social life. Cultures are sensitive enough that when one suspects the world, including its economic and political arrangements, is changing, cultures are where one might first find signs of the purported change. This is especially the case when the change is so great as to entail the breaking up of modernity.

Yet, you might ask, what then is *culture*? A reasonably simple way of describing culture is to say that it is the complex of socially produced values, rules, beliefs, literatures, arts, media, penal codes, laws, political ideas and other such diversions by which a society, or any social group, represents its view of the world as its members (or at least the members in charge) believe it is or ought to be. Madonna, like it or not, is part of culture. As are your local mosque and temple, the rhetoric of all political parties, the finest poetry, John Updike's latest novel, TV ads for Air Jordan shoes as well as Michael Jordan himself, and much more. Though itself a complicated thing, culture possesses one attribute which is relatively straightforward, even though it is seldom discussed. Any collective attempt to represent, or express, what a group of people think the social world ideally is must also, and necessarily, exclude those worlds the people disapprove of. Madonna is the expression of a cultural view that the world ought to invite all sorts of outrageous sexual experiences. The culture that has produced Madonna, and a good bit of today's popular culture is, therefore, a culture that frowns upon the more traditional and puritan sexual values; just as certain religious conservatives produce a culture that intends to exclude the likes of Madonna. So, simply, cultures are means whereby a social group says what it likes and what it hates. Though the former is easier to spot than the latter, it too can be found with a little poking around.

So, we might say that postmodernism is a culture that believes there is a better world than the modern one. In particular it disapproves of modernism's uncritical assumption that European culture (including its diaspora versions in such places as South Africa, the United States, Australia, and Argentina) is an authentic, self-evident, and true universal culture in which all the world's people ought to believe. Postmodernism is a culture that prefers to break things up, to respect the several parts of social world. When it speaks of culture it prefers to speak of cultures.

This is readily seen when one looks at those aspects of culture most famously associated with postmodernism — architecture, for example. One of the most frequently cited representations of the postmodern is the famous AT&T (now SONY) building at Madison Avenue and 55th Street in New York City. This midtown Manhattan building, like most in that section of the world's most famous city of skyscrapers, is a tall, imposing structure. In this sense it is purely and classically modern. The skyscraper is said to be the architectural symbol of modernity's brash self-confidence — rising above common things to dominate the urban world. Yet, this same building is evidently weird. There is, for one thing, a Chippendale flourish at the pediment, or top-most part. Chippendale is a seventeenth-century furniture design which includes two rising angles which are broken at their apex by a wide circular opening. Many have seen such figures in their grandmother's bedrooms. But for those unfamiliar with this emblem, the top of the AT&T building could just as well appear to be an old-fashioned telephone cradle. Either way this surprising design feature makes those who view the building wonder: What am I to think of this? More odd still, at the base of the building, there are columns reminiscent of classical Greco-Roman temples and an entrance with a prominent semicircular, Byzantine arch recalling still another culture from another time. What exactly are these ironic design features doing on such a modernist structure? Was the building's architect, Philip Johnson, playing a joke on the city of New York?

Even if you have never seen this building, there are few American cities, even smaller ones, where there is not some postmodern building adorned with figures of architectural speech from differing eras and contrasting forms — copper flashing typical of small town farm houses askance modernist corporate headquarters, triangulated cupolas protruding at surprising angles atop tall buildings. Thus, just like the odd throwing together of the ancient and modern I experienced in Kyongju, Korea, most

Americans live with something similar at their local malls or downtown centers.

Or, to suggest still another category of illustration, think of the most striking personalities of popular entertainment. What do Michael Jackson, Madonna, Snoop Doggy Dogg, and the-artist-formerly-known-as-Prince have in common? Each has a uniquely composed public persona. True, many entertainment personalities assume stage names and identities. But with these four something different is going on. The personae they have invented are made out of absurdly contradictory elements juxtaposed to each other to create, not just shock, but irony. Michael Jackson has remade his body into a sexually ambiguous form through which he expresses powerful, but confusing, erotic messages. At one moment his face is girlish, coy. At another he demonstratively grabs his crotch in the most masculinist of gestures. Yet, in the end we hear a child's voice. Madonna, it hardly need be said, presses the very limits of heterosexual provocation, while frequently blurring the visual and sensual line between heteronormative and lesbian sexual desire. Snoop Doggy Dogg is a play on names in which a child's cartoon figure names a music that samples the most extreme forms of political and sexual expression. In fact, hip-hop music's use of sampling is a near perfect illustration of the postmodern form. Here elements from differing musics, from political discourse and TV sitcoms, from artificial street sounds and the manipulation of the recording discs themselves are packed into a dense, mixed-up sound effect through which a nonetheless clear message line is conveyed.

Whether one looks at public architecture or these invented personalities and musical forms, such cultural forms are the kinds of things those who take postmodernism seriously look to. Each of these examples suggests that the postmodern entails a playful aggression on the modernist ideal that the world we live in is reasonable and responsive to the human desire for progress and a better world. To be sure, postmodernism involves jokes of various kinds like the AT&T building, but it is also an entirely serious criticism of any innocent modernist ideal that all things work together for good.

At the same time, the postmodern also uses the modern alongside other cultural forms. Whatever Madonna and Michael Jackson are doing, they are unmistakably also highly successfully popular music performers, just as the AT&T, or SONY, building is still a very tall, thus very modern building with all the efficiencies required to satisfy its corporate clients. Whatever may be the relation of the postmodern to the modern, that relation is not one of simple progression and criticism. Common sense alone suggests that the world in all its major structural features is still very much the same — if not exactly the same — world that emerged politically, culturally, and economically over the last half-millennium since Europeans first set out to explore and conquer the new world. If the world is postmodern (and many think it is), then it is also somehow still modern.

Social Theory — What Is It?

Before turning at last to postmodernism itself, it is prudent to say a few words about one of its most ubiquitous and disturbing cultural forms — the one with which this book is principally concerned: social theory. Those who are upset by postmodernism's beastly and freakish epiphanies are usually upset most by postmodernish theories of social life. I have personally never heard of any who dislike postmodern architecture becoming as foolishly enraged as those who hate postmodern social theories. True, there are people of certain moral and political sects who are quite besides themselves at the very idea of Madonna, but they usually have bigger fish to fry than MTV (though of course some have tried, without success, to fry its more extreme mediations).

But postmodern social theory seems to be uncommonly able to arouse the worst fears of its opponents, who themselves may or may not be social theorists. Many of those who hate postmodernism can be found to be among those who hate social theory itself. Alan Sokal, for example, bases his disgust at postmodernism in part on its studied indifference to true, scientific theories, which are something other than social theories. There are, after all, many different kinds of theories, of which social theory is but one. Just how a social theory (let alone a postmodern one) might differ from, say, the scientific theory of a physicist, or an economist, or a scientific sociologist is therefore a matter of some importance to an understanding of postmodernism itself and the trouble it causes.

Since social theory is not a name brand among the many forms by which cultures express themselves, an ever so small digression into its unique nature may not be a waste of the reader's time — especially not since, for better or worse, among the most aggravatingly interesting forms of postmodern culture are its social theories.

Simply put, *social theory* is any theory of society or social life that distinguishes itself from scientific theories by its willingness to be critical as well as factual. Though the distinction between social theory and, say, "sociological theory" is often blurred today, there is a difference. Many sociologists, for example, believe that sociology is a science like others and must, therefore, obey strict rules and protocols — above all others, they want to obey rules that, in their opinion, are able to assure *objectivity* (the idea that facts, once analyzed, can be considered valid indications of the objective nature of the things they represent). A sociological theorist (that is, a sociologist who thinks of himself as a scientist) might, thereby, look for objective measures of, say, the number of individuals who espouse favorable attitudes toward the idea that the economic world encourages a progressive improvement in the social prospects of those who work hard. If a measurably significant number of persons interviewed in, say, the Republic of Korea, admit that they hold this attitude, then (if there is similar confirming data) a sociological theorist might be willing to assert that South Korea *is* a modern society. A social theorist, by contrast, would be very interested in what a sociological theorist claims as objective fact, but she would tend to be more skeptical, even critical of the idea that objective measures can be found. A social theorist is more inclined to say that the attitudes people claim to hold, and report to interviewers, are themselves mediated as much by what people are taught about their social situation (perhaps by television and other media) as by any certifiable prospect that the world they live in is hospitable to their attitudes. This is just one example of the way social theorists are, usually, respectful of scientific description, but wish to add to it a more critical, or imaginative, dimension that cannot be fully verified. Social theorists are, in short, more relaxed in their science and more intense in their politics.

The tradition of social theory is, if anything, even longer than that of the more scientific sociological theories. It is reasonable, for example, to say that the great nineteenth-century radical thinker Karl Marx was an important social theorist. His monumental study, *Capital*, was based on the most current evidence and concepts available in his day. It was, in this sense, scientific. But Marx made no secret of his intention of writing this book in order to produce what many have considered a devastating criticism of the social effects of capitalism. Marx made no pretense of objectivity, even though much of what he said is indeed a reliable description of the capitalist world. On the other hand, early sociological theorists like Emile Durkheim, who wrote in France in the late nineteenth and early twentieth centuries, believed that sociology could be, and must be, a science of social things. His scientific procedures were among the most rigorous of his day. His study *Suicide*, for example, was based on careful empirical analysis that led to a theory of suicide which holds up pretty well today. Yet, even though he considered himself a scientist, Durkheim did his science because he was critical of a society that seemed to leave so many people lost as to the rules they should follow in daily life. He was as deeply concerned about people who committed suicide as Marx was about those exploited by the early factory system. Scientific sociological theories are not uncaring, even though they are more cautious.

Conversely, social theories are less cautious with respect to facts in order that they may be more bold with respect to human values. This should suggest why those who attempt to explain, promote, or attack postmodernism, are more likely to be social theorists. The more scientific sociologists consider the argument, at best, hogwash; at worst, dirty business.

You can see why social theorists are interested in phenomena like postmodernism. It is their business to concern themselves with anything that suggests something is wrong with the world. And this is why, as I have already said, there are at least two different groups of postmodern social theorists, and one large group of modernist social theorists who worry about the postmodern even while believing it is a terrible thing. Social theorists gravitate toward controversy. They do not agree with each other because they deal with subjects, like postmodernism, that are beyond hard factual proof but are of evident importance to an understanding of the world we live in.

Postmodernism Is Not What You Think

I intend two meanings by the title of the book. Postmodernism is not what you think, that is: Not only is it not what you might suppose it is, it is not *primarily* something one thinks. In fact, one of the most crucial ways in which postmodernism is not what many people think it is that it is not *principally* (and certainly not exclusively) a form of social thought. True, it has spawned a great deal of important social theory. But this fact alone must be interpreted with respect to the more interesting question: What does the remarkable appearance of postmodernism in fields as seemingly different from each other as social theory, architecture, and popular music say about the world?

It is always important to distinguish between a theory or cultural attitude *about* the world and the facts of world reality themselves. This distinction is inherent in the difference between speaking of *postmodernity*, a purportedly new state of world affairs, and postmodernism, a theory or cultural attitude toward those affairs. This is not an uncommon distinction. We are well accustomed to speaking about modernism as the culture of modernity, and there is very little reason to doubt that such a state of world affairs as modernity, or the modern age, has existed for the better part of the last half-millennium. Modernity, thus, is the dominant reality in the worldly affairs of Europe and North America and their vast imperial systems across the globe from the first age of explorations in the late fifteenth century through at least the two decades following World War II. Thus, just as modernism would be the culture of that age, so postmodernism is the culture (including the social theories) of an age that is alleged to be after, against, but still mixed up with modernity. Thus, postmodern social theorists are usually pre-occupied with events occurring in the last half-century and especially those that made the 1960s such a notorious time. It was then, postmodernists believe, that the world began to change. It was then that modernity, they think, started visibly to come apart.

It is important to keep in mind the distinction between theories about the world and events in the world when studying postmodernism. One should first inquire into the nature of the world itself before taking the theories of that world too much at their face value. This is the fundamental sense in which postmodernism is not what you think. Postmodernism has spawned many social and cultural theories about the world, but their plausibility should be tested against the "facts" of the world itself. To be sure, this is tricky business because they are social theories of a subject that is beyond factual proof. Still there can be plausible social theories, even when the facts are not as robust as one might like, or one might think possible in the first place.

So, to say that postmodernism is not what you think is to challenge the idea that this idea could be just an idea. The reason it is so difficult to overcome the notion that postmodernism exists apart from a possible postmodern world reality is that the appearances of the idea are so alluring in and of themselves. In fact, one of the most notorious strains of postmodern cultural theory is the one associated with the French social theorist, Jean Baudrillard. Those who agree with Baudrillard believe that today the world of culture is entirely cut loose from any necessary basis in reality. Social life, according to this school of postmodern thought, is much more a spectacle that simulates reality, than reality itself. People, they say, get their reality mostly through media. There is something to this but, I should warn, it does not necessarily mean that the world does not exist — only that it exists in some strange new form.

By the time many American children enter school they will have already watched more hours of television than the total number of hours of classroom instruction they will encounter in their school careers. The media, notably television (more recently its extension and transformation in the many new forms of cyberreal technologies), are surely one of the most pervasive cultural forces in most societies, worldwide. (What *do* those Buddhist monks in Kyongju watch through their satellite TV hookup?) A simple fact such as this has been analyzed by writers like Baudrillard into a general theory of society as *hyperreality* in which simulation of reality is more real than the thing itself. Baudrillard has actually said that

Disneyworld replications of a mythical America are the real American thing — more real than any actual American village.[2]

What is it about the world itself that produces a theory like Baudrillard's and what inspires so many people to find it wholly plausible? To propose an answer, let us return to Madonna.

What exactly is Madonna? The Madonna we viewers of MTV know and love is so far beyond a "who" that it hardly makes sense to use the expected pronoun. Surely, we assume, there is some real, beautiful and talented, outrageous still-young woman behind the name and persona. But to those (and their number is considerable) who get their sense of sex, love, gender, and sexuality from the MTV star, it hardly makes any difference who the girl was out of whom Madonna has been invented. Like it or not, one of the first facts of culture today is that its influence on the shaping of one's sense of herself and her place in the world is *more*, not less, powerful to the *very* extent that culture itself is *less*, not more, real in the usual sense of the word. As we will soon see, "reality" is itself very much at issue in discussion of the postmodern. But, for now, to say that culture is "less real" is to acknowledge that, like Madonna, culture itself is seldom exactly what it seems to be.

But, what does it mean to say that the world is "less real" because it is hyperreal, or "super-real"? This strange notion can be so because, today, culture is, as cultural theorists would put it, mediated.[3] The media, notably television, are literally media (or, more simply, tools) through which we gain a "sense of the world." That sense may be expanded, displaced, distorted, perverted, intensified, and more. It may be, in our view, good or bad. But the important fact is that when we live in a culture where culture is mediated our sense of reality is, to some important degree, mediated; hence indirect; hence (further) susceptible to intrusions and perhaps corruptions through the process of mediation. Several times I actually watched an NBA basketball game in person at the old Boston Garden. The seats were in the first balcony. As a result, the players (most near seven feet tall) actually appeared very small indeed. But I knew who the stars were, and what to expect of them. When Larry Bird hit an impossible three-pointer while falling behind the base-line I *knew* what was going on. But I knew it in spite of the fact that, at such a distance in the first balcony, I could hardly make out the details. How did I know what I knew? I knew because I had seen them close up many times on television. I knew these men as others know Madonna because I saw them through a very articulate medium. So powerful is that medium that, one supposes, the real person hardly matters. What matters is the show, and the show I know because I saw it on television, mediated.

I have never met Larry Bird though I once visited French Lick, Indiana, where he grew up and still has a home. There is little about this faded, once-grand tourist town that helps me explain who Larry Bird really is. For those who don't know basketball, one of the best-known "facts" about the real Larry Bird is that he is said to have been the hardest working white-guy in basketball history. He practiced and practiced, long after he had become one of the game's immortals. In sports culture, the legend is that this is what made him great and it was the values of small-town Midwest life that accounted for Bird's basketball genius. Perhaps, but not likely. This is just another mediated story, one that gains currency through the avaricious talk of the sports media (again the word). Whatever made Larry Bird great almost surely had only the most accidental relation to that small town. I have lived in small Midwestern towns. Most of the white guys are like young white-guys everywhere. They don't practice much of anything. In fact they spend much of their time drinking beer and talking about how small-town life made men like Bird different. When we know what we know about culture, even the heroes of sports culture, we know it today in mediated form, behind which it is awfully hard to find the real thing.

The same is true, more true, of characters like Madonna, who is almost purely an artifact of televisual culture. Televisual media are unlike others. Radio, by contrast, is usually said to be a medium that invites the listener to expand his or her imagination. I am old enough to have listened as a boy to the Cincinnati Reds baseball games on radio broadcast in the days when broadcasters seldom traveled with the team. So, when the Reds were in St Louis, the account of the game was transmitted from the radio station in Cincinnati by a broadcaster who literally made up the action he described from teletype facts. From a telegraphic code something like: "2out/2:1/29StL at bat, K," we heard "Blackwell winds, holds the runner at first, throws. Another blazing fastball, inside corner. Strike. He's got his stuff tonight." Radio (before today's top forty and talk-a-thon formats) was like that. One had to imagine to get it.

Movies are more different still. One "goes to" the movies, and there enters into a darkened environment in which a story is projected from behind on to a huge screen, so huge that one loses oneself in the images and sounds. I hate to admit it, but *Bridges of Madison County* made me cry, and I can't say why. The film is about longing and lost loves. But I saw the film with the love of my life who was right there crying with me. We passed the same popcorn napkin back and forth. What is the power of the movies to evoke deep feelings in such an artificial environment, bad popcorn and all? Somehow this is a medium that by projecting images before us causes us to project ourselves into those images, drawing out feeling from our unconsciousness. But the movies, like radio, are not, for the most part, the least postmodern. When a movie is over we leave, and leave behind the feelings. I can remember still crying a little two miles out from town on the way back home. But when we got home, I am further embarrassed to say, we flipped on the TV to check the Yankees game, and all we had felt ten minutes before was gone, completely.

Televisual media are different because they are *in* our lives. I once saw Madonna's memoir film, *Truth or Dare*, two nights after its release in a remote vacation village. It was a Sunday night. In the sparse crowd, I recognized the famous feminist journalist, writer, and organizer, Betty Friedan, author of the classic work of American feminism, *The Feminine Mystique*. I never got up the nerve to ask her what she thought of Madonna's gender politics. But, her presence made the setting and the film itself all the more bizarre. There was Betty Friedan, an icon of modern feminism, watching Madonna, an icon of postmodern, postfeminism. Madonna plays so wildly with images of female sexuality that the issues feminists care about are at once oddly accentuated and blurred. The movie was a documentary. Its portrayal of Madonna's behind-the-scenes activities revealed a style that seemed to me little different from the concert performances or the videos. She had no particular "real life" story to tell. Movies are meant to tell stories with beginnings and endings. Television, by contrast, immerses the viewer in a sea of loosely organized, provocative images. Madonna is a product of television. She enters our lives and hearts as we channel surf from this to that, make trips to the bathroom or the fridge, or tape stuff so we can occasionally go out into the "real" world to do whatever — attend a class, rake a few leaves, shop around.

This is the nature of televisual culture. It is composed in large part by us *in the very course of the life* in which we are composing our daily lives. Thus, as MTV video lasts, at the most, a few minutes, because televisual "events" must be fitted in, by the channel surfing viewers, among other tubal attractions and events occurring without interruption around the house — cats or babies crying, thunder storms, gun shots in the hallway, whatever. You cannot make a movie of Madonna because there is not story there. She's a TV thing, about five minutes at the most. She's good enough to get us to stop for those minutes, but there is not much there, after or before. This is what makes televisual and advanced televisual media like video games and the Internet different from other media and so effective in the course of world affairs. They are not *unreal* or even *irreal* (that is, extreme distortions of the real). Hyperreality is some other dimension of reality that borrows its images and contents from a purported real world which then remakes them in vastly more complex mediated forms than one ever experiences in the so-called real world. The *hyperreal* is, literally, more real than reality itself. It is highly unlikely, for example, that there is a real family anywhere as "super-real" as that of Ozzie and Harriet or of the Huxtable–Cosby's.

It is pervasive experiences such as those we have had through exposure to televisual culture that lend plausibility to the idea of postmodernism, and they lend it even when we are unable to provide a proper theory of the culture's effect on us. But, please note, I said "the plausibility of the postmodern." The postmodern cannot be proven, as I have said, because, if it exists, it exists as a world order that exaggerates the world of real facts and evidence. As a result, social theories of the postmodern are not so much arguments from undisputed facts as representations of a way of understanding the world. This does not mean, however, that postmodern social theories are uninterested in the real world. On the contrary, they take "reality" with, you might say, extreme seriousness because they begin from the assumption that in a televisual culture the reality of the world is always *mediated* — that is, not directly present to those who live in the world.

This, then, is the sense in which the world is seen as *post*modern. Postmodernism is the culture that takes seriously the breaking apart of the world, which, if this is what is happening, is clearly a question of just how hyperreal is reality? It is thereby a question to which evidence of a sort can be brought, if only to provoke one's thinking about what is going on.

The Claim That the World Might Be Postmodern

It cannot be proven, as I said, that the world has become postmodern. In fact, one of the central tenets of postmodern philosophies is that nothing can be *proven*, everything is open to argument, everything is more a truth-claim than a stable argument.[4]

Not only this, but it is all too easy to forget that whenever one is talking about massive changes in world structures it takes several hundred years before any considerable number of people will agree that the change has indeed taken place.[5] Consider, for a moment, just how long it must have taken for moderns to realize that the traditional feudal world was irretrievably gone. Even today people are searching for some way to return to the simpler times of agrarian, village life. Vermont and Montana are, as you read, filling up with urban migrants doing just that. And no one would visit the world's ancient sites, like Kyongju, were she not enchanted by the past before the world had changed. So, one does not have to be a determined modernist in order to be cautious before the claim the world has changed.

Thus, if postmodernism is not what one thinks, it is important to state the evidence for its reality, even if that evidence will not do much more than explain the prior and intriguing question: Why are so many people, often against their wills, concerned about postmodernism? It is impossible to go anywhere in the world without encountering intellectuals, artists, or politicians wondering about postmodernity. I have on my shelves, at latest count, some 35 books on postmodernism. This is an interesting number because, to the best of my recollection, I have purchased no more than two of them. All the rest were sent as unsolicited copies by various publishers. If so many appear without asking how many others must there be? More interesting yet, two of the most frequently cited books on the subject are by authors who take a decidedly negative attitude towards postmodernism.[6] If the subject occasions such feeling, and causes people who are not postmodernists to write about postmodernism, then we know, virtually for certain, that something real is going on out there. But what might be the evidence, so to speak, for it?

One does not have to be a postmodernist to grant that the world is changing. At the least it is obvious that the world which for a long time has been thought of as "modern" is experiencing a crisis of grave and global proportions. What the changes mean exactly we cannot know for certain, but it is clear that they are disrupting the most fundamental structures that underlie the modern world — structures that were built up and have endured for nearly half a millennium. Though one could describe the changes in various ways, I suggest just the three most obvious and serious:

1) The Euro-American world colonial system has collapsed, suddenly and completely, within the very short world time of a third of a century or so. The collapse began with the successful decolonizing movements in the late 1940s and 1950s in which, first India, then China, were liberated from direct or indirect colonial rule. Through the 1950s most of Europe's African colonies were struggling toward liberation. By 1959, Cuba threw off American rule and, by the end of the 1960s, most of the Caribbean, Asia, and Africa were free of European political control, however much many continued to rely on economic relations with the West. Most notably, the defeat of the Americans in Vietnam marked the most impressive decolonizing event of the 1970s. But the similar defeat of the Soviets in Afghanistan somewhat later was, though less noisy, more important because the Soviet failure in this colonizing war sapped too much moral and economic capital from an already weak Soviet system. Here was a notable instance in which failure to colonize led directly to a collapse of the colonizing regime itself. By 1990, it was not just the Cold War that had ended. More important, far more important, is that by then the colo-

nial system that had begun half a millennium earlier in the 1490s was at its end, at least as a formal world political system.

In the simplest of terms, the collapse of the colonial system has destroyed the foundational economic base for the so-called modern world. Obviously, this does not mean that all that went before has disappeared. In fact, a newly structured world system has come fast on the heels of the original modern one. But the fact remains (even if we do not agree on what it means) that the classic modern world system, one based on a half-millennium of colonization, has collapsed.

2) One of the most enduring features of that classic system was that there was always one, mostly unrivaled, imperial center.[7] In the sixteenth century it was the Iberian powers, in the seventeenth it was the Dutch; by the nineteenth it had become the British, by mid-twentieth century it had become the United States. References to Pax Britannica or the American Century were references to the days when Great Britain and the United States were the guarantors of the world order such as it was. It hardly needs to be said that such imperial power (even when the term empire was studiously avoided) meant also that these great nation-states were as much the center of world culture as of the world economic and political system. But not any more.

The so-called defeat of communism and the triumph of the capitalist societies in 1990 have left the world without an unchallenged center. The United States is still the world's most powerful economy by volume, and US military might is without peer. But such a qualified power this is. The size of its economy is limited by its economic and social debts — debts so severe that no one quite knows how to settle them. Shortly after the turn of the millennium, Japan will likely pass the US in GNP. Still, to be sure, no other nation rivals America's military capability. But what use is all that technological finesse in wars like the one against Iraq in which, afterward, Kuwait was "liberated" but the real target, Sadam Hussein, remained securely in power? And what can military sophistication do in a world where a chemically treated pile of manure is sufficient to destroy a federal building in Oklahoma City?

Today the world lacks the center it always had in the modern, colony-based world economy. The new arrangement for world domination (or, if you prefer, world order) is at best one in which a group of North American and European states plus Japan, consulting guardedly with Russia and China, rule the world economy. They do not agree with each other and are seldom able to impose their political will where, in places like Bosnia, Somalia, or the Middle East, regional interests are sharply defined. The most pervasive fact of the world order today is that the plight of the most hungry and most poor is so much worse than once anyone would have imagined and that there is no world center of power willing or able to do anything about it. At least, under the colonial system, the great power centers claimed to care about their subjects and believed they could do something about their supposedly inferior states of learning and well-being. Today, fewer care, and hardly anyone believes that good can really get done.

The absence of an unchallenged political and economic Center in world affairs since the collapse of the American post-World War II hegemony is the most striking fact of today's world order. It is indeed a new world order, but not a very promising one and, without much doubt, it is *not* very similar to the system that ruled the world during the modern era. In the absence of a dominant core state, the definitive structure of the modern world has lost its classic form.

3) Along with the collapse of the center, the world has experienced the rise of dramatic, vital, and persuasive opposition to the very idea of a uni-fied and universal world culture based on Euro-American values. The modern world is itself a pervasive culture based on a compelling theory of the world. In the simplest of terms, that theory was that the West was best and that the culture that took definite shape in Europe and North America in the eighteenth century was, in the famous words of the American Declaration of Independence, the self-evident truth of "all men." Life, liberty, and the pursuit of happiness are fine values. Though I would personally like to see more assurance of equal distribution built into the happiness ideal, this is a good list of virtues to which indeed all men and women might aspire. But the culture of the modern world was one in which it was assumed that these truths were not just "self-evi-dent," but were the hard and fast universal ideals to which all *must* aspire. What else could explain the naive self-confidence with which Europeans and Americans felt they could and should descend anywhere in the world both to teach their ways to the natives and take home what-ever they found to be of economic worth? The universal right of self-evident truth was so closely mixed up with the presumptive right to extract ("steal" if you prefer) wealth from other people of other cultures that one hardly questioned it. Leaving aside for the moment the slave trade and related means of stealing other peoples' lives and labor, the modern world system was (or, is) one that entailed the principle that the truth was so obvious that the stealing could not really be stealing. There is little reason to believe that the Romans were interested in their colonies for anything other than pure imperial motive. They left behind aqueducts, civil codes, and administrative practices because colonizers always leave something behind, not because it had been the Roman moral mission to redeem the world. But the British in India and the

Americans in Vietnam actually thought they were doing good by right and responsibility of the superiority of their culture. That is the way of modern culture.

But the once supreme confidence of modernist cultures is no longer respected, as but a short list of all too real events suggests:

- the resistance by New Social Movements (such as feminist, race-based, or gay rights movements) within the North American and European nations;
- the reemergence of ethnicities, as opposed to nationalities, as a primary basis of social identification, particularly in the collapsed sphere of influence of the former Soviet Union (Chechnya, for example);
- the reappearance of traditionalist cultures as a basis for opposition to American and other modernist cultures in the form of various religious fundamentalisms (Christian in the United States, Muslim in the Middle East and parts of Asia and Africa).

Modernity's long-standing claim to be THE universal culture of human progress lacks the global legitimacy it once demanded and, to a surprising extent, was granted.

This list could be much longer, or arranged differently, but this one is sufficient for present purposes. As you can see, there is more than enough reason to suspect that the co-called modern world has changed, or is changing, with respect to three of its most fundamental features: the colonial system from which core states extracted natural and labor resources;[8] the organizing centers from which they administered world politics and exploited world markets; the presumptive culture on the basis of which the Euro-American centers successively and collectively constructed interpretive principles to account for world dynamics or, one might say, "world history."

In other words, three of the most essential characteristics of the global system that emerged in the late fifteenth century with the first systematic and continuing European intrusions into Africa, the Americas, and Asia are in a state of flux, if not outright collapse. One might even speculate that the change is in the direction of a reversion to what were once called primate social orders. But whichever the direction, and nature of the change, something is changing, and the world thus changing is the world that was once called, without serious controversy, "the modern world." *That* it is changing accounts for the fact that the question is asked everywhere one goes, even by those who still believe in and seek to defend modernity. That it is changing in ways that involve the breaking apart of the 500-year-old structure based in a colonial system (or its analogues) controlled by one or another Euro-American state creates the distinctive impressions that are associated with postmodern theories of the world.

It would be hard to ignore the coincidence between the world's actual structure as it is changing and the main features of postmodern theories. As we will see in the next section, most postmodern theories argue that a once linear and well-defined world has given way to one that can be characterized by such terms as fragmented, decentered, playful, anarchical, ironic, indeterminate. Where the modern world was allegedly well-organized along a linear history yielding straightforward meanings, the postmodern world is thought to be poorly organized in the absence of a clear, predictable historical future without which there are, at best, uncertain, playful, or ironic meanings.

Postmodern Social Theories Today

There are, as I said, three compelling, and inherently important, positions with respect to the postmodernism question. They are: *radical postmodernism*, of which Jean Baudrillard's theory discussed above is a good example; *radical modernism*, which objects to theories like Baudrillard's while granting that something has changed but not enough to consider modernity dead; and *strategic postmodernism*, which in its way shares aspects of the former two — a postmodern readiness to think of the world as transformed by a strategic and appreciative reconsideration of modernist culture.

Radical postmodernism

Radical postmodernism considers modernity a thing of the past because it believes the present situation is, again, hyperreal. This, the first of three positions in the debate, has already been introduced briefly above, where Jean Baudrillard was first discussed. To understand postmodernism one must understand why a serious social theorist like Baudrillard would come to the ideas he holds about the mediated, spectacular nature of today's social world.

Baudrillard has written some books in which he appears to be perfectly frivolous. One of these is *Cool Memories* (1990), a journal of aphorisms drawn from visits to the United States (mostly California) in the early 1980s. But, such excursions aside, Baudrillard's thinking is deeply rooted in the classics of social thought, Marx and Freud especially. For example, Baudrillard's early writings in the late 1960s and early 1970s are quite original and, in my opinion, rigorous interpretations of the consumer society based on ideas drawn from Marx's theory of values reinterpreted partly through a Freudian view of the fetishized desire to consume commodified objects. Among Baudrillard's early books was *For a Critique of the Political Economy of Signs* (1972) in which he persuasively demonstrated the value of *semiotics* (the social study of signs and sign systems) to Marx's theory of the economic values of consumable commodities. Though in these early writings Baudrillard already displayed his penchant for the original, even perverse, insight, his writings were a reasonable and compelling contribution to the sociology of post-industrial society (an early, modernist precursor of the postmodernism idea).

So, one might ask, why might his thinking have changed from the scholarly study of Marx to the writing of aphorisms on California? Without going into the details, it is easiest to suggest the reasons by noting that in 1968 Baudrillard was professor of sociology at the Nanterre campus of the University of Paris. It was on this campus, in the spring of 1968, that the famous student rebellions broke out, soon spreading across Paris, eventually to most of the urban centers of France. Of all the student rebellions worldwide in the 1960s few had a more paralyzing effect on their society as a whole. There was a moment that spring when, quite literally, all of Paris was consumed by the spectacle of pitched battles between police and students and workers, by public demonstrations and debates about the quality of life in France, and eventually by the remarkable drama of the President of France, Charles de Gaulle, quitting the homeland in order to rally the French foreign legion to retake Paris just as, almost a quarter of a century before, he had led the Allied troops as the Nazis fled France. De Gaulle's 1968 heroics turned out to be laughably unnecessary. The whole drama of *mai '68* was a replaying of France's historic dramas. For the young radicals it was in part a renewal fantasy of the storming of the Bastille in 1789 and the revitalization of the dream of a new society.

At about the same time many thousands of Baudrillard's generation in the US participated in civil rights and anti-war demonstrations, often recalling the sacred texts of the American revolution of 1776. These movements were deadly serious business. Hundreds were injured and some died. But they also had the aspect of a huge national drama — if not a game, at least a public theater. This effect was heightened in two ways: first, by the ever-present television cameras which altered the events themselves as a consequence of being watched;[9] second, by the ultimate failure of most of the actions which at the time seemed certain to be true revolutions. Both of these secondary effects lent to social participation an aura of what later came to be called hyperreality. Social experience was incredibly intensified, making it seem all too real, yet in the end not tangibly real at all.

Many of those active in politics in the 1960s came away from it all with a qualified sense of accomplishment. There were some real changes, but most of them faded into caricatures of the original dream. Civil rights gains are today being reversed. The war in Vietnam was ended, but the militarism continues. Poverty in America was discovered anew, but the number of hungry and homeless has grown. Far from being producers of a new social order, we were destined to become consumers of a culture that was subjected to an ever intensified recommodification. The very culture of the 1960s is today repackaged and resold for a generation of youth born well after the sixties were over. Sixties happenings like *The Grateful Dead* and *The Rolling Stones* — for that matter the very form of the rock concert itself — linger on as bizarre simulations behind which all the original political and cultural ideals are barely intelligible, if at all.

You can see the likely correspondence between the events Baudrillard experienced in his relative youth in the 1960s and the ideas he came to articulate with greater and greater intensity in subsequent years. He was far from alone. In 1967, just before Baudrillard published his first book, Guy Debord published what has since become a kind of radical post-modernist manifesto, *Society as Spectacle*, which began:

> In societies where modern conditions of production prevail, all life presents itself as an immense accumulation of *spectacles*. Everything that was directly lived has moved away into a representation. . . . The spectacle is not a collection of images, but a social relation among people mediated by images.[10]

If you find these remarks a bit obscure, just reread them with the following questions in mind: In your opinion, how often do most people get their information about "what's really happening" from representations and images produced by televisual media rather than from direct experience? How much do the people you know live directly? What role does the culture represented in their media (television, Internet, CD-ROM, VCR) play in their lives? You do not have to believe this is a good thing (as some naive radical postmodernists seem to suggest) to see that it captures a compelling truth about the world we live in.

Radical postmodernists like Baudrillard and Debord are the writers opponents of any kind of postmodernism love to hate. Unfortunately, even such a radical position as theirs is not as simple as it may seem. This discomforting fact is illustrated by reference to a writer whose ideas are taken seriously be radical postmodernists and some less radical ones; even by some modernists. It is possible that the most frequently quoted of all philosophical discussions of postmodernism is a book by Jean-François Lyotard. In his essay *The Postmodern Condition: A Report on Knowledge* (first published in French in 1979), Lyotard provided an influential summary of a radical postmodernism. I quote just two statements from an otherwise complicated argument: "Scientific knowledge is a kind of discourse" (p. 3) And: "I define *postmodern* as incredulity toward meta-narratives" (p. xxiv). The argument that connects these two statements is this: All knowledge, including science, has a social basis and is supported by the shared culture of the society in which the knowledge is produced. "$E = mc^2$" may be true scientifically, but it is also an article of cultural faith to those who believe the legends about Einstein and modern science, even to those who have no idea what it means. The culture by which science itself, as well as its particular knowledges, is a widespread, social faith in grand stories — in metanarratives, of which the legend of Einstein is a part.

Lyotard's argument continues: Science and other forms of knowledge depend on the legitimacy in which the culture holds them. Modernity, thus, is that culture which believes certain *metanarratives*, or widely shared stories, about the value and "truth" of science, and truth itself. This is an important way in which science is discourse. In short, then, post-modernity is that culture in which those metanarratives are no longer considered completely legitimate and, thus, are not universally held to be completely credible.

One of the consequences of such a theory as Lyotard's is the assumption that if what modern knowledge says about reality is no longer held to be automatically true, then in this sense "reality" itself is held in some doubt. Postmodernism is about this incredulity and its effects throughout society. One could say that Madonna and Michael Jackson exhibit a certain inexpressible incredulity toward modern sexual morality — by making themselves the be-all and end-all of sexual and gender possibilities they point beyond themselves to something more real than reality. Baudrillard, for example, has said the following of Michael Jackson:

> He has constructed himself in every tiny detail. It is this which makes him a pure, innocent child — the artificial androgyne of the fable, who, better than Christ, can reign over the world and bring reconciliation, because he is better than the child-god: he is a prosthesis-child, an embryo of all the forms of mutation we have imagined to deliver us from race and sex.[11]

As you can see, when it comes to doubting reality Lyotard and Baudrillard are not far apart. Indeed, Lyotard is often seen, as I said, as a radical postmodernist. But Lyotard's postmodernism is in fact more complicated and cautious than Baudrillard's.

The English edition of Lyotard's *The Postmodern Condition* ends with the cryptic statement: "Let us wage a war on totality; . . . let us activate the differences and save the honor of the name."[12] What he means is that in modernity the power of those metanarratives created the illusion that the world was itself whole or, in the language of philosophy, a totality — a myth that had the effect of suppressing differences. Though, as I said, postmodernists of both kinds wage war on totality — on cultures that want to unify the human race around grand but artificial ideas and, in some instances, fascist politics — so too do many modernisms. This is why one cannot understand postmodernism without studying the more radical modernists as well.

Just to show how complicated this debate is, Lyotard's statement is one that could be supported by prominent representatives of *both* radical modernism and strategic postmodernism, as we shall now see.

Radical modernism

"Let us wage war on totality" is a slogan the meaning of which depends mostly on what one thinks about the world itself. For most postmodernists (radical and strategic alike) it refers to the deceptions of modern culture by which the dream of a universal humanity based on Western ideals imposes itself and thus restricts human freedom. Behind all the humanistic idealism of modern culture, postmodernists find a deeper desire to suppress the unspeakable social differences that disrupt the ideal. This is known as the critique of *essentialism*, or the critique of the cultural ideal which holds that social differences are at best incidental variances on one, universal, true and essential human nature.

Radical *modernists*, on the other hand, believe that this critique, while sensitive to important political and moral issues, is itself dangerous. Instead, they view the sad effects of totalization as a *social* failure under certain historical conditions, but not as an inherent flaw of modernity itself. Today, the single most important tradition of radical modernism is the German school of *critical theory*, often known as the "Frankfurt School" after the city in which its original institute was located in the 1930s. One need only reflect on the time and place of this school's founding to imagine what its most formative historical experience was. The Nazi reign of terror in Germany and Western Europe was nothing if it was not the imposition of a totalizing system of culture and politics. The Frankfurt theorists were among the first to see that the Enlightenment ideal of a true, universal humanity was also at risk of being distorted into the kind of evil Hitler actually unleashed. Hitler wanted to eliminate human differences, to create a pure, universal master race.

From the beginning, the Frankfurt School was intent upon rethinking the classic texts of the Enlightenment tradition as well as the social theories of Karl Marx, Max Weber, and Sigmund Freud. The idea was (and is) to produce a social philosophy that could both draw on these sources *and* remain actively critical of both of them and of modern society. Hence, the appellation "critical theory." Critical theory could just as easily be considered that school of social theory most devoted to "waging war on totality," at least as much as any postmodernism. Indeed, Lyotard's line is very nearly a rephrasing of the classic idea of Theodor Adorno, one of the founders of the Frankfurt School, who once said that "Auschwitz demonstrated that culture has failed," and who believed that the whole is always untrue.[13]

One of the consequences of the historical situation of the critical theorists was that, by the end of the 1930s, most of the original Frankfurt School members had fled Hitler's Germany, mostly for the United States. There they continued their work, often applying it to other sociological subjects in which the problem of totalization is evident. One of these was mass culture. It is well known that, among other of his evils, Hitler was a master manipulator of the masses. It is not surprising, therefore, that the critical theorists, once they were ensconced in the United States, turned their attention to such subjects as the mass media — radio, Hollywood movies, even jazz and other forms of popular music.

It is safe to say that Adorno, were he still living, would be no fan of Madonna, hip-hop, or Michael Jackson. His critical theory was profoundly suspicious of any form of culture with mass appeal which, because of his direct historical experience with fascism, he considered inevitably a totalizing force destructive of human freedom. "The culture industry," Adorno once said,[14] "intentionally integrates its consumers from above." In other words, Adorno would have seen phenomena like Madonna as anything but a liberating playing out of *popular* desires with respect to sex, sexuality, and gender. He would have been far more inclined to view them as, to use his word, the intentional manipulation of popular consciousness by a totalizing industry serving elite corporate interests for which the media, especially television, are the most important instruments for manufacturing consumer tastes for goods and services.

Another critical theorist, Herbert Marcuse, developed a version of this idea in his book, *One Dimensional Man* (1964). This book became one of the "must reads" of 1960s cultural radicals who also believed that the dominant powers in society had made ordinary people one dimensional, that is: lacking in the critical capacity to stand outside the cultural forces shaping them. If you wonder what this might mean, just ask yourself the next time you're hanging out watching MTV what most of those videos are really saying to you about who you are supposed to be? And how easy or difficult is it for you, on those occasions, to be critical of their effects on your life, even if the only "critique" is that, while you were hanging out you could have been reading a book, not to mention organizing a political rally?

Today the most important critical theorist is the German social theorist, Jürgen Habermas. Like others in this tradition, Habermas's voluminous writings usually dwell on depth reinterpretations of the classic texts of modernity. Also like his predecessors, Habermas is critical of the Enlightenment tradition with its dangerous temptations to essentialize all humanity into a one-dimensional totality shorn of real differences. Yet, this position is a radical *modernism* because it seeks critically to discover the liberating potential in modern culture. It would be impossible here even to begin to demonstrate the details of how Habermas does this. But it can be illustrated by quoting from one of his most straightforward definitional statements of the basic concepts of social thought:

> I call *culture* the store of knowledge from which those engaged in communicative action draw interpretations susceptible of consensus as they come to an understanding about something in the world. I call *society* (in the narrower sense of a component of the lifeworld) the legitimate orders from which those engaged in communicative action gather a solidarity, based on belonging to groups, as they enter into interpersonal relationships with one another. *Personality* serves as a term of art for acquired competences that render a subject capable of speech and action and hence able to participate in processes of mutual understanding in a given context and to maintain his own identity in the shifting contexts of interaction.[15]

If you have not read Habermas previously, this may seem a little abstract (and, indeed, his writing is abstract in the sense of being highly theoretical). But even so, you can see that behind the concepts is a deep, abiding respect for the liberating and community-building potential of human beings. Culture, far from being merely an imposed integration (as Adorno put it), allows people to communicate in ways that can build consensus. Society, far from being a totalizing abstraction, is rooted in the life world of ordinary people coming into relations with each other. Personality, far from being a passive vehicle of the subjugating force of totalities, refers to the art of participation and of keeping true to one's identity. You can see, at least, that Habermas's radical critique of modernity serves the purpose of radically rethinking modernity to serve the ideal of human freedom and community.

If you still find this abstract, remember that this tradition of radical modernism was originally forged in the terrible furnaces of the Holocaust from whence comes its steadfast commitment to protecting the human spirit. This also is one of the reasons radical modernists hold to the grand humanistic principles of the modern age. The business they are about is far too serious, in their experience, for them to sacrifice known principles of emancipation for the whim of a fractious postmodernism that presents itself too often in the spectacle of popular culture. Where, really, is the common humanity you or I share with the-artist-formerly-known-as-Prince or Michael Jackson? It must be there behind the show, but radical modernists are too sober to play. One must respect their reasons.

There are quite a number of radical modernisms today.[16] At their best, they share this sense of sober regard for the human values of the modern age. One of them is a line of contemporary feminism which, like the earliest critical theorists, writes social theory out of a very clear sense of the oppressions women have suffered and, consequently, the urgent need to protect some universal principles of ideal humanity with which to wage war on totalizing attempts to ignore the differences sexism has imposed on women's lives.[17] Some consider this position still too essentialist. But the important fact about radical modernism is that, far from dismissing postmodernism, it is engaged with it in order to redefine the modernist ideal.

Strategic postmodernism

There is a category of thinkers who are commonly lumped together with the radical postmodernists even though there is little evidence they would (or would have) accepted the designation for themselves. This is because when social theorists try to understand postmodernism they quite naturally gravitate to the writings of figures who have justifiably strong reputations and whose thinking *seems* to be postmodern. The most famous of these are three French social thinkers: Michel Foucault, Jacques Derrida, and Jacques Lacan. (Of these, only Derrida still lives but I will speak of them nonetheless in the literary present tense.)

Foucault, Derrida, and Lacan share the following general theoretical views: 1) a commitment to reinterpreting the modern classic social thinkers (Nietzsche, Husserl, and Freud, respectively — among many others); 2) a conviction that language, or discourse, is fundamental to any science of the human; 3) a rejection of any version of the ideal of a universal essence, totality, or center as a basis for social thought. You can see immediately that the first two of these three points fails to distinguish them from either of the two groups of radicals. All three of the groups are devoted to rewriting the classics in one fashion or another. And all three are involved in what Habermas and others have called the "linguistic turn" in social theory. Only the third of the three general attributes of the strategic postmodernists can be said to be a distinctively postmodern social idea. This is, in fact, the principle that most strongly separates post-modernists of both kinds from modernists of all kinds. Yet, when this principle is examined closely enough, it is plain that it is also a point of demarcation between the two kinds of postmodernism.

Strategic postmodernists differ from radical ones in the way they attack the totalizing aspects of modernist essentialism — that is, in the way they wage war on totality. They are far less inclined to take for granted that the world has yet changed. They might, in fact, be properly accused of wishing the world were changed or acting as though it had. But in their writings, they take a more modest attitude toward culture and world reality than the radical postmodernists. Like the radical modernists, strategic postmodernists are less concerned to imagine the new world, than to rethink and rewrite modernity itself. In this sense they too are critical theorists of a special kind.

Here is where the most famous of the words associated with postmod-ernism must be mentioned: *deconstruction*. This is a more difficult term to use correctly than many realize. Notice please that the word is not "deconstruction*ism*." Strategic postmodernism is most emphatically opposed to any "ism" because it considers ideology one of the most tricky and debilitating features of modern culture. Nor is the word meant to be a sly cognate for "*des*truction" — though some of the word's abusers jump to this conclusion because they view deconstruction all too simply as a "taking apart" of modern culture. There is nothing destructive or, as it is sometimes said, "nihilistic" about strategic postmodernism (though this might be said more accurately of some radical postmodernists). Nor should the word be used casually in the infinitive form, "to deconstruct," which suggests a transitive action, as in "Madonna deconstructs sexu-ality." Deconstruction is not a new method, though it is taken as such by those with a loose understanding of Jacques Derrida, the originator of the idea. Deconstruction is more an attitude, a way of working with culture in order to reconstrue it.

Derrida's basic ideas were first presented in two early and very difficult books (both originally published in 1967, just before the student and worker rebellions in France): *Of Grammatology* and *Writing and Difference*. One of the reasons Derrida's writings are so difficult for the first-time reader is that he writes in an unusual manner, but for a purpose.

Derrida believes it is impossible even for the critics of modernity to abandon the culture and the language of modernity. Thus, the only way to be critical of modernity is to subvert it by using its own language and ideas against it. In his early writings, therefore, Derrida often spoke of putting language under erasure — of using the words and concepts one *must* use, but to put an "X" through them, literally in some cases, figuratively in most. To give an example of my own making: How is it possible to criticize Reason (one of modernity's most sacred cultural ideals) without being "reasonable" or using the word "reason" and speaking in the "logic" of reasonable people? In order to be critical of the concept one must use the term critically. While the radical modernists would seek (to put it simply) to improve modernity's concept (as in the case of Habermas's attempt to give a more reasonable and emancipatory definition of "culture"), the strategic postmodernists seek to use the term just as it is, but, by various literary means (like erasing it while keeping it visible), to call attention to its limitations and problems. As a result, Derrida's writings ooze with various stylistic ironies of this sort.

A somewhat easier to understand irony used in deconstruction is the *double entendre*, or "double meaning." The most famous of those used by Derrida is also the one that best illustrates his basic theory of modernity. In the French language, the words *différence* and *différance* sound exactly the same when spoken. But, in writing, their meanings are distinct. The former means what it means in English, but the latter, *différance* with an "a," means "the act of deferring," or "of putting off for a later time." Now you might wonder what in the world do "differences" have to do with the act of "deferring"? The answer is quite surprising.

The two terms (and the cultural concepts they convey) refer to the most fundamental facts of modern society and culture. To explain this, I will use ideas that are faithful to Derrida but are a somewhat free interpretation of his thinking. As we have seen, the postmodern critique of modernity's essentialism is an attack on modern culture's inability to tolerate or even to recognize the importance of actual social differences. Social theorists who rely on Derrida would say that the fact of differences is so fundamental that it appears even in the most subtle aspects of culture, most especially in the very language with which we speak.[18]

One of the ways, says Derrida, that the fact of differences is masked and ignored is by the privilege modern culture accords to speech over writing. By this he does not mean that Western culture has no appreciation of great writing. Rather he is referring to the assumption made in Western culture that speaking is presumed to be the "most original" and "most basic" form of communication. Think about it. We are suspicious of relationships and communications that are not "face to face." Our culture does indeed place a very heavy emphasis on "direct" talk, which is taken as the "more honest" and "more human" type of communication. One of the reasons we are suspicious of lawyers is that they reduce everything to writing. Conversely, perhaps one of the reasons we are seduced by televisual media is that they create the illusion of "being there" in some primary way (which of course we know not to be so). Visual media allow us to "see" and "hear" what people are "really" saying. Lincoln's Gettysburg Address would have been a flop of TV. In fact it was a flop at Gettysburg when spoken. But it was a brilliant success when published. Why? What is at issue is the difference between speech and writing.

Derrida believes that the difference (take note) between speech and writing is that in writing the meaning of what is being said is "deferred." Americans really did not get the meaning of the Gettysburg Address until long after it was spoken. Most of those present on November 19, 1863 at Gettysburg could not even hear Lincoln. But, and this is important, the meaning of the address itself was dependent on its reference, most of all, to the horrible battle in which 51,000 men were killed. The Civil War was, still is, the worst nightmare in American history — worse even than Vietnam. At Gettysburg, as we know, the hope dawned that the tide had turned — that the Union would be preserved, the slaves emancipated. A follower of Derrida, thus, might say that Lincoln's address was actually a piece of writing that called forth at a later time the "historical writing" or "inscription" of the moral meaning of the Civil War and its most famous battle in the American psyche. If you doubt this, visit the battlefield and see whether or not something is not inscribed there, even now in the quiet hills and monuments. In other words, Derrida argues that human culture and history are the primary "inscriptions" of human meaning — written, if you will, in the monuments, battlefields, village and urban plans, on literally the whole of culture which always imposes its visible markings on the landscape of a nation. But, these meanings are *deferred*. We get them after the fact, with some work, if at all.

Against this, compare the illusion of the "primary meanings" associated with speech. Of course, they are very slippery. A speaker can always say (as politicians do), "Oh, but I didn't mean it." But when something is written — whether on the back of an envelope, or on a battlefield — its marks remain, and its truth is definite. Writing, in effect, cannot ever be completely erased. Thus, again treating Derrida somewhat loosely, we can say that a strategic postmodernism is based on a critique of Western culture's privileging of "primary speech" as an illusion that broadcasts true meanings as though their truth were derived from their immediacy.

It is the illusion that social meanings are immediately available which, among much else, masks the fact of differences.

Likewise, the spoken words *différence/différance* are indistinguishable in speech, while in writing their important differences are evident. Modernity, therefore, could be said to work its cultural effects by centering culture on the ideal of primary, essential meaning (idealized in the face-to-face speaker, the truth-giver). In this, modern culture has hidden all the many subtle, complicated, and embarrassing meanings of its history. Not the least of which is the fact that modernity struggles with the reality of social differences just as it seeks to bring all meanings into the present moment. The problem is that if social differences such as those of class, racial, and gender divisions are real (as they surely are), then the meaning of those differences will be "deferred" or postponed and put off in the pious platitudes of the politicians. But, to anyone who "reads" the writing of urban ghettos torn by economic misery, of women bruised by violence, of neighborhoods pocked by dilapidation, or of monuments to dead young warriors, the painful reality of differences could not be more evident.

This is why, in the spirit of Derrida, strategic postmodernism can be understood as more cautious than radical postmodernism but more critical even than radical modernism. Thus, one could say that a very great deal of this line of postmodernism is engaged in the process of rewriting the history of modernity. Derrida himself is a philosopher, so his rewriting is directed at philosophers (from Husserl, the subject of his first book, to Marx, the subject of one of his latest). Beyond Derrida, this kind of post-modernism has had an important influence on feminism, gay-lesbian, African-American and other of the new forms of social knowledge. While not all African-Americanists consider themselves postmodernists of any kind, nor followers of Derrida, they do enjoy a certain similarity of purpose. African-American studies, like feminism and queer studies, are in large part attempts to rewrite the history of society in ways that are explicitly critical of the culture's exclusion of blacks, women, and gay and lesbian people.

This reconstructive style appears in another of the strategic postmodernists. Michel Foucault is perhaps somewhat easier to understand than Derrida because his subject matter is more historical and within the range of common experience.

Foucault, who died in 1984 of AIDS, wrote books on an amazing range of topics — on madness and the rise of modern psychology (for example, *Madness and Civilization* in 1961), on the emergence of modern medical practice (*Birth of the Clinic* in 1963), on the history of the social and human sciences (*The Order of Things* in 1966), on the early modern penitentiary (*Discipline and Punish*, 1975). What these studies have in common is that all are about the histories of the most distinctive institutions of modern society. Many scholars agree that one of the most unusual features of modernity is its attempt, and claim, to treat all persons in a more humane way by doing away with the terrors often associated with feudal societies. This is one of the reasons we associate the culture of "humanism" with modernity itself. All of the institutions Foucault wrote about were notable for their apparent commitment to using gentle, humane, and liberal (another word associated with modern culture) means to heal the ill, understand social life, and rehabilitate the criminal. Like Marx long before (though Foucault was not a Marxist), and his contemporary Derrida, Foucault's social theory of modernity refuses to take modernity at face value. Appearances are in fact the very opposite of reality.

Let us consider an example from Foucault's last, and very controversial, project, *The History of Sexuality* (1976). In this book, the introductory volume to a series of studies on sex in the West, Foucault provides a succinct summary of his most famous concept, *power/knowledge*. Before going into the concept, however, let me first explain his method and how he proposed to apply it to the history of sex and sexuality in the modern age. Many historians are infuriated by Foucault's studies because he presents his ideas without the usual heavy footnoting of his sources and facts. Though he did his own archival research on original documents in France's national library, his literary style and his ideas are filled with surprises. Often he begins with a shocking claim that runs entirely contrary to what most people think (like Derrida, Foucault also deals in irony and literary tricks — though not in so obscure a manner).

In the beginning of his book on sexuality, Foucault immediately attacks (but in an understated way) two general concepts that are typical of modern thinking: that power is the effect of strong elites consciously and overtly crushing ordinary people; and, that Christian morality and its secular successors were determined to repress all talk of sex, not to mention sex itself. Most of us are inclined to believe, for example, that the fabled prudishness of the Victorian age in the late nineteenth century is simply a fact — plain and simple. Foucault disagrees. In his view, if one looks more skeptically at the facts, it appears that the Victorians talked a great deal about sex. Foucault points to a number of documents that were widely read in the Victorian era. If you doubt this, just think of the romance novels that became popular in the mid-nineteenth century and continue to be popular today. Charlotte Brontë's *Jane Eyre* is a classic instance of a book on romantic longing. In this novel, true sex is not described as it would be today, but the book is very much about sexual desire, sexual tragedy, sexual conquest, and abandonment. Or, in an early era, consider Jean-Jacques Rousseau's *Confessions* from the eighteenth century. Though written in a very high language, the book is very hot indeed. Rousseau liked sex and had a lot of it. These, of course, are just two famous classic writings of modern culture. Foucault refers to lesser-known writings, usually ones he discovered hidden away in the French archives.

Take as an example one of the stories he reports in *The History of Sexuality* from a lost document he found somewhere on a dusty library shelf: In 1867, Juoy, apparently a retarded person (perhaps the village idiot), was arrested for what we would consider the sexual abuse of a young girl. What he had done, apparently, was to persuade her to exchange sexual touches under the guise of a game he had seen children playing in the village. Children everywhere play with sex in this way. The man did not realize he was not a child. Today, Juoy would have been thrown in jail and severely punished, as he might have been prior to modern times. But in this small, still rural nineteenth-century village, he was sentenced, in effect, to become a subject of study and investigation. The man had his brain pan measured, his facial anatomy examined, his personal history taken down, and more. He was studied in the most minute detail. The then new methods of the medical and social sciences were applied to the end of "understanding" this man. The basic fact was that he *was* indeed punished but by the extraordinarily gentle means of being subjected to examination — just as today mental patients and criminals are, first of all, processed through diagnostic procedures that classify their exact illness according to carefully defined rules of medical or criminological evidence. By contrast, in the feudal age, the insane, the confused, the poor, *and* the criminal were locked up without distinction, often thrown into the same prison cell as though there were no differences between the criminal and the ill.

So, you can see, Foucault's idea is that in the modern age the knowledge of the new human sciences was used to control individuals, including those like the simpleton Juoy who deviated from accepted adult sexual norms. In this case, Foucault drew his conclusions from an archive, originally a very public document taken from much-discussed legal and medical hearings. In other words, in that small village the sexual offense of the man was talked up all over town. Not very prudish. Foucault's larger argument is that throughout the history of the West the Christian prohibition against sex, and talk of sex, was actually quite contrary to the practices of daily life. Even in feudal Christendom, the Roman Catholic confessional was, in fact, a place in which the penitents were (as today) *encouraged* to talk about sex, just as at a later time in the twentieth century junior high school manuals about "dating" encourage sex talk and giggles, or, for the more sophisticated, psychotherapeutic counseling sessions today induce people to talk about their sexual feelings and activities, among other things. Remote as it is from our day, in which every part of culture is saturated by sex talk, these seemingly more innocent occasions for talk of sex were actually precursors of today's situation. Foucault suggests that the confessional was actually the origin of the West's preoccupation with sex — a preoccupation that grew more and more (*not* less and less) intense through the Victorian and post-Victorian eras.

How does Foucault link sex to power? Here you can again see the irony in strategic postmodernism's method. Modernity appears to be prudish, when in fact it is very sexy. Why this encouragement of sex talk? Foucault says (in a more subtle argument than this) that talk about sex is the method by which modern culture teaches people to control their sex in a definite way. What the modern world had to do, in the nineteenth century, was to control a dramatically changing population of people who were migrating from rural towns to the new factories. For the factories to function in an efficient and productive way, those new workers had to be disciplined into a new form of life. Since the rules of modern culture are that people must be considered free and not forced to work and live according to imposed rules, workers had to be *taught* to organize their lives in a certain factory-like way. With respect to sex, it was a matter of some urgency that the waves of new workers from the country-side be taught, let us say, to have just enough sex to produce new generations of baby workers but not so much sex that the population would overwhelm the social system's ability to provide.

Obviously, such a system must accomplish two tasks: produce a reasonable number of workers; but do so by reasonable, gentle, and human means. Thus, argues Foucault, modernity is interested in teaching people about sex and everything else, hence its interest in knowledge and education. It must use moral and formal instruction to discipline because its own cultural values prohibit force. These methods were so successful that ordinary people were, and are, among the most fervent believers in the teachings by which they were disciplined. This is one reason why the working class in industrial societies is often the most patriotic.

You now can see the importance of Foucault's concept *power/ knowledge* and his surprising criticism of the usual assumption about power as a force that works from the top down. Power in modernity mostly operates through knowledge — through the teachings of judging priests, prudish school marms, prying guidance counselors, officious boy-scout leaders, ambitious authors of dating guides, probing therapists, and so on. Modernity must use knowledge to discipline; and, discipline is an exercise of power that works through the (seemingly) gentle means of teaching. This is why, according to Foucault's thinking, the invention of new forms of knowledge in medicine, mental health, criminology, sociology, and sexology were fundamental to the establishment of modern culture.

Once again, you can see why this is a strategic postmodernism, one parallel to, if not the same as, Derrida's. Foucault's main work was to rewrite the history of modernity in order to expose the ways power worked, not overtly or from the top down, but through the popular effects of *knowledge* — through the (apparently) benign means of education for the masses. Though Foucault upsets quite a few people with his daring and unconventional methods and ideas, he has served as a model and, in many ways, an inspiration to social theorists who seek to rewrite the histories of oppressed people with whom they identify.

Foucault himself was openly gay in later life, and is considered one of the classic figures in what today is known as *queer theory*, that is: the politically radical but intellectually demanding social theories of gay, lesbian, or bisexual people who take "queer" as a sign of their refusal to be disciplined by the standards of heterosexual society. Once a stigmatizing term, "queer" is used by queer theorists to challenge modernity's appallingly sacred beliefs about them. Foucault, so far as I know, did not use the term "queer" for his own politics, even though his ironic method was clearly a forerunner of this and other radical social theories. You might also be able to imagine the parallels of the strategic use of "queer" with Derrida's own play on words.

The last of the three great strategic postmodernists is the French psychoanalyst, Jacques Lacan (who died in 1981). Just as Derrida rewrites philosophy, and Foucault rewrote the history of modern knowledges, so Lacan rewrote classical Freudian psychoanalysis, as in his famous (some say, notorious) paper on the *mirror-stage* in a child's development.

The concept of the mirror-stage is not so much a criticism of Freud as a radicalization of psychoanalytic ideas in order to explain a crucial moment in the normal development of a child. About the sixth month, most infant children have the experience of "discovering" themselves in a mirror. This may be the first moment when they, literally, "see" themselves and formulate in their minds what they look like. According to Lacan, this is often a shocking experience because it so contradicts the infant's actual experience. In the earliest months of life, when the developing child lacks an "image" of what she looks like, her experience is dominated by feelings — anger, affection, fear, desire, and the like. These feelings are usually associated with very concrete objects — the mother's breast, wet or soiled diapers, hunger pangs, too much light, loud noises. These experiences, being associated in primary process with objects the child herself cannot appreciate as real objects, produce an overriding sense of fragmentation. In the earliest months, life is not integrated in the least, and the child has no sense of herself as a whole thing. Then, according to Lacan, she looks in a mirror one day and sees something remarkable: Herself, a whole, coherent thing!

Thus, according to Lacanian social theorists, the mirror stage is crucial for the child's development because here she develops the necessary illusion of her completeness. In Lacan's words, this is the "moment that decisively . . . tips the 'I' [the self, or ego] into that apparatus for which every instinctual thrust constitutes a danger."[19] What happens, in effect, is that, from this stage on, the individual encounters her own real feelings, always fragmentary, as a danger to the illusion of her "whole self." Where, however, does the *social* theory come in?

One of the most famous (though poorly done, and even more poorly understood) uses of Lacan's ideas is that of the late French Marxist social theorist, Louis Althusser. In a widely read essay, "Ideology and Ideological State Apparatuses," Althusser makes the connection between Lacan's ideas such as those on the mirror stage and the role of ideology in modern social life.[20] All too briefly, one of those connections is that ideology arises in social life at an early moment in its life just as the false sense of the whole of the ego, or self, arises in the early months of a child's life. And, both have the same effects. Ideologies, such as the modernist dream of the Good Society, are the illusions by which society wards off the dangerous feelings of fragmentation in the reality of social life, just as the illusion of the self wards off the feelings that fragment emotional life. This is the famous *imaginary* of Lacanian theory — the idea that all of culture (at least modernist culture) is fundamentally an imaginary of the whole truth of the Good Society, that is: a defense against the more painful truth of differences. Many cultural theorists have used this connection, in much more sophisticated ways than I am able to present here, to uncover the deceptions of modern culture.

Conclusion

The differences among the three types of postmodern social theory are perhaps clearer now. *Radical postmodernism* tends to believe that modernity is utterly overthrown by a new social arrangement in which reality is a virtual reality, in which the differences between fact and fiction no longer apply, and in which there is little basis for defending any specific idea or ideal as more real than any other. *Radical modernism* believes that, though modernity has produced social evil, modern culture remains the only discernable basis for human liberation from those evils. It holds fast to the principle that to give up on the modern world is to give up any hope of finding values and principles able to criticize and correct social evil. *Strategic postmodernism* believes that modernity is too clever, too subtle in its workings, for any one to be able to criticize it from the point of view of its own ideas. Yet, this third position also believes that we have no sensible choice but to use modern culture, that is: to subvert the culture, to overcome its denial of differences, its deceptive deployment of *power/knowledge*, its self-denying ideologies.

Or, one might summarize by returning to Lyotard's line about totality. *Radical postmodernism* wages war on totality by moving beyond the real to the hyperreal. *Radical modernism* wages this war by radicalizing the most powerful critical weapons of modern culture to attack real totalizing effects. *Strategic postmodernism* neither gives up on nor overrates modernity's power. It wages war on totality by working within the modern, as modernity works within us. As modernity deceives us into ignoring painful differences, this last postmodernism seeks to subvert those deceptions by its own tricks.

Whichever position you prefer in the postmodernism debate will depend to a large extent on your historical interpretation of the present age. In the end, as I said, postmodernism is about the extent to which our world has changed. Social theories of the postmodern are interpretations of that world, the reality (or hyperreality) of which is much more in the experience of living than thinking.

3

An Impossible Glossary of Social Reality

Some people, I admit, think of me as belonging to a small, but persistent, if unorganized, group of sociologists who are considered qualified to speak and write on postmodernism. Whether I deserve this consideration is one thing. Whether it is a compliment is another. Just the same, I am occasionally asked to give my account of postmodernism. One of the more surprising invitations of this type, proposed to a very large publishing company by a colleague I consider sincere and respectful, may in fact have been a compliment. The invitation led to the writing of a long article for a corporation with a commanding stake in the lucrative college market.

Thereupon I began a brief, but instructive, relation with lesser, but decent, managers of the corporate world who, of all things, wanted me to write, on behalf of their shareholders, an explanation of postmodernism. I was immediately and uncharacteristically seized by an attack of caution, if not humility. How could I possibly explain this subject in a manner acceptable to those so invested in one of modernity's most ubiquitous cultural products, the college textbook? The caution soon lifted, taking with it the last misty traces of humility, when I compared my situation to that of the famous architect Philip Johnson. He, a vastly more talented man than I, had found a way to design and build a postmodern skyscraper for the American Telephone and Telegraph Company in the days when AT&T was undividedly one of the mega-giants of corporate capitalism. Johnson's accomplishment is considered ironic because the skyscraper is the architectural genre most commonly thought to be the icon of modernism's heroic, robust, and rational reach for the skies. Yet, somehow, Johnson's building in New York City has become, instead, an icon, not of modernism, but of postmodernism. This perverse attribution arises upon amusement given by the building's many decorative jokes imposed upon an otherwise sober and functional modern structure complete with elevators, offices, bathrooms, and all that is efficient to economic progress. In Johnson's case the postmodernish aspect is less in the various historical flourishes and allusions than in the putting together of these surprises into an operative modernist structure. Notwithstanding the extreme disparities in talent and compensation that will forever make us different, I felt that, if Philip Johnson could do what he did, I ought to be able to produce something such-like in relation to an ever more modest modernist structure like the textbook.

I found the work surprisingly pleasant and corporate resistance virtu-ally nil. The textbook's editors were less interested in what I said than in the clarity of its presentation and its accessibility to students in (to use the industry term) "lower-level classes" (a phrase that cries out for closer scrutiny). Though I had always supposed that whatever was being said affected the clarity with which it could be presented, I at least understood the commercial interest in accessibility. What I comprehended less well was, as it turned out, one of their more insistent demands. Having not ever read very many textbooks, I had forgotten that such books are expected to contain, among the bells and whistles, a list of definitions of terms used — or, as my publishers properly called it, a glossary!

It ought not to be possible, I supposed, to write a glossary of words used by or about postmodernism. Yet, having ultimately lost all but a wisp of caution, I set about doing it. To my further amazement, it could, in fact, be done, which is to say that I did it without official objection. I wrote definitions and comments appropriate to various terms that had appeared in the essay I'd written (a version of which is present as chapter 2, preceding). The "definitions" just came — easily and (to me) clearly as though I had been granted some magical authority to define. Whether the definitions and glosses (which appear at the end of this chapter) are clear to anyone else I cannot (and dare not) say. But they did pass muster at McGraw-Hill. The only definition in my glossary that was objected to was that of "ideology," to which an editor proposed I add, immediately after the word-entry itself, the qualifying redundancy: "in the postmodern sense." Why she believed that my gloss on "ideology" should be thus uniquely marked I do not know, any more than I can imagine why a defi-nition of "ideology" might be more disturbing of modernist sensibilities than the comments I made upon the remaining 27 entries in the glossary. I returned the revised typescript to the publishers without making the change suggested.

At last word the essay was making its way through production and, by now, is likely to be available for, as I understand it, downloading from its home in a database who knows where. As it turns out this textbook is not really a book in the usual sense of book. Rather, it is a series of encyclopedia entries available for purchase from electronic storage. The idea is that the textbook in question is in reality a possible book available for making according to taste. This advance in the form of a book open to the buyer's tastes is, therefore, to a surprising extent, postmodern. Such a volume of potential chapters is again comparable to Johnson's AT&T building, which, though decorated at the top with what many imagine to be a telephone, just as readily suited the tastes of the purveyor of a more advanced line of technologies, the SONY Corporation, which bought the building in the days after AT&T broke into its several competing pieces. As I said, postmodern things have less to do with what one thinks than with taste, hence with desire, hence with a reservoir of feelings free of attachment to the bound book, the built space, or any other concrete object to which the taste of human significance might be attracted. Postmodern products are, thus, commodities of various sizes and prices which are capable of floating across a world of semi-detachable meanings. This is why it ought to have been, but was not, impossible to write a postmodern glossary.

An experience like the one just described, instructs on a point more grand than it may seem. Anyone with the will to do so can write a glossary which, strictly speaking, is nothing more than a series of glosses upon a list of words. More precisely, the most esteemed of all dictionaries, the *Oxford English Dictionary* (*OED*), defines a "glossary" as: "A collection of glosses; a list with explanations of abstruse, antiquated, dialectal, or technical terms; a partial dictionary."[1] Mine is, in principle, a list of "technical" terms explained in order that some might not believe them to be "abstruse"; and, since it comprises no more than 28 items, it is obviously at best a "partial dictionary." But what is a dictionary? The same Oxford English source, if it is to be trusted to define itself, defines a "dictionary." But what is a dictionary? The same Oxford English source, if it is to be trusted to define itself, defines a "dictionary" as: "A book dealing with the words of a language (or certain specified classes of them)."[2] Even with the limiting parenthetical phrase, it is clear that a dictionary, as opposed to a glossary, is obliged to list, in principle, *all* the words of a language or some class of words which, being approximately exhaustive of the one recognizable kind, constitute a universe of their own (such as a dictionary of slang).

Hence, the difference between a glossary and a dictionary. A glossary, being partial, seems to invite the efforts of just about anyone able to compose a list of terms applicable in some or another realm in respect to which he or she has passable authority. My first precise instructions as to the practical details of heteronormal sex and the organs and actions appertaining thereto were provided me at the age of 9 years or so by two neighborhood girls. What they offered was truly a partial list of this class of terms, but they offered them, stirringly, as glosses — as interpretations of certain terms and their referents. Curiously, the first *OED* definition of "gloss" is transitive: "to insert glosses or comments on; to comment upon, to explain, or interpret." Those girls, to whom I innocently ceded authority on the arousing subject, did in fact insert comments on my latent but active curiosity, but they did so in keeping with the *OED*'s secondary meaning of the transitive verb: "to veil in specious language." It took some time before I fully realized just how specious their insertions were when it came to the practice of my first, sweaty sexual acts in the presence of an undressed body not my own. But, the informal, spoken glossary established by these girls served then present purposes well enough — as do, in other settings, the commands of drill sergeants, the safety rules of playground supervisors, the lessons of Sunday School volunteers, and the stipulations of others with at least provisional authority to gloss the meaning of words and their correspondent things. The benefits of the defining office usually include the presumption that the definer is in the right as well as the know.

A dictionary is simply the more encompassing document. A dictionary of sexual terms would be expected to cover all the terms applicable to the universe of the subject in question, as distinct from those available to the ill-informed experiences of neighborhood girlfriends. One expects a reliable dictionary to cover all the terms of a language and to deal with them convincingly. A dictionary, thereby, is supposed to possess the authority of the abstract value of the definitions listed in proper order, normally (in modern times) alphabetically. Thus the very A to Z of the terms implies that the whole of the language is well represented. But, it turns out, this assumption is open to doubt on at least two counts.

First, the normal use of dictionaries is limited to the practice of an occasional, if urgent, consultation. I have heard of only one person who is said to have read a dictionary of the English language from cover to cover. Malcolm X claimed he did so while in prison which effort, he said, opened his eyes to learning, even as the exercise, conducted through long nights in the dim light of the prison corridor, ruined his eyes such that we remember him as a revolutionary with spectacles.[3] Most of us do not ever read dictionaries in this way, even though we rely on them in emergencies — though seldom convincingly so, as when students writing papers in the middle of the night feel they must account for a concept of importance in the material they had been asked to read but did not. Otherwise, save for the resolution of arguments while playing board games like *Scrabble*, dictionary definitions are consulted in private and seldom used (as I am doing here) to gain the upper hand in public discourse. This observable fact of dictionary use is off-limits to systematic discussion, perhaps because close scrutiny might open doors better left closed.

The second count against the naive assumption that dictionaries are authoritative uncovers a further reluctance to inquire — this time into the authority of those who write them. The first comprehensive, authoritative dictionary of the American language was written by Noah Webster. Webster's 1828 *An American Dictionary of the English Language* was based on a 1755 revision of Samuel Johnson's dictionary of the English language. Webster's, which is still used in extensive revision, added many terms to Johnson's English ones and was particularly authoritative for its coverage of American meanings and pronunciations. I have heard it said that Webster, thus, imposed upon the American tongue the bland regional pronunciations of the Connecticut River Valley from Amherst, Massachusetts (where he taught) through Hartford (where he grew up) to the lower Connecticut (where he spent his later years). We know very well that he did not eradicate many, if any, of the various dialects Americans use, but he did succeed in producing a most authoritative dictionary. But, who was he to have done this? While a learned man (though not as learned as Samuel Johnson), Mr Webster, like Dr Johnson, was not a man whose personal manners could stand as testimony to the character of his definitions. Both men were, it seems, odd, opinionated, even careless in many things, as one would expect of anyone who would attempt so impossible a task as to define the universe of terms constituting a language. The work is not for the overly fastidious. Yet, they did their work, personal deficiencies notwithstanding, and produced, at least in Webster's case, an enduring dictionary of the American language.

Still, one wonders, just how does a dictionary happen, and why does it possess the authority it does? Whether a dictionary strictly speaking, or a glossary, it does not appear that the authority of definitional lists rests reliably with their authors. From Dr Samuel Johnson, a paragon of erudition, to the girls in my neighborhood, paragons of childhood confusion, the range of qualifications for the work is broad and indifferently patrolled. Though the authority of a published dictionary may be enhanced by the name of Dr Johnson, to say nothing of Oxford University Press, the authority is not in the name. Though Noah Webster had a good name, it alone was sufficient neither to cause the book to sell as he would have liked nor to prevent it from becoming a bestseller after Webster's estate sold the rights to George and Charles Merriam who, being commercial publishers not scholars, possessed no definitional authority whatsoever. Plus which, as every parent of small children knows, there is no barrier to anyone in the world producing a glossary, at least, of words and things one is asked repeatedly to explain.

How do words get their meanings? That is, how does it come about that meanings are pronounced with sufficient local or cosmopolitan conviction that, over time, their meanings are agreed to? Neither Dr Johnson, nor Mr Webster, nor Oxford University Press, nor certainly my 9-year-old childhood girlfriends, was the definer of the terms. Each was instead a collector of meanings in use. Thus when the *OED* provides us with "to veil in specious language" as a secondary meaning for the verb "to gloss," it is reporting, in its admittedly authoritative language, a meaning that has come into practical use. Try as some might, it is impossible to keep some words and meanings out of use. I know quite a few persons who occasionally use "interface" as a transitive verb when referring to a specific interaction they may have had with another person. Yet none who say they interface in this way are truly connected by cable to their intersubjective others. It is not possible these days to keep "interface" from exceeding its abstruse technical applications, just as it has not been possible to keep "pissed off" out of polite and public talk. If "interface" and "pissed off," then "faxation" and "asshole" cannot be far behind.

Words and their meanings are social conventions. They come into use and refine their meanings in the common, not well-thought-through, practice of ordinary talk. How individual speakers learn to perform competent speech, thus to deploy the words and meanings they hear on the streets, is (so far as I know) still not exactly understood. But this is a question for linguists. All a sociologist needs to bother with is the prior certainty that the words themselves are social in origin, which is known with sufficient assurance by the fact that their meanings change, often against the expressed will of the authorities. This in itself is bother enough.

The discovery of the social foundations of words and meanings was an important occasion in the early history of what came to be known as postmodernism. This involves the story of structuralist semiotics and the well-known linguistic turn that some abhor. The story, which I previously introduced when discussing Derrida, and which will be told at length in the chapters following, requires further mention here.

To speak optimistically of postmodernism is to refer, as I have said, first of all to a dramatic shift in the structures of world events such that it is tempting to believe that, in simple terms, "things are not what we thought they were." The last half of the twentieth century is hardly the first time when people may have entertained such fears. But it *may* be a time when, relative to other periods of rapid social change, there was no obvious, nor even possible, grand scheme to account for "the way things are supposed to be." In recent centuries, the only other such time I can think of might have been in the early fifth century when, in AD 410, the Roman Empire gave way to Alaric and his Goths. We speak of the years following as the Dark Ages, as though they were a void, when in fact the system of Roman administration remained well secured, soon to be taken up by the Roman Church which, in time, reconstituted it as the Holy Roman Empire. In any case, the Christian Church was well formed during this time, giving those anxious about the culturally dangerous Goths an explanatory retreat. Historians may well be able to name other such periods. But, lacking the close comparison, the prospect implied in the idea of the postmodern is that, whatever in fact happens, things have changed in a direction that has undermined the certitudes of modern culture and, very possibly, the prospect of socially agreed upon certitudes of any kind.

Though the media of which I spoke in the previous chapter *may* be a cause of this change, they are at least as much an effect of it. People who have allowed themselves to be exposed to the televisual environment in all its forms (not excluding the Net and e-mail) think of themselves as knowing more (or in a position to know more) than they can ever possibly use. Hence the irony of the circumstance: As information is made more available, people are in a position to feel as though they know less well how to use what they know.

Such a cultural environment as this surely turns back upon the most basic moral aptitudes for well-considered action, creating the most striking difference between a postmodern and modern ethics. If modernist ethics were those rational and future-oriented attitudes that took the place of traditionalist, past-preserving habits, then postmodern ethics are those in which rational choices are less calculable in inverse ratio to the vastly increased number of choices, many of which are disconcertingly at odds with each other. Watch CNN, order airline tickets, check one's e-mail, catch some MTV, buy a nose-ring, take a pee, consider the state of one's abdomen, pay the bills, and more — all these without leaving home. When Georg Simmel wrote in 1903, in "The Metropolis and Urban Life," of the psychological bombardment to which one is exposed in the modern city, he had in mind the out-of-doors, public life which, though changed from then earlier times, was still understood to be heading somewhere. Those who take seriously the mediated culture of today have more in mind an environment in which so many incongruent facts of out-of-doors life are brought not just indoors but into the personal consciousnesses of those addicted to them. As a result, the world, such as it is, is both a presumed fact of the external global situation and a state of internal feeling. All the fuss about the "social construction of reality" has, I suppose, less to do with reality in a philosopher's (to say nothing of physicist's) sense than with the social psychology of a disturbingly possible postmodern life. So much is real that one hardly knows just how to judge the more real from the less. Who, indeed, is to say that the man Ronald Reagan was more real than the presidential character he portrayed with great success? And how do we determine that Bart Simpson, the cartoon, is less real than the grown-up children he portrays? Or is it that some of them portray him?

Questions about the meaning of social reality are not to suppose that there is no difference in categorical kind between a cartoon character and a flesh and blood one, but that there are so many borrowings back and forth that the line between is more than fine. Someone might say, as Alan Sokal has, that when I jump from a building I know what reality is, but who is to say what reality is when Americans elect as their President a man who, for much of his second term in office, wasn't? In order not to diminish, or exaggerate, the effects of the disease that impaired Mr Reagan's own sense of reality, one could just as easily ask the same of any character with respect to whom we form an opinion solely on the basis of televisual and other mediated information. Who knows who is what, really?

One might suppose, as those on the political Left might, that these confusions are unique to the comfortable classes. But this expectation surely is a class-specific error. Is it not probable that, even and especially, the poor are no less exposed to mediated meanings? There are some very good empirical reasons to suppose that, being unable to afford the high price of public entertainment, they are more dependent on television for distraction, not less. Among the more disconcerting reports by Robert Kaplan from his voyage to the ends of the earth is that the most poor in the shanty towns of Africa and Asia very often are found with television sets somehow rigged for reception in shacks made of cardboard, brush, or metal scrap.[4] For them, one supposes, uncertainty as to what is real is more, not less, acute than it is for those of my well-provided-for students who clamor to write all too serious term papers about Madonna, for which they increasingly generate footnotes taken from home pages on the Internet, the reality of which is, truly, beyond understanding.

Such a view of things (which I emphasize can only be a provisional view) is, of course, accompanied by numerous social theories — the three main groups of which I have described in the previous chapter. Those theories caught at least some of their impetus in the early years after World War II from writers who took an extreme and provocative interest in language. Postmodern social theory is, generally speaking, the current state of a line of thinking that began, first, with structuralist semiotics in the 1940s and 1950s and which led in turn to a rebellion of sorts, poststructuralism. Though postmodern social theory, when it applies itself to culture, has now lost much of its interest in technical linguistics and semiotics, one does well to examine, at least, the most elementary of the principles of that first linguistic turn.

When in the early 1950s Claude Lévi-Strauss, Roland Barthes, A. J. Greimas and numerous others first experimented with a science of social things from the perspective of their linguistic or semiotic properties, they were, in effect, attempting to reinvent sociology. Though only Lévi-Strauss considered himself in one of the traditions of professional sociology, the early semioticians, and those who learned from them, toyed with the notion that the most parsimonious and powerful science of society would be one based on the principle that societies are obedient to the same or similar formal laws as those governing language use. Today the very mention of this idea drives some people absolutely nuts. But then it seemed interesting enough to inspire a number of studies of which, as it turned out, only Lévi-Strauss's work on myths and, perhaps, Barthes's brilliant book of essays, *Mythologies*, survive as enduring classics of the tradition. Soon enough many in the tradition applied the principle to cultural interpretations of cinema and literature. In many places, this practice is still followed. But, even early leaders like Barthes abandoned the more scientistic versions of structuralist semiotics by the mid-1960s.

Though the more grandiose extensions of this early semiotic sociology have been swept under one or another rug of academic specialization, the important idea of sociology derived from the relations of words to things remains both appealing and of more potential utility than it has been accorded. The original idea drew heavily on a number of thinkers of whom one of the most important was the early twentieth-century Swiss linguist, Ferdinand de Saussure, who almost certainly was directly influenced by Durkheim and, in any case, was Durkheimian through and through. Though many linguists still do not embrace Saussure's ideas, his thinking exercised a considerable influence in the early years of the linguistic turn. In the simplest of terms, Saussure's most controversial idea was that the meanings of words bear no direct, natural, or necessary relation to the things they signify. The word "cow" cannot be derived from any observable connection with actual cows in the field. This we know, Saussure argued, because the words themselves can vary from language to language while the thing itself is much the same everywhere. I have seen cows in fields in France where the word for them is *vache*, not "cow." It is true of course that when languages are historically close to each other the words may be similar. In France a "cat" is *un chat*. Close enough. But the similarity in words for cats, like the difference in those for cows, cannot derive from anything in the nature of cats or cows. The correspondence of the words in the one case is due more to the historical and social relations between English and French people than to the essence of the things themselves for which the two groups merely agree to use different words.

The inference that was taken from Saussure's social theory of words was that the relation between words and their meanings is arbitrary. Nothing between them is fixed or necessary. But this, of course, does not mean that there are no meanings. On the contrary, Saussure's, and other linguistic theories of this kind, insisted that the meaning of words derives only and exclusively from a social contract among speakers in a particular speaking community, that is: People speaking a common language decide over time what the things in their real worlds mean. In effect, they agree to assign certain arbitrary words, or signifiers, in order to permit meaningful communication about these realities.

I once tried to order in a Sushi bar in Hiroshima, Japan. True, I was able to point and thus be fed. But, not knowing Japanese, I was surprised to discover that what I thought was shrimp was something else. My older son, who was with me, actually tried to mime a shrimp. As it turns out this practice works tolerably well when ordering chicken, but fails miserably when one must imitate a shrimp and, even more so, when (as we discovered the next evening) what one wants is a piece of cow, that is: *boeuf*. Any social communication depends on a prior linguistic competence which, in turn, depends on paid-up membership in a social group from which the speaker acquires both training and permission to speak by borrowing words from the official (if second-nature) list of meanings agreed upon. Linguistic competence is a question of social membership, not sophistication, learning, or even age — as my son and I well understood from the barely restrained amusement his imitation of a shrimp inspired in a very young Japanese boy at the adjoining table.

So, it might well be asked, in what sense do words refer to "real" things? Clearly social things are not real in the sense that the pavement toward which Alan Sokal proposes postmodernists might jump is real. My son Matthew and I got ourselves fed and bedded well enough, so the reality of social conventions determining social communications is not an uncompromisingly hard one. There are ways around social realities (though, of course, we can all imagine circumstances in which being unable to find the word to name a looming reality can be life threatening). Still, the reality of "words" is the reality of the conventions we agree to. This is why, where there is disagreement as to the official language in a community or nation, political turmoil can and usually does break forth.

People must agree on the meanings if they are to make sense with each other and they must make sense if they are to live in at least tolerable social peace. This is why, far beyond the importance of their languages, the majority of people in a society are also strongly inclined to create, over time, other cultural accords by which they organize themselves for the complicated task of making things work. The rules, maxims, ideologies, beliefs, threats, and such like that constitute cultures serve the same purpose, and work in the same way, as do words. This affinity for grand and reconciling ideologies was the reason for being of the original semiotic sociologies. That they were unable to establish and maintain the scientific discipline necessary to demonstrate the exactness of the comparison ought not to detract from the saliency of their most elementary principle.

When it comes to the meaning of social things, reality and its corollary, truth, are in fact arbitrary in the rigorously sociological sense: They are conventions of the social community, thus real so long as the community agrees to uphold them, and something other than real whenever the community loses its ability to exercise authority over the truth of social things.

A glossary of postmodern terms ought to be impossible not because the postmodern is itself any more impossible than the modern. Rather it is impossible in the sense that the intimations of postmodernity that some find disturbingly real are, among much else, public murmurings about the possibility that even the modern is not so real as modernists would like it to be and, for a number of centuries, believed it was.

If, however, Noah Webster can compose a dictionary of the American language based on the meanings he heard people associating with the words they used, then I can at least compose a glossary of interpretations of the words I have heard used in attempts to explain postmodernism. Not any more than Webster invented either the words or meanings in his dictionary, did I invent the terms on the list that follows. Like Noah Webster, and Samuel Johnson before him, I too put the meanings I think I have heard in my own words and, in so doing, it is unlikely that I have not changed their senses. Webster, it is known, was free and nasty in his redefinitions of many of Dr Johnson's words.

All dictionaries and glossaries are, therefore, impossible only if what one seeks to find in them is the hard reality of things. A glossary of postmodern terms may be in this sense, perceptibly more impossible because there is detectably less accord as to the nature and thus meaning of postmodern things, the reality of which some trust, others deny. A postmodern glossary is still more impossible in another way. It is the purpose, if not the nature, of a postmodern glossary to define the startling extent to which the reality of the meaning of words and things is arbitrary. The meaning of social life is necessarily arbitrary. The meaning of words used to describe a purported postmodern world are doubly so by virtue of the arguable idea that the words to which we have grown accustomed have, like modern social things themselves, somehow fallen into controversy.

If postmodernism makes any sense, now or eventually, it will make it, Lord knows, not out of any glossary, nor even of any particular theory or thought, but only if and when it is determined whether or not, in the absence of a prevailing ideology, the majority of folks in a place can learn to tolerate the most basic fact of social life: Things certainly are not what they seem to be. They are only what we say they are. Is this reality enough?

The Impossible Glossary (in the postmodern sense):

critical theory: a feature of all social theories whereby they are distinguished from theories of the "pure" sciences which vainly attempt to avoid value judgments; the tradition of radical modernist social theory associated with the German school of critical theory or the Frankfurt School.

culture: the complex of socially produced values, rules, beliefs, literatures, arts, media, penal codes, laws, political ideals, and other diversions by which a society, or social group, represents its view of the world as it is and ought to be; the complex of mechanisms by which societies, or social groups, justify their exclusions of realities they find intolerable; see *imaginary*.

deconstruction: a social-theoretical attitude that has led to the use of irony to rethink, rewrite, and reconstrue the basic features of modernity and modernism; the most misunderstood and misused term associated with postmodernism; a term owing vaguely to Jacques Derrida and concretely to his followers; not an "ism," nor a method, nor a "destruction."

différence/différance: (English: difference/deferral): French-language words that sound the same in speech but have differing meanings in writing; ironic terms used by social theorists affiliated with deconstruction to critique the modernist (and essentialist) ideal of primary and universal cultural meaning.

Enlightenment: the high culture of modernity which was first developed in the eighteenth century to advance the still influential ideology that reason is sufficient to human progress which, in turn, is considered the distinctive characteristic of the modern age; the state of belief in which the individual considers himself (and, less often, herself) struck to good effect by the light of reason; an essentialist culture, or belief, devoid of irony.

essentialism: a social theoretical term used to describe modernism's cultural ideal whereby social differences are considered secondary and non-essential variances on universal human nature; as in: "We hold these truths to be self-evident, that *all men* are created equal . . ."

hyperreality: a radical postmodernist concept that describes the world as being so much under the sway of mediated cultures that the sense of reality is intensified such that simulations of reality (like Disneyland or television) are experienced as *more real* than the realities they simulate.

ideology: an ironic concept whereby modernism both expresses its belief that truth must be free of distortion and recognizes (though indirectly) that its own claim to truth is itself a distortion; related to modernism's faith in reality, as in the belief that truth reflects the real order of things, while ideology is a motivated distortion of reality.

imaginary (noun): the complex of means whereby a society, or social group, unconsciously represses intolerable feelings, facts, and histories — such as the reality of differences; associated with the ideas of Jacques Lacan and his followers; see *culture*.

irony/ironic: a literary device (or, trope) used to call surprising attention to the usually ignored by means of reversal or negation, as in Foucault's oxymoronic ideas: sexy Victorians, gentle power; a typical literary and theoretical device of strategic postmodernists.

linguistic turn in social theory, the: refers to the remarkable fact that, since the 1960s, a great number of social theories of different origins (France, Germany, Russia, the United States, Finland, notably) rethought social theory by emphasizing the role of language, or discourse, in social life.

media: any socially or technologically produced means by which reality is communicated indirectly; see *mediated culture*.

mediated culture: any cultural form that communicates representations of reality by indirect means, as in the culture produced by prolonged mass exposure to television and other televisual media.

metanarratives: widely shared cultural stories by which a society, or social group, sometimes expresses the most fundamental ideals, or "truths," of their culture; as in: the metanarratives of modernism whereby scientific truth is considered to be objective and, simply, "true."

mirror-stage: a psychoanalytic term describing that stage when the developing infant (at about six months) first recognizes itself in a mirror, thereafter to think of itself as a whole and well-formed self, notwithstanding primary feelings that tell it (usually in the unconscious) that it is in fact fragmented; the most famous concept of Jacques Lacan.

modernism: the culture, including the theories, of modernity.

modernity/the modern age: the historical period that arose around 1500 with the era of European exploration and colonization of the world, the high culture and social foundations of which were formulated in the eighteenth and nineteenth centuries, beginning with the Enlightenment; see *Enlightenment*.

postmodernism: the culture, including the theories, of postmodernity; any culture or theory that studies, practices, celebrates, or otherwise takes seriously the breaking apart of modernity.

postmodernity: an historical period that is believed by some to mark the end of modernity; the complex whole of a real social historical period; compare *postmodernism*.

power/knowledge: a concept composed by bringing together two others as though they were one in order to express the social theoretical idea that, in modernity, power actually works indirectly *through* knowledge, rather than directly as overt abuse, domination, and control; the most famous concept of Michel Foucault.

queer theory: social theories that subvert the epithet often hurled at gay, lesbian, or bisexual people in order to call attention to the queer nature of modernity's abuse of queer and other people whose differences many modernisms officially consider deviant; a variant, if not self-conscious, form of strategic postmodernism.

radical modernism: a group of social theories that strive to be simultaneously critical of and loyal to the highest values of modernism and modernity itself.

radical postmodernism: a group of social theories that consider modernity a thing of the past, or, at least, in its last historical moments; social theories that consider the present situation to be characterized more by hyperreality than reality.

reality: a modernist concept representing modernity's willingness to suspend disbelief in the originality of the things of the world.

semiotics: the social study of signs and sign systems, usually according to formal rules derived from linguistics; the study of codes, as in the semiotic study of the "language" of traffic signs or fashion culture; for present purposes, different from, but equivalent to, semiology.

social theory: any theory of society or social life that distinguishes itself from scientific theories of society by a willingness to be critical as well as factual.

strategic postmodernism: a group of social theories that seek to reconstruct the cultural, social, and political history of modernity in order to expose the deceptions of the modern age; neither hyperrealists, nor realists.

totality: a concept used by social theorists to describe one of the most essentialist characteristics of modern culture, namely: the cultural urge to think of social life and world reality as being (and needing to be) complete, whole, and constant; frequently, and notoriously, converted into a political idea, as in Hitler's intent to purify Western culture by eliminating Jewish people; one of the most common objects of criticism by radical modernist and postmodernist social theories.

Part II

Beginnings

4

The Political Reality of the Linguistic Turn

As everyone knows, politics is the real thing. Politics brings home the most fundamental life and death issues of social life. Who gets what, in which proportion, of what is needed for survival? This is the final question of life with strangers. It is the rock that makes all serious politics a hard place from which to deny the reality of social life.

The seriousness of politics, and of those self-conscious about their politics, is often involved in the hostility to, or fear of, postmodernism, as we have seen in the case of Alan Sokal. Objections to postmodernism and its various precursor and affiliated movements usually, therefore, call bitter attention to postmodernism's lack of seriousness. This most often takes the form of demeaning epithets, among which those considered most devastating are: nihilistic (the most common), narcissistic (the second most common), relativistic (third), pseudo-history, obsessive, apolitical, and comic.[1] For some reason, no one of my acquaintance has ever reported an alleged postmodernist being more than annoyed by the names. It is even possible to imagine some of them taking, if not delight, modest satisfaction in being the brunt of empty oaths.

One of the most important reasons for this gulf of attitudes between the *pro* and *con* forces in the postmodernism controversy is that both sides consider themselves equally serious about politics, even those whose seriousness takes an ironic turn. With rare exception this aspect of their differences turns on the role of culture and language, broadly conceived, in social studies. For the most part, opponents of postmodernism (especially those of the political Left) consider the famous linguistic turn in social studies a disastrous turn away from the sober attitude one must assume in order to understand the terrible inequalities of modern societies.

So, why the linguistic turn? Does not the idea that interpreting society and culture as though it were a literary text, or even a language, or perhaps a sign system, deflect attention away from the raw reality of daily life? Do the poor worry about literature? Is their suffering, however Dickensian, truly understood in even the finest literary text? Is not culture, including literature and language, secondary to the more fundamental effects of economic exclusion or, stretching Marx's idea, of the brutality of political force? These are legitimate questions to which a general outline of the answers has been provided. If postmodernism is not what you *think*, then it must be that which arises from some prior structural condition in the world at large. If so, then the justification for the linguistic turn (when it is serious, even if ironic) must be that there is something about the social, economic, and political conditions in the second half of the twentieth century that invites a linguistic or, more broadly, a semiotic analysis.

But what could those conditions have been to have justified such an odd turn of analytic events? They were (and are), as I tried previously to show, a decline in the nature and prospects of the world economic and geopolitical structures within which the modern world had thrived and by which modernity produced and effected the very idea of a world culture. Even the immediate post-World War II years in the United States, so reminiscentially affluent and happy, were ones in which attention was paid to structure of social things and of the role of the United States in world affairs. The Cold War, the idea of a triumphant social technology, and eventually the intrusions of decolonization in the Civil Rights Movement were among the defining events of the early years of the second half of the century. Each, and most others, was an adjustment to the social reality brought on by the terrors of economic depression, holocaust, and world war that required further adjustment in modernity's culture in the form of closer attention to the effective reality of structures. Politics through those years, and since, has been more rigorously a politics founded on a recognition that the individual moral actor is an insufficient unit of analysis or agent of progress.

But why, given the attention to structures, should language and culture seize the upper analytic hand? The answer, simply (but only in part), was that a good bit of the earliest attention to structures by social thinkers was skeptical in the extreme. There was, even in the late 1950s and into the 1960s, a rival sentiment to the arrogant, liberal faith in the American Century — in the power of the American State and way of life to bring the modernist dream of progress to a new, perhaps ultimate, level of fruition. Though the liberal ideas of the American century were themselves a structural revision of the nineteenth-century doctrines of *laissez-faire* individualism, there was quite early (but at the time little noticed) a powerful rival idea taking shape. Its central suspicion was, indeed, that the most sacred of modernity's progressive ideas had exhausted themselves. This brooding alternative was founded in the second thoughts of many in Europe who were old enough to have identified with the Resistance to Hitler's occupations but just young enough to doubt with equal emphasis both the Gaullist triumphalism and the Sartrean existentialism. This was a generation that counted among its numbers those who eventually called into question the very idea of the acting, deciding, knowing individual as the basis of progressive history and, in so doing, cast a broadening shadow over the very idea of history itself.

Hence the turn to language and its entailments in social thought was, in part, a deep structural skepticism. The first structuralist of world reputation was the French anthropologist Claude Lévi-Strauss who, in addition to his famous attacks on Sartre's existentialism, was one of the first to claim that a thoroughly skeptical consideration of social structures required a reconsideration of the very nature of social structures. From this came Lévi-Strauss's famous reworking of Durkheimian sociology in which, instead of praising the moral virtue of society, he turned to the analysis of culture from the point of view of its myths interpreted systematically as though cultures were, for all intents and purposes, obedient to the same rules as language itself.

Lévi-Strauss himself has never been known for his politics, in the usual sense of the word. Just the same, his structuralist method was fashioned out of the wreckage of liberal politics — that is: out of the then, to many, obvious weakness of the individual moral subject, whether buttressed by the normative core of society or not, as the cause of the evil of the earlier half of the century or the promise of a renewal of modernity. Though Lévi-Strauss may properly be called the aboriginal social-theoretical post-modernist, the term "postmodernism" was not current in those days as it is today — except of course in various cognates among liberal thinkers like Daniel Bell, John Kenneth Galbraith, and most influentially Walter Rostow and the modernization theorists who, in their attempts to account for transformations occurring *after* full modernization, projected a "mature" modernism which, by dint of its being more consumption that production oriented, was really a post-industrialism or a post-modernism. The intimations in Lévi-Strauss of what would come to be postmodernism as it is known today, were, by contrast, at once more empirically modest and theoretically aggressive than these liberal usages. Structuralism, or semiotic structuralism, was, even in those early days, a serious turning away from the idea that human history is distinct from the natural, and its corollary that human history pushed along the gently inclining line of progress toward a vaguely promised but vividly desired teleological good ending. Anyone who doubts so profound and glorious a proposition as this must examine the language and culture by and in which it was composed, taught, and believed.

But still: Why, simply, the linguistic turn in a time of structural politics? Because, simply, social structures are by their nature reconstructions of reality *after the fact*. No one ever encounters the reality of structures as such — not markets, not states, not stratification systems. Real people encounter, rather, insufficient pay-checks, impossibly excluding bureaucratic rules, and particular slights and injuries, but not the structures themselves. The reality of social structures is always, unavoidably, composed in the sociological imagination, whether well-trained and mundane. Thus, in a time when the structure of world things is widely called into question for good, perhaps even sufficient, political and economic reasons, *one* sensible turn is to give primary heed to the language of culture in which those structures are widely known and knowable.

This is why the structuralist semiotics of which Lévi-Strauss's anthropology of human culture is a first, famous instance was one of the more influential moves from the analysis of social reality as such to the analysis of signs, languages, discourse, and talk — the media through which social reality comes into being and disperses itself across and through a body politic. In the years following the structuralist return to culture and language, there followed any number of refinements and alternatives in the growing preoccupation with signs and discourse. A healthy tradition of radical modernism, that of Habermas in particular, eventually turned to language to reestablish the ideal of a practical but universal basis for human emancipation in the ideal of dialogue-constituting universals. And, as is well known, the structuralism of Lévi-Strauss and the early Roland Barthes, soon gave way to the poststructuralist generation of Derrida and Foucault, not to mention the later Barthes and Jacques Lacan and many others. But the terms of the linguistic turn can safely be drawn in some good measure from that early experiment of structuralist anthropology which itself arose, in some quarters, from the political conditions of an already dawning disenchantment with the structures of the modern world.

The linguistic turn was, and is, part and parcel with the renewed seriousness with which structures must be taken. To discuss social structures is sooner or later to discuss the languages, signs, spectacles, discourses, rhetorics, images, and all the other media by which structures are conjured up and held enticingly before the believing or unbelieving public. Skepticism with respect to the world must come up against the discursive practices by which social worlds are structured in the first place.

There is no good reason even to discuss the question of modernity's status, or of a possible lapse in a postmodern dispensation, unless what is put at issue is the global structure of things social. None of those, whether academics or public speakers, who hate postmodernism, whether called by that name or by one of its virtual cognates, would bother to voice their feelings were it not for their concern that so-called postmodernism is a foolish or otherwise dangerous way of talking about the world. Radical modernists, the most sensible of the opponents of postmodernism, take the world very seriously, as I have tried to demonstrate. Likewise, post-modernists of both the radical and strategic kinds would have nothing to say — at least nothing worth the bother they are accorded — were they not pronouncing a fundamental change in the structure of things. The debate, though preoccupied with details of many interesting kinds, is ultimately about structures — most especially those considered likely to provide a degree of intelligibility to what we innocently call "the world." Modernists, generally speaking, believe the world is structured with respect to, or for the sake of, common and hopeful, universal features of human social nature — ideals of freedom, reasonable practices, community-making competencies, and the like. The more sensible post-modernists, being generally respectful of much in modernity, are rigorously skeptical of the prospects that modernity's grand ideals ever will, or ever were truly meant to, become the true *manifest* structure of world things.

Though structures have been the unavoidable focus of most in recent years, they have been the professional responsibility of some for a longer time. For nearly a century since its founding as a discipline in the late nineteenth century, the analytic care of social structures was assigned, often by default, to sociology. Though in different ways, the earliest sociological thinkers — Marx, Spencer, Durkheim, and Weber — were principally engaged in the practice of studying, explaining, or proclaiming the truth of the changed structures of industrialized, urbanized, and bureaucratized modern societies. It is not surprising, therefore, that when, in the years after World War II, structuralism emerged in Europe as a general philosophy of social life, sociology in the United States was similarly engaged in a rethinking of the classic traditions of structural reasoning. The famous schools of grand and middle-range sociology, associated more or less properly with the writings and leadership of Talcott Parsons and Robert K. Merton, were above all else attempts to dispel the idea that anything less than a thoroughgoing structuralism could justify academic sociology's claims to account for the dynamics of changing societies. In their two great writings of the late 1930s, Parsons' *Structure of Social Action* and Merton's "Social Structure and Anomie," the leaders of post-war sociology explicitly turned sociological reasoning away from classic modernity's idealization of the autonomous individual as the source of social action. In this respect these revisions of sociology were, at the least, politically sensitive. They, like their more philosophical European counterparts, were well aware that the terrors of war, economic failure, and holocaust rendered the free-standing and free-thinking individual ever thereafter constrained by the structure of things.

Though the parallel is seldom taken seriously, the structuralism within American sociology was executed in a virtual shadow dance with today's more notorious European structuralisms from which postmodernism drew so much of its early intellectual momentum. The poststructuralist wave associated in memory with important writings by Michel Foucault and Jacques Derrida in the late 1960s drew its energy, in part, from the head of steam that had been worked up by the early writings of the great structuralists of the 1950s, notably Claude Lévi-Strauss and Roland Barthes. I will account for the specifics of these relationships in the chapters that follow. But, for the moment, it is important to observe that Derrida, in particular, and Foucault, to a degree, worked out their schemes in response to the ideas of Lévi-Strauss who, in turn, was a self-conscious Durkheimian, especially in his earliest writings on kinship, about which more later. At the same time, the postwar sociological structuralists in America, the descendants of whom consider Derrida and Foucault quite beside the point, actually borrowed directly from Lévi-Strauss. This is especially so of Peter Blau's exchange theory and Harrison White's own influential structuralism of kin and other networked relations.[2] Though the academic sociologists, and their students, quickly enough parted company with their European structuralist counterparts, there was a moment in the 1960s when the two passed each other in the night, the one taking at least some conceptual comfort from the other.

To make matters even more complicated, beyond these two structuralisms, there are several more. There are, indeed, at least three, very probably four (perhaps more): the structuralism associated with Lévi-Strauss, that of the American sociologists, the poststructuralism that replied to and revised Lévi-Strauss, to say nothing of the postmodernism and, possibly even, the radical modernisms which today sustain the central argument in social theory.

That argument necessarily is drawn into the deeper argumentative morass of language and signs because the very history of this controversy has been shaped by challenges thrown down originally by structuralist semiotics. One of the more interesting of the challenges to sociologists is the one systematically ignored and thus the one constituting a principal point of demarcation between the French and the American structuralists in the years following World War II. Lévi Strauss and Roland Barthes, among numerous others, turned to language, myth, and sign-systems in general as the primary basis for the study of social structures, while Parsons and Merton, and their numerous students and intellectual affines, never once took language seriously except as an innocent medium of social communication. For Parsons language was but one of the observable media of social exchange, while for Merton it was the means, the graceful deployment of which allowed his writings the wide influence they have enjoyed. Otherwise, neither of their traditions gave the least formal scientific regard to language, signification, myth, or literature. These matters were summarily regarded as aspects of a more primary sphere of structures: culture. Hence, the difference between the two founding traditions of recent structuralism.

The Europeans, by contrast to the Americans, considered language itself a social structure as such. In this they were in the tradition of the crypto-Durkheimian Saussure, whose original structuralist linguistics devolved on the crucial Durkheimian principle that *la langue*, the system of linguistic contents and competencies upon which speakers draw, is itself a social contract reliant on the secure, but arbitrary, culture of the social group. In the simplest of terms, this line of social theory, now so controversial and prominent, began in a fine, but telling, distinction as to the structure of the social world. The world the French structuralists believed in was not a primary social thing, as the early Durkheim of *Suicide* seemed to have thought, but was every bit as much a representation of social experience, as the Durkheim of *The Elementary Forms of the Religious Life* believed. Thus, it is not too far wrong to say that the two great traditions of contemporary structuralism both go back to one or another Durkheim. Though both Parsons and Merton, in their earliest structuralist writings, were thoughtful readers of the whole of Durkheim, neither rose to the semiotic bait of Durkheim's *Elementary Forms* wherein he argued that collective life is not merely represented by cultural things but created by them. Consciousness of the social world, to say nothing of thinking itself, was for this Durkheim the representation of social structures. Just after offering his famous tag line that "Society is a reality *sui generis*," Durkheim said:

> Collective representations are the result of an immense cooperation, which stretches out not only into space but into time as well; to make them, a multitude of minds have associated, united, and combined their ideas and sentiments; for them, long generations have accumulated their experience and their knowledge.[3]

Society, and thought of society, result from and create the collective representatives, the systematic mass of social communications. Durkheim's sociology was a semiotics of a crude kind. This is the idea Lévi-Strauss understood very well. This was the idea that, thereby, buttressed structuralist semiotics as it developed a half-century later.

Even in its original, weakly-developed form in Durkheim, semiotics was a project of intense political moment. Durkheim's grand moral strategy of reconstructing the social life of modern society against the ravages of industrial conflict was intimately dependent on his invention of a sociology capable of justifying and explaining the new amoral social division of labor. Modernity's anomic propensities were avoidable, he thought, only to the extent that a new moral solidarity could take over where traditional religion had declined. Though too much knowledge of the individualizing kind was thought to promote a dangerous removal of individuals from the social whole, social knowledge as the core element of a societal culture was considered a sufficient antidote to anomie and egoism. Durkheim's politics were those of the educational reforms he led, revising the French schools into a system whereby they could promote and transmit cultural representations of French social life. Collective representations, though abstract in *Elementary Forms*, were more concrete and urgent in Durkheim's reformist politics. In this sense, at the time of its founding in France, semiotics was inherently political.

When structuralist semiotics reappeared after World War II, it reappeared in an even more overtly political form. Structuralist semiotics was born by the hands of Lévi-Strauss and Barthes, among others, just when the very culture Durkheim had sought to resuscitate was engulfed, on one side, by the hot wars of colonial liberation and, on the other, by the Cold War struggles among the great colonizing forces of the postwar era. When structuralism gave way to poststructuralism these two political forces came together with unmistakable effect in the 1960s in the form of revolutionary-like struggles *within* the colonizing societies in America and Europe. Poststructuralism, a semiotics of a less self-conscious kind, was one of the important responses to the clashes which then disrupted everything — clashes prompted largely by the freshly understood deceits of the colonial system and the deceptions upon which the Cold War was founded. It is not, therefore, by accident that the postmodernism controversy, a still more refractory response to structuralist semiotics, rages on alongside the faults that are breached by the acute confusions attendant upon the West's inability to assert (much less achieve) its claims to moral superiority and the final collapse of the Cold War which was, it is now apparent, a grand Manichean projection of the worldly pretenses of the good and evil sides of modernity's failed aspirations.

Behind both structures and structuralism — that is, behind the reality of world disorder and the various theories of social order — lurks the nasty suspicion that the meaning of things is, once again, or still, in grave doubt. How those doubts are resolved, or accounted for, is the business of sociologies of all kinds, including those that emerged outside academic sociology from structuralist semiotics. Structures must be treated with mindful care because it is all too easy to deny or otherwise disrespect the fact that today we cannot speak of them without taking a political stand, on one side or another.

Much the same can be said from the point of view of the modern history of structuralist semiotics, which is a history that turned uncannily, but precisely, on the most important world political events of the postwar era.

In an autobiographical essay, Roland Barthes, one of the founders of modern semiotics, described the three decisive moments in the history of the semiotic challenge as hope, science, and text.[4]

Hope, the first of these moments, was the dominant attitude in the early 1950s. It was, Barthes recalled, the initial phase of discovery and, in his word, amazement. This was the period of Barthes's own defining semiological explorations, *Mythologies* and *Le degré zéro de l'écriture*.[5] It was also the period of Lévi-Strauss's first important writings, *Les structures élémentaires de la parenté* (1949) and *Tristes tropiques* (1955) — the former a bold first experiment in sociological semiotics, the latter still today a compelling journal of anthropological travel back to the most elementary forms of cultural life. In a phrase made famous in Derrida's critical reflection on Lévi-Strauss's earliest writings, the period of the 1950s was indeed the dawning of a time in which language first began its invasion of the universal problematic.[6]

Science, the second moment of Barthes's short history of modern semiotics, is assigned to the period of the late 1960s, which was, according to Barthes, a time "of science, or at least of scientificity."[7] For Barthes himself this was the period during which he defined and experimented with the formal scientific possibilities of semiotics in *Eléments de sémiologie* (1964) and *Système de la mode* (1967). "All around me," says Barthes,[8]

> semiological science was being elaborated according to the origins, movement, and independence proper to each investigator (I am thinking of my friends and companions Greimas and Eco); certain junctures were made with the great elders, such as Jakobson and Benveniste, and the younger investigators such as Bremond and Metz.

A. J. Greimas's *Sémantique structurale* appeared in 1966 and the first Italian version of Umberto Eco's *A Theory of Semiotics* was published in

1968 as *La struttura assentee*. These two works, linked by Barthes, belong however to two different currents in the history of semiotics. Greimas's was decidedly an important statement of scientific semiotics.[9] Eco's *Theory of Semiotics*, in spite of its formalized presentation, belonged as much to the third moment which was already gathering force late in the 1960s.[10]

Barthes's third historical moment, that of the Text, came surprisingly into its own in 1968, one of the most remarkable years of intellectual and political ferment in the postwar era. Barthes characterized this as the moment when the text replaced all other considerations in the exploration of signs and signification. With the text, writing became an open, political practice directed precisely and politically against one of the more central convictions of Western culture: the idea of an original, organizing Center.

> The Text, in the modern, current sense which we are trying to give this word, is fundamentally to be distinguished from the literary work: it is not an aesthetic product, it is a signifying practice; it is not a structure, it is a structuration; it is not an object, it is a work and a game; it is not a group of closed signs, endowed with a meaning to be rediscovered, it is a volume of traces in displacement.[11]

This, of course, was the period during which Foucault, Derrida, Lacan, and Julia Kristeva notably dominated the literary scene in France. It was also, outside France, the time when intellectuals quite unrelated to the activities in Paris initiated a worldwide movement away from belief in a positive science and its truth and into the uncertain pragmatic truths of language. Habermas's *Knowledge and Human Interests*, the foundational work for his linguistic turn, appeared in Germany in 1968, the year after Harold Garfinkel's *Studies in Ethnomethodology* appeared in the United States, and the year before John Searle's *Speech Acts: An Essay in the Philosophy of Language*.

This was truly a decisive moment in the linguistic turn in the social and human sciences. Thereafter, especially among the then younger intellectuals and academics who turned to writing and teaching after the political movements of the 1960s, it became increasingly difficult not to encounter the idea of the text, as Barthes wrote of it, as a "signifying practice" or, even, as a "volume of traces" in which the politics of the streets were in fact displaced in order to open up the meaning of a formerly closed culture. What Barthes said of the moment of the text in semiotics is a reasonable reflection of what thousands of young scholars — even those who came to hate the ideas Barthes and Lévi-Strauss inspired — were in fact doing.

It is not likely to have been mere coincidence that the three crucial moments in the history of semiotics corresponded to three crucial moments in post-World War II politics. The moment of semiotic hope in the 1950s came just when world politics was freezing into the ice-hard terms of cold war. Did not McCarthyism in the United States and the establishing of NATO in 1949 and the Warsaw Pact in 1955 define a political juncture when even the politicians used words as weapons to wound, define, and condemn?

The moment of semiotic science in the 1960s came during a particularly conclusive period in the by then more than a decade of wars of colonial liberation. Were not Castro's revolution in 1959 and the Algerian truce in 1962 decisive signs that decolonization could strike close to home, thus requiring a fundamentally different attitude toward the soon-to-be-former world colonial system in Asia, Africa, and the Caribbean? If that different attitude did not eventuate in a change in the official "science" of the diplomatic world order, it was, just the same, a difference of attitude that had to recognize, if not admit, the flaws in the Cold War's sphere of influence doctrine. President Kennedy's small victory in the Cuban Missile Crisis, like his memorable speech at the Berlin Wall, were more the benedictions of the old order than the invocations of a new, as the war in Vietnam would soon thereafter make clear. Even today, Europe and the United States struggle to make political sense of their simultaneous reliance upon and hostility toward immigrant workers from and in their former colonies.

And, thirdly, Barthes's moment of the Text, beginning in 1968, occurred just when the two formerly divergent forces of cold war *and* decolonization veered sharply toward each other only to clash not in the far reaches of the world system but in virtually every major capitol *in* the Westernized world. This was, as the saying went, the time when, in politics, the Center did not hold, or so it seemed. It certainly was a time when, as the truth of many civil rights movements joined the reality of Vietnam, public opinion shifted gradually out from under the idea that the troubles in Berkeley, Paris, Chicago, Tokyo, Mexico were communist inspired. The moment of the Text in semiotics was also the moment of increased and shocked realization that the well-defined cultural verities to which most had adhered were less self-evident. Meaning was indeed, for a good number of years, and perhaps still, cut loose from the old centered scheme of things such that, again in Barthes's phrase, politics was a signifying practice because the cultural and political centers no longer imposed themselves with impunity. The politics of the Text might thus be seen as the politics appropriate to the lack of an unquestionable cultural authority.

Semiotics cannot be, and did not become, a general science of culture, just as many now realize that Barthes and others of the day required the Text to bear too much responsibility for the changed political and cultural situation after the 1960s. Yet, the moment of the Text must be credited with having advanced understanding of the delicacy with which, as we now would put it, power intrudes gently upon even the most refined expressions of our knowledge and discourse. Again quoting Barthes (though one could just as well quote Foucault or Derrida to the same effect): "It is the responsibility of semiotics . . . to question its own discourse: as a science of languages, as a datum, a transparency, a tool."[12] The burden of any practice that questions its own language is that it must be not just post-scientific but necessarily political. Who would have thought in the early public days of Lévi-Strauss and Barthes that within a mere quarter century good liberal philosophers would echo their ideas? "The heroes of a liberal society are the strong poet and the utopian revolutionary," as Richard Rorty put it in 1989.[13] But then who would have thought in the early 1950s that the Cold War would not only collapse at about the same time Rorty and others were recasting liberal politics as poetics, but collapse so severely that the former spheres of their influence are today caught up in economic struggles so severe as to make them seem vastly more Malthusian than Marxian?[14]

Structuralist semiotics, including even the politics of the text, had their limits to which they soon enough arrived. They were not the cause of the new geopolitical order, to be sure. Yet, they were part, and a vital part, of the larger changes, just as their successors, not excluding postmodernism, are also among the attempts to come to terms with the lack of a convincing, enforcing Center to world affairs. There is misery still, to be certain; as there are pretenders to centralizing power seeking to bully the world into conformity with their selfish interests. They succeed. The world is more, not less, unequal. The poor are more, not less, hungry and shelterless. But, even the political bullies must realize that they are in fact pretenders who make their selfish ways as much through the bluster of their commercial broadcasts as through the truth of the way of life they once claimed, against surprisingly little protest, to embody.

5

Letters From Brazil: Structuralism's Zero Signifier

March 12, 1996

Dr Maria Lucia Andrade
Somewhere in Brasilia
BRAZIL

Dear Maria,
I received your e-mail and immediately set about to reply. This, it turns out, was a mistake. Somehow, I pushed a bad key and eliminated not only my reply but your message along with your address. It is unlikely that, after all these years, you would be able fully to understand just how much of a loss this is to me.

First of all, and needless to say, it means the loss of the contact with you. The words I had typed on the screen just before my electronic accident were: "Hearing from you is one of the most wonderful . . ." I would have gone on to say that I was truly surprised at just how much I felt hearing from you. Yours was not the first e-mail message I have received, nor the first I have erased more or less accidentally. But it was the first of such unexpected and uninvited communications that so promptly brought back kind memories of the pleasures of a long-lost friendship. Most of the e-mail I get is from people who want something from me, or at least want to tell me something of importance to them if not to me. Otherwise, it is from people so far out of my past I can hardly, if at all, remember them. How, exactly, you and these others find my electronic address, I do not understand. Nor is it that these voices from some incomprehensible e-world are unwelcome. The plain fact is that I do not have, at least not yet, the will or desire to engage in correspondences of this sort. But the message from you was different.

It brought back the days in Paris, nearly twenty years ago, when, I now realize, I had begun to think differently about life, work, and the world. With your now lost note, those years came back with a force that had been *dormant for a long time. I remember (or imagine I remember) walks in the early Spring through the Quartier Latin. I do not, curiously, remember which language we spoke. It must have been French — or was it? I remember seeing* Fellini's Roma *with you at a cinema somewhere in one of the* arrondissements *tourists seldom visit. The film was with Portuguese subtitles but I do not recall that the language of the subtitles made any difference. Until Armarcord, I never understood any of Fellini's films and never supposed they were meant to be understood in the usual sense. What I understand about that evening and the few other times we passed together is that they were a comforting interlude at a time when I felt utterly uprooted from nearly everything that before had been familiar and obvious.*

Why were you in Paris? Wasn't it that you were training as psychoanalyst — Jungian, right? (But, then, we talked a lot of Lacan. Were you working at a Lacanian institute?) I loved this rare opportunity to discuss such strange ideas with a person not less an outsider to them than I. It was, I think, the uncertainty of grasp that may have provided the medium of communication. Paris, even then nearly a decade after '68, was to me like dream language. What people were saying and writing was absolutely true and beyond refutation, yet never quite definitive and certainly not absolute truth. This was my Paris experience that year — fresh and exciting but also strange and disconcerting. I did not have the sense that you were in any way as badly unhinged by it all as I was. Yet, we flourish it seems.

Since those days I have been unhappily divorced and now happily re-married. The boys (I think you met Noah once when I picked him up from the Ecole maternelle *at the* Eglise américaine*) are both grown, or at least both out of college and finding their ways, reliably, in the world. I teach at a smallish school not far from New York City. I write books and essays still somewhat influenced by what I learned that year in Paris and find that what I have to say is generally of interest to sociologists younger than I but specifically annoying to almost everyone older. The reactions of those younger are encouraging but still I entertain the fantasy of trying my hand at something else — something more directly human. I trained for a brief while as a psychoanalyst, but gave that up (I am unable to sit still that long). I toy with writing different kinds of books, ones that might be read outside colleges; and I have even thought of once again becoming a parish priest (of the married, Protestant kind). But, I imagine I will in the remaining years still do some of what I do now.*

Oh, how I wish I could find your postal address. I want to learn just how you have gotten from Paris to Brasilia and how you are settling into these years of later life. I have a colleague and friend who visits Brazil quite often, perhaps he can help me find your address through some e-mail or regular mail listing or another. I would so enjoy a correspondence with you. I wonder what it is like living in Brasilia? Wasn't it chopped out of the world's second most famously dark jungle? And I wonder what an analyst finds in the talk of patients living in a modern city against that history of pillage of the natural world? You can see that loss was already much on my mind. This

*may be part of aging, or of trying to live in and understand a world that,
having been built on the destruction of all the precious pasts of natural and
human worlds, now offers itself as though it were growing closer, smaller,
more singular. This when anyone who stops to think must realize that what
is offered is offered in passing. There one minute, lost another, just like your
e-mail message.*

*I lost your e-note because I do not know how to use the system. More
honestly, I have refused to use it and the best way not to use it is not to learn
it. My students are not sure what to think of this. My colleagues find it
irritating. Others don't say. They just don't write. Though I occasionally
browse the few e-mails I receive (mostly local notices of blood drives or of
down times in the e-mail system), I answer, if at all, through the regular
mails. As a result, I receive relatively little mail of any kind since almost no
one writes real letters any more. This I do not mind. But losing your message
and address makes me realize that I am living in a most fragile world.*

*Why this occurs to me just now in life, I do not know. Take regular mail,
for example. I never once completely understood how it happens that the
postal services work, that all those millions upon millions of tiny pieces of
paper find their ways to almost any place in the world except, I am told,
parts of Italy and Afghanistan. The only thing I know for sure about this is
that the postal system relies on actual, as opposed to virtual, human beings
— not all of them reliable. My local postman is a miserable soul. He comes
by late in the day because, my neighbor tells me, he would have to go home
after lunch if he did his rounds promptly. It seems he is bored at home, but
what kind of a person gets thrills from other people's mail? Yet, even with
lost souls like this one delivering it, somehow nearly all the mail gets
through.*

*But e-mail is something else. Wherever your message to me went first —
to some satellite I suppose (could there actually be wires connecting you to
me?) — the only human hands in the process were yours set purposefully
to your keyboard and mine set clumsily (and disastrously) to mine.
Otherwise, the message was sealed within some electronically derived and
driven machine vulnerable only to my ignorance of my keyboard (and, in
principle, to the evil of some terrorist anywhere on the planet). Electronic
messages, once sent, cannot get lost except by the stupidity of the receiver,
while postal messages — which are totally dependent on frail, usually
walking and weary, human beings — are completely vulnerable to loss. It
happens, of course. We had a famous case of millions of letters being lost
in the Chicago post office. But the miracle remains that, relatively speaking,
so few are normally lost in a system so fragile. I wonder if, in the end, e-
mail does all that much better than human mail? Or, if the world is all that
much better for having deprived so many humans of honest work sorting
and delivering? Or, even if there will always be humans delivering paper
and cardboard, if the result of new electronic media is merely that there are
infinitely more messages than are needed? I have no doubt that much of the
e-mail sent (if mine is any indication) would be better unsent, or sent after*

the deferrals and delays of actually putting pen to paper (so to speak), then trudging through the snow or rain to the post office. As a psychoanalyst you surely appreciate the importance of deferral and delay, of simply waiting and thinking and then speaking only when the feeling or thought is well formed. What if, as in the nineteenth century and all the centuries before that, all serious human communications over space were sent only under the rule of waiting for the right words at the right moment and measured against the effort and inconvenience of getting them written and posted? Rousseau's wealthy lovers would invite him to that evening's soirée by notes hand-delivered to his cottage within view of the main house. Whether or not his love was better, I am tempted to believe such a world was, or would be, a better world.

Well, I should say this is what I thought until I received your lovely note, which I am sure I could not have received other than through the e-mails. Even if you had saved the address book from when we last wrote, I have been away from Illinois for nearly seventeen years. It would have never been forwarded. But, I will test this assumption by sending this letter to the last address of yours I have, if I can find it in a box in the garage.

Since we last saw each other in Paris I imagine you have changed. I know I have, and I believe the world has in ways that then even two people alert to the world, as we were, could not have imagined. Or, has it? This question haunts my work and my life. I worry about my boys and my students. Will they be able to survive in a world so much less welcoming than the one that allowed us, neither of us wealthy, to spend those years in Paris, thus to meet but for a few days? I wonder just how much all the mass of humanity is still balanced on the edge of some deep void of silence against which we keep ourselves alive by saying what comes to mind? Are we better off now that the void is the emptiness of cyberspace filled as it is with digitalized codes than by the dark forests of life out of which your city in Brazil and my village in New England were once, long ago, ruthlessly carved?

Well, as you can see, I have gotten far from the original point of my letter which was to tell you that I got your message, that it brightened my already bright day, that it made me think about loss and the world, and that it made me long for things I never really had in the first place. It added life to life. I hope you get this, somehow. But even if your e-message was the last I shall hear from you, I trust that you,having been good enough to send it, are otherwise enjoying the blessings of a life in which you must have touched others, including your patients, as you once touched me and did again by your note.

With affection and abiding friendship,

Charles

Personal Business

The letter to Maria was actually sent. I do, in fact, write letters of this sort on occasion, especially when moved as I was. Whatever the reader thinks of the letter, it might well offend academic sensibilities that I would use it to introduce what will soon become a rather technical discussion of an aspect of structuralist semiotics.

Only recently has the use of personal material begun to appear in writings read by academics and many readers wonder about such things. Once, not so long ago, in a colloquium of scholars whom I had not previously met, someone remarked that the use of autobiographical and other personal material was, he said (as though it were self-evidently true), "a typical postmodern device." The idea that postmodernism is pre-occupied with the personal holds currency especially among those who hate it. This, no doubt, is a slightly more polite version of the allegation that, among other terrible things, postmodernism is "narcissistic." Yet, such a complaint does not account for the fact that writing that is not in any obvious way postmodern is also highly personal, whether or not it is self-referential. Rousseau's *Confessions* was highly personal and perhaps self-referential, and justifiably a classic in spite of this. Kant's famous *Critique of Practical Reason*, written not long after Rousseau's book, was not in the least personal though it founded a self-referential theory of knowledge (and led to an ethics of the same sort). Why does no one call Kant "narcissistic"? Could any philosophy have been more so? Much more recently, Patricia Williams's *Race and the Alchemy of Rights*, while occasionally narcissistic, is considered a point of departure for the studied use of memoir in critical legal studies, while Henry Louis Gates's *Colored People*,[1] a very intimate personal memoir, is not, so far as I can tell, self-referential. Personal references of whatever kind are hardly a domain property of postmodernism.

Yet, it is true that considerations of the relationship between one's personal, even private, circumstances and the structure of the world as such, are a part of today's culture. It is a reliable suspicion that this un-settling attention to personal business may have been due not so much to an epidemic of narcissistic disorder as to events that transpired in the world order — events which have made "the personal" everyone's busi-ness, like it or not. Such world events — that is: events like the decolonization of world politics, globalization and the particular effect of televisual media on personal and economic life, the class wars and the disappearance of industrial work, the new social movements and the rise of identity politics, the seeming collapse of common regard for Western "values" — are most clearly events transpiring quite outside any academic circle. They are also indisputably events that have, each in its own way, made the personal the business of world discussion. Yet, in the short history of their occurrence since the early years after World War II, events like these have affected not just how the media, the politicians, and ordinary persons view the world, but, to be sure, how the guardians of academic culture think. Thus, it is not at all a leap to suggest that among the new traditions of opinion with respect to world events and world culture, the social theories of culture to which this book is devoted are important, if not instrumental, to our general understanding of the events themselves. Postmodern social theories are one, though not by any means the only or most important one, of these events.

Postmodern social theory today is, in fact, a recently occurring dispensation of a much longer tradition that goes back to a beginning in the late 1940s in the first blush of writings that began the structuralist — more properly, the structuralist semiotic—movement. As I said in the previous chapter, the origins of what today we call postmodern ideas were in a complicated, earlier time when social theories of many kinds (including those of scientific sociology) were undergoing a necessary adjustment to a world transformed by war, economic failure, and the holocaust. Thus, as I said, to refer to the foundations of structuralist semiotics is also to refer to a fork in the social-scientific road from which the formal social sciences, including sociology, took one path and the eventually-to-become postmodern movements took another. This irony of ironies is evident in the very texts which are indisputably central to social science as they are to structuralist semiotics — texts like Claude Lévi-Strauss's *Elementary Structures of Kinship*, which was at once a going back to the earlier ideas of Emile Durkheim and a step forward toward the transformation of cultural sociology into a rigorous study of the meaning of cultural things under the aegis of their semiotic (as opposed to factual) properties.

In the simplest of terms, structuralist semiotics arose from the idea that the meaning of human structures was not merely mediated by the descriptive totems and rites by which human groups represented their worlds. Rather, the structures meant something in their own right. In the early traditions of semiotics, Lévi-Strauss's elementary kinship relations, like Durkheim's elementary forms of religious life, were considered meaningful by their very nature. They did not so much *convey* meanings held somewhere in the collective consciousness of group members as they *were* those meanings — their only and irreducible source. Readers of Durkheim's *Elementary Forms of the Religious Life* will readily appreciate his anticipation of such thinking in his later writings, as they will understand why, in 1949. Lévi-Strauss took up and advanced what Durkheim had done just shy of a half-century before.[2]

But what is easily forgotten, or was never seen in the first place, is that by joining language (or sign systems) to human structures this early structuralism necessarily dislocated the personal or subjective side of the traditional epistemological couplet. It is all too simple an error to reduce structuralism to, say, Lévi-Strauss's famous controversy with Sartre's alleged subjectivism.[3] It may be the case that Lévi-Strauss had stumbled onto something the implications of which his own system could not explain. But he did seem, even in the early years, fully to appreciate that the structural study of cultural things stimulates a lingering uncertainty as to one's hold on the personal. If indeed there are universal structures in the human mind, then one must wonder what is to become of the private deviations of the individual? No modern thinker who has studied the most elementary social groups from a structural perspective could help but wonder what these people actually thought and felt about their totemic and kin arrangements. Was it truly possible for them to wish he were a *wartwut* instead of a *wurant*, to be hot wind instead of black cockatoo? Reading Mauss, Durkheim, and Lévi-Strauss, it always seemed to me improbable that such structures permitted deviant and ultimately destructive aspirations of this sort. But, if they did not, or if they only controlled the impulse to be other than black cockatoo, it would be necessary to ask what then would be left of the universal human structures that ought to unite us even with the Australian aboriginal Wotjobaluks of whom Mauss and Durkheim wrote in *Primitive Classifications,*[4] thereby providing Lévi-Strauss an important clue to his semiotics?

I say that Lévi-Strauss understood this dilemma not just because he exhibited a keen regard for it in many of his writings, but because he exhibited a healthy confidence in the universal significance of *his* personal experience by writing a memoir of the years of his formation as an anthropologist. *Tristes Tropiques*, surely one of the most enduring classics of social-scientific memoir (and a book Susan Sontag called "one of the great books of the century,"[5] was published in 1955 as a memoir of Lévi-Strauss's first and only extended trip to Brazil in 1935. *Tristes Tropiques*, sad tropics, written well before the postmodern era, is a book about the disappearance of things — of the tribal societies he encountered in his four years in Brazil in the 1930s, but clearly also of the European civilization that in the 1950s was just emerging from the trials that challenged its most important articles of faith, especially those as to its capacity to renew itself endlessly. The book is an intensely personal one because it is the memoir of Lévi-Strauss's coming of age as an anthropologist and because of its deep, almost painful, revelations of his feeling of loss for the modern world which in 1935 was already reverting to its most savage instincts.

He concluded *Tristes Tropiques* much in the style of travelogues of that day, with a sadly voiced farewell at the setting sun:

> The brotherhood of man acquires a concrete meaning when it makes us see, in the poorest tribe, a confirmation of our own image and an experience, the lessons of which we can assimilate, along with so many others. We may even discover a pristine freshness in these lessons. Since we know that, for thousands of years, man has succeeded only in repeating himself, we will attain in that nobility of thought which consists in going back beyond all the repetitions and taking as the starting-point of our reflections the indefinable grandeur of man's beginnings. Being human signifies, for each one of us, belonging to a class, a society, a country, a continent and a civilization; and for us European earth-dwellers, the adventure played out in the heart of the New World signifies in the first place that it was not our world and that we bear responsibility for the crime of its destruction; and secondly, that there will never be another New World: since the confrontation between the Old World and the new makes us thus conscious of our selves, let us at least express it in its primary terms — in the place where, and by referring back to a time when, our world missed the opportunity offered to it of choosing between its various missions.[6]

The personal memoir had become a meditation on the end of the human order — or, at least, though he did not use the expression, of the *modern* world, as it was conceived during the half-millennium in which European modernism ruled. And the meditation owed its moral convictions, curiously, to the systematic study of the passing structures of Brazil's elementary social groups — those whose land would open itself to the construction of Brasilia and later to the capitalization of the natural riches of the deeper jungles and beds of the Amazon.

The day of structuralist semiotics is now passed. Its earnest experiments in the semiotic interpretation of modern cultures, though they achieved impressive theoretical heights, never advanced in any convincing degree beyond Roland Barthes's early essays in *Mythologies* (published just two years after *Tristes Tropiques*. Semiotics, once it was seized upon by young academics in America, soon froze under the cold, long-tenured pressure of scientific regulation. Structuralism, on the other hand, endured a while longer. It even outlived the tragic end of Louis Althusser, serving a good purpose in sociology's revision of social movement theory, world systems history, and crypto-Marxist political sociology. One still notes with respect the faint lines of its effect, visible on the horizon where Marxism slowly sinks. Structuralist semiotics, as such, is gone. In the place where it stood ever so briefly one can still feel the chill of its ghost.

Somewhere still there are signs organized by the space from which came

Maria's e-mail message, itself sent from a prior space in human time where she works things through with her patients who live over the remains of the sacred forests of a part of the New World the Old destroyed. These point, one supposes, to that which is suddenly now exposed. The void from which we get mediated messages out of pasts we can only dimly recall is no different from that which Lévi-Strauss explored — both in his travels to Brazil and in his first structural investigations of the zero-signi-fier of human culture.

Semiotic Politics

In the generation of the 1960s which, in Europe considered itself post-structuralist, many took up where Lévi-Strauss and the early Barthes and even the younger Althusser left off. As some early feminist theory, especially Julia Kristeva and Luce Irigaray, self-consciously sought, for a while at least, to work out an engendered semiotics, more broadly the earliest wave of feminist activists around the world began by, simply, talking through the hidden meanings of their gender in thousands upon thousands of meetings in bars, bookstores, centers, bedrooms, and living rooms. Much the same was true, though perhaps without the self-conscious semiotics of Kristeva, in the decolonizing and race movements in Africa, the Latin Americas and Asia, Europe and the American South, in the early gay and lesbian rights movement, and most explicitly in the student movement which was in name and tactic first of all a "Free Speech Movement." A quarter century later it surprised the pundits of world politics that the revolutions in East Central Europe were as non-violent as they were. Others who had been reading between the lines of sensationalizing news accounts knew that the many new social move-ments were, first of all, based on talking, preaching, acting, singing, writing, marching, and dancing things through. Though, to be sure, blood was shed and lives lost, these were largely movements based on a reinterpretation of culture. Those who had participated in, or watched closely, these other new movements might have been less surprised by the role played by leaders of great eloquence — Vaclav Havel in Czecho-slovakia and Nelson Mandela in South Africa most notably — in leading a tired and beaten people to redefine the meaning of their political cul-tures. The communists and proponents of apartheid fell because, in large part, they ran out of things to say that made any sense of the contradic-tions everyone could see.

This is not to suggest that the world had become or is becoming nothing but a cultural spectacle, as some believe; nor to propose, foolishly, as not even Derrida ever did, that there is nothing but text. It is merely, and simply, to say that we live in a world changed by movements that transcend the existential method while trying still to answer its question of meaning. Since the decolonizing and civil rights movements, the sustained feminist and queer politics, the emergent movements of ethnic pride — not all of which are to be admired in equal measure — we can reliably say that those aggrieved with the world as it is are inquiring into the meaning of life, though without the naive existential sense that it could ever be sufficient to change it by the quality of personal choices one makes. Semiotics, in this broader sense, is not so much a metaphor for cultural studies and cultural politics as the most astute way to describe those politics. They are, in the most precise sense, attempts to rethink the meaning of the world, by retalking the world's meaning. This is why all of the new social movements are, without exception, attempts to create, as it is said, a new discourse. But those new discourses are nothing new. They are, rather, attempts to put into words, and other discursive media, the stories of peoples — blacks, women, gays, natives, subalterns of all kinds — whose stories had been hidden. This is what Lévi-Strauss seems to have vaguely realized he was doing in his fateful voyages to Brazil and the New World.

But there is one character, or social type, whose story has not yet been told, and may never be tellable. It is the character who stood in the place of "Man" himself — the man of humanism, of proud liberalism, of universal reason. His story had been, may still be, the purported story of the West, of the longish history of modernizing culture that arose in Europe at least by the eighteenth century, was projected back onto Greece and forward onto the New World, and thus onto the human Universal itself. At the center of that story was generic Man who, it is now realized, was always as gendered as those who suffered by his hand had thought. Could he be the zero signifier of modern culture? Of modern politics? Could he be the one whose story, so insusceptible to the particulars of narration, must be told, if it can be, in order for the world to discover, truly, whether it is post- or just plain still-modern?

Man as Zero Sign?

As a white, europeanized male I am member to a social category that is object of most of the radical political currents of protest expressed, in part, in the aftermath of the "linguistic turn" deriving from structural semiotics. I am, in other words, member of that category marked today by the oppositional force of those whose differences are signs of the oppression wrought by members, if not the whole, of those belonging to my most visible and undeniable social affinity. Such an affiliation, once earnestly desired, now is possessed of at least uncertain, and in many instances certain least, value. Those who are joined with me in this designation are comparably marked, frequently against their will, by the racial, gendered, cultural, and world positional signs of the evil at whose hands others have suffered.

Somewhere on a fine line between the recognition of a personal circumstance and acknowledgement of a general social category, the distinction between personal and general fades. The personal complicity need not, perhaps cannot, be disregarded.[7] Yet, acknowledgment of the categorical circumstance somehow eludes the power of the subject to explain the politically decisive relation of the category of white, europeanized, males to the "Others" whose oppositional consciousness is formed against "It," the category (if not always concrete individuals within it).

Were I to shift voice abruptly and assume the technical attitude of a semiotician in analyzing this social category, I would in effect be describing a familiar term in the science of signs. I am describing, thus, a term the significance of which owes not to an inherent attribute, nor to a definite relation between its particular meaning and phenomena in a real world. This social category, thus described, signifies entirely by its location in relation to other significant and signifying terms. More specifically, there is good reason further to classify this term as bearing a unique relation in its proper system, though this additional analytic step requires that the hitherto synchronic and historically neutral analysis be now supplemented by a diachronic judgment, taking into the account the evolution of the term.

We are discussing, thereby, not simply a significant term in an equivalent but differential relation to others, rather one with a unique history. This term, as yet unmarked, has never in its history been merely equivalent and not, until recently, considered with enough critical focus even to be understood as differential.

The social category significantly constituted of (among other elements) white, europeanized males was generally an unmarked, silent term in the discourse of world politics because, prior to the 1960s, it was *the* significant term to such an extent that its difference was not commonly inflected or otherwise glossed. In this usage the term was pure by virtue of its signifying power. In the past generation, with the historical recognition of its difference, the term has assumed a technically different purity owing to a sharp shift in signifying valence associated closely with the discovery of its differential power. Political movements based in the oppositional consciousness of people of color, women, former colonial subjects, the

sexually stigmatized, and others now could be said to use the term as a
zero signifier in political discourse.

Is the social category of which white, europeanized, heterosexual males
are member the zero signifier of contemporary political discourse? Is that
category necessary to a system of oppositional politics without which the
system could generate no articulated differences? Do zero signifiers exist
in any signifying system, much less a political one?

These questions are shocking because they bear all the defects of any
structural analysis applied to historical matters. They seem to eliminate
the subjective force of the term or terms. In this case, they would seem to
excuse members of the purported category from responsibility associated
with their social status. Quite apart from the prospect of their defensive-
ness when stated by a member of the category, the questions could be
taken, on the other hand, as a kind of technical joke, thereby unserious.
Thus is required further analysis of the concept of a zero signifier in political discourse.

The Zero Signifier

The zero signifier occurs prominently at several junctures in the recent
history of semiotics. At each, a crucial step in the politicization of semiotic discourse was taken.

The first appearance of the zero signifier was at the virtual first moment
of the modern history of structural semiotics, the beginning of Lévi-
Strauss's *Elementary Structures of Kinship*. Here, as Derrida comments
in an equally important first text,[8] Lévi-Strauss introduces himself with
reference to two important subjects of the book's two introductory chapters: nature and culture, the problem of incest. In effect, Lévi-Strauss here
introduces and transcends Saussure by referring the science of signs to the
most general of problems. Incest plays the crucial role of being the one
fact which confounds the almost naive definition he provides for the
difference between nature and culture (the former being that which is
universal, and the latter that which is particular, hence normative, in the
human circumstance):

> We have been led to pose the problem of incest in connection with the
> relationship between man's biological existence and his social existence,
> and we have immediately established that the prohibition could not be
> ascribed accurately to either one or the other. In the present work we
> propose to find the solution to this anomaly by showing that the prohibi-
> tion of incest is the link between them. . . . But this union is neither static

nor arbitrary, and as soon as it comes into being, the whole situation is completely changed. Indeed, it is less a union than a transformation or transition. Before it, culture is still non-existent; with it, nature's sovereignty over man is ended. *The problem of incest is where nature transcends itself.*[9]

The problem of incest is that incest, as a fact of human nature, is at once *both* universal, hence natural, *and* normative, hence cultural. It, incest, thereby throws into disarray the very distinction it constitutes. Lévi-Strauss seeks, hereby, to make a new departure in the human sciences, one that recognizes yet seeks to discredit that crucial distinction upon which the idea of a human or social science is founded. He sought to make of the human sciences a true science by the very act of removing, or displacing, the essential condition of its original scientific claims.

It is well-known that this reading of Lévi-Strauss's structuralist program is that of Jacques Derrida, rendered at a crucial moment in the post-history of semiotics — the one at which Lévi-strauss's structuralism was read simultaneously in and out of legitimacy. It was, in fact, the founding moment in poststructuralism. Derrida's play on Lévi-Strauss (to which I shall return shortly) is a double play on Lévi-Strauss's own double trick: that of simultaneously bringing linguistics up to date while using it to turn anthropology back on its own central riddle.

At the one moment, Lévi-Strauss brings Saussure into modern discourse, but with a supplementary appeal to Roman Jakobson in which he seeks to resolve the fundamental dilemma in Saussure's scheme: its inability to explain strongly the social origins of the arbitrary sign. This attempt at resolution now of two riddles (the social origin of the sign, the nature of anthropology) is just one of the many, sometimes maddening, plays on texts and words for which poststructuralism has become famous. But what Derrida does, in his reading of Lévi-Strauss, is to demonstrate that once the semiotics of discourse enters the picture of social science even the great structuralizing master cannot resist its demands of intertextual play. Thus, in effect, Derrida's reading of Lévi-Strauss requires first Lévi-Strauss's (silent) reading of Saussure. The founding of poststructuralism entails the founding of structuralism in a curious way that makes it worth the while to look at each move.

The earliest mention of the zero signifier in Lévi-Strauss appears in a 1945 essay, "Structural Analysis in Linguistics and in Anthropology," his first major professional publication.[10] Here is the surest evidence that Lévi-Strauss used the Russian tradition and Jakobson to supplement Saussure from the very beginning. The essay is a general discussion of the "close methodological analogy which exists" between linguistics and anthropology in which he makes the extraordinarily strong claim that "structural linguistics will certainly play the same renovating role with respect to the social sciences that nuclear physics, for example, has played in the physical sciences."[11] Two pages thereafter Lévi-Strauss illustrates this bold claim with reference to the analogy of structural oppositions taken from linguistics to the study of kinship. Immediately, Lévi-Strauss refers to the zero signifier:

> Following an analogous method, the anthropologist might be tempted to break down analytically the kinship terms of any given system into their components. In our own kinship system, for instance, the term *father* has positive connotations with respect to sex, relative age, and generations; *but it has a zero value on the dimension of collaterality, and it cannot express an affinal relationship.*[12]

Importantly, the sentence preceding this extract ends with a reference not to Saussure but to one of Jakobson's articles on the phonological classification of consonants. The importance of this very early prior appeal to the authority of Jakobson is evident in the defense of this, and other early discussions made thirteen years later for their collection into *Structural Anthropology.*

Here, Lévi-Strauss addresses directly the limitations of Saussure. His argument is that Saussure's rigid separation of synchronic and diachronic linguistics led structural linguistics to a falsely abstract idea of the sign:

> The arbitrary character of the linguistic sign is thus only provisional. Once a sign has been created its function becomes explicit, as related, on the one hand, to the biological structure of the brain and, on the other, to the aggregate of other signs — that is, to the linguistic universe, which always tends to be systematic.[13]

But there is another move in this discussion, one that — not surprisingly — depends on Jakobson. Following Jakobson, Lévi-Strauss downshifts from the sign represented by the lexical union of a mental concept and sound image to the phoneme. This, he claims, is the most parsimonious route to an understanding of the identity that might exist between "the laws of the universe and those of the human mind."[14]

This piece, published in France in 1958, like the 1945 article it defends, is not closely argued. The difference seems to be that in the later piece Lévi-Strauss drops the analogical quality of the relationship between social science and linguistics. The linguistic model is now taken for granted as the solution. Between the two articles Jakobson remains the constant link by which a Saussurean structuralism is brought into history, then beyond through the phoneme to nature. In the same intervening period Lévi-Strauss published *Elementary Structures of Kinship* (originally 1949) and the "Structural Study of Myth" originally (1955). The former, as Derrida pointed out in 1966 [1971], seeks to mediate the nature/culture dichotomy with reference to the universal/particular elements of the incest problem. The latter, perhaps Lévi-Strauss's mostly widely read piece, is amazingly a near purely Saussurean discussion.[15]

Thus, Lévi-Strauss can be turned on himself. He too, in this early period, can only be read structurally in his Jakobsonian sense. His theory is incomplete at any one diachronic slice. *The Elementary Structures* omits language, includes nature/culture; the "Structural Study" includes language, omits explicit reference to nature/culture. While the 1945 and 1958 programmatic pieces include both, but in a relationship in which, in the former, language is prior as the analogue to structural anthropology while, in the latter, anthropology is prior as the general theory of relationships. It would seem reasonable to propose that in this early period Lévi-Strauss himself was deploying (or, perhaps, being deployed by) a series of scientific riddles that oscillated uneasily around, among other things, the one almost inaudible term uttered in 1945, the father as zero signifier without affinal competence.

The zero signifier is what Derrida picks up in his reading of Lévi-Strauss.[16] Derrida must make more of the zero signifier in Lévi-Strauss because it is invoked in a crucial way in his own poststructuralist theory of the supplement which he presents in this surprisingly positive reference to Lévi-Strauss. Thus, at the beginning of "Structure, Sign, and Play in the Discourse of the Human Sciences", Derrida announces a portentous "event" in the "history of the concept structure,[17] which event is immediately described as an event in world politics. "This moment was that in which language invaded the universal problematic; that in which, in the absence of a center or origin, everything became discourse . . ."[18] These words, announcing the now famous political concept decentering, were uttered in 1966, published in France in 1968 — just as the free play of discourse in Europe and the United States was, in fact, decentering the eurocentric world. Derrida pronounced this political moment in an ironically cool discussion of technical matters in Lévi-Strauss's structuralism. Cool irony was the only trope available to refer to the politics of a zero signifier, to define an event that is neither natural nor cultural, but both, yet neither.

Thus, behind Derrida's double play on Lévi-Strauss, stands Lévi-Strauss's double play on Saussure, and we are left with the "politics of free play." In the 1960s that play unsettled one aspect of the strong cultural center, the imperialist intent of world capitalism of which the colonial liberation movements and resistance to the war in Vietnam are signs. In the 1990s the seemingly same play has destroyed the grand ideology of postwar imperialism, the cold war. Politics of such magnitude cannot be conducted simply within history or nature; they must call the fundamentals into question — even if only for a moment of our time.

The zero signifier, therefore, played a necessary role in the evolution of semiotics and, thereby, of world politics. Without it the arbitrary absolute of signification could not have been conceived. By means of it, semiotically informed politics has called (is calling) into question the foundations of world politics.

The Lost Centre

The zero signifier is and is not the Center that is decentered. This is the irony required of both Lévi-Strauss and Derrida; the irony, therefore, central (though largely unarticulated) to the history of modern semiotics. Saussure prepared the way for modern structural semiotics by the ironic move of destroying an epistemological Center (the realism of the sign), while founding significance in the zero signifier of the historicized social community without a history. Lévi-Strauss articulated the zero signifier in the play of nature and culture in incest, and the theory of language whose only history is the diachrony of sound. Derrida founded post-structuralism on the ironic event of a move within and against Lévi-Strauss's structuralism which, contrary to appearances, is not just a technical debate, but *the* event of world politics. And world politics, since the 1960s and through the current moment, turns to the pen to destroy the sword, to words to overcome the centuries-long domination of eurocentrism.

In each of these successive turns, gradually a political semiotics has emerged. Each entails a simultaneous move against a center — epistemological realism, historical realism, political imperialism — and each move entails use of a zero signifier — history without time, the zero point of nature/culture, the free play of signification.

Are not, we must ask, the zero signifier and the Center the same? The first, formal answer is of course to point out that the question is asked within a philosophy of identity, the very philosophy the political semiotics of differences attacks. The second, more substantial answer is that a social theory of difference decenters by means of a center which is not.

The white, europeanized, straight, and bourgeois male is the lost Center, the zero signifier that, having been outed from the closet of cultural pride, is, in today's cultural politics, still the zero signifier. This categorical Man functions now, less as an imperial Center, and less as the silent zero sign of the modernizing culture of which he was the unspeakable source of all meaning. But he functions nonetheless. Unable to tell his story, it having been the purported story of all, he stands, just the same, as the sign against and upon which the politics of difference articulates itself. Yet, it hardly need be said, he is increasingly feeble in both the categorical and actual political senses. His newly come upon frailty is a direct correlate of a weakening of the persuasive force of modernity itself. Modernity was, or is, as you wish, the culture that dreamt, or dreams, of a common, true, and universal humanity.

This ideal, noble in its own right, was, or is, one that, to this point in human history, never once conclusively was able to make itself politically or economically real in measurable terms. If all "men" are free and equal then, at least, most of them (and their sisters) should after this long time have some reasonable expectation of these desirable goods. No one can deny that they do not. Indeed, at the near end of the twentieth century, particularly in the most affluent societies, the number of those denied equal benefit of law and income is indisputably growing in direct proportion to the widening gap between their real prospects and those of the most blessed. Modernity's answer to this dilemma has always been to refer those who suffer to hope. This is fine and good for the short-run moral sanity of the social body. But, through the cold eye of social analysis, hope is not what was originally promised.

Universal humanity implies, as it must, a goodly prospect of fair access to a decent share of the political and economic goods the few have in such stark abundance. Even, or especially, the more conservative version of the promise of Universal humanity — that we are offered only an equal chance, and no other specific promises — fails to read plausibly among the most hungry, shelterless, ill, and impoverished. It is not that I or any other particular white guy of straight inclination and relative privilege can be held to a specific responsibility for this failure (though surely some of us could be and most of us might be). Whatever is done about the real political and economic injustices no one of fair mind can deny, and surely doing something is the first order of business, the fact remains that resistance to doing what can be done is largely bound up in the unreadiness of those who have shared this categorical power to relent in their insistence that the culture our kind founded in the eighteenth century and before is the one, true culture. There is no logic or method that can assert the truth of what we once believed with impunity. It was never, in the first place, anything more than a well-meant political idea.

Thus the irony that in these late days of the power of modern culture, we realize (or, can realize if we will) that this culture of ours, like all cultures, was founded on a zero signifier that allowed us to make sense of our world. Now, when the world makes less obvious moral sense, we see the zero signifier for who he was, and is. Some will call this "nihilism," but, if it is, it is the nihilism of the privileged order. It might be too early to call it "realism," for, if it is more real than that to which people are accustomed, few are ready truly to say what will take its place.

Just as Lévi-Strauss sent us his sad message from the tropics of his youth, the world today is one in which we must face the prospect that in the dark jungles and river beds of our civilization those strange voices that sing at night, or come to us along the pathways of our e-world, sing to us of the truth of things we do not understand. The final logic of any culture is that, ultimately, no cultural logic can out-run nature, into which at any moment the human can slip. Culture is talk, often talk of hope. At its best, it is talk of hope measured against fungible promises. Today the talk is about what we will do without a Center, even the Center so many had, with good reason, grown to hate. If there is a dawning postmodern world, it might well be one that transcends the older cultural logic, one in which there is no zero signifier. To some this is a terrifying prospect. To others it is a great relief, however frightening. But neither knows, or can know, whether it is so that the human might be drifting toward some new state of affairs in which the dream of common man slips over into a dream-like world in which the cockatoos and hot wind, the jungles and the concrete cities, the e-mails and postmails, and all the other signs of the world settle, finally, into their true, conclusive, and not exactly meaningless equalities.

6

The Uses of French Structuralisms
in Sociology

Some years ago, Raymond Boudon, one of France's most distinguished sociologists, published a critique of structuralism with the title *A quoi sert la notion de "structure"?* In English the French title translates, "What use is the notion of structure?" However, the book's eventual English-language publishers, presumably afraid of killing their product with such a negative title, named the book *The Uses of Structuralism.*[1] Boudon's book was indeed quite negative. He argued that French structuralism was not useful because it was little more than a reincarnation of all structural logics back to the Greeks. Writing in the sixties, when poststructuralism had not yet fully surfaced, Boudon saw only one side of the then very new movement. The uniquely different features of structuralism were invisible, hence useless, to him.

Most of the troubles American sociologists experience with French social thought, to say nothing of postmodernism, are condensed in this reflection on Boudon and his title. The structuralist movement, indeed, is a moving target. At first, as structuralism pure and simple, it appeared as a formalism that seemed to reduce the human sciences to pitiful abstractions — Lévi-Strauss's universal binary oppositions, Althusser's scientific Marx, Barthes's zero-degree writing and formalistic semiology.[2] At a second moment, between roughly 1966 and 1970, poststructuralism burst on the scene, incorporating strange Nietzschean and psychoanalytic concepts. The target was different, yet it retained clear affinities with the structuralism it attacked. Then, a decade or so later in the seventies, postmodernism gathered force from numerous sources, presenting still another target both different from and continuous with the earlier structuralisms. It is difficult to take accurate interpretive aim at such a thing which is simultaneously different and the same.

To make matters even worse, the thing itself is, seemingly, intentionally obscure. It challenges what many believe to be true. Michel Foucault understood quite well the problems his interpreters faced: "I understand the unease of all such people. They have probably found it difficult enough to recognize that their history, their economics, their social practices, the language (*langue*) they speak, the mythology of their ancestors, even the stories that they were told in their childhood, are governed by rules that are not all given to their consciousness."[3] This is an important reason why no school of post-structuralist thought has fully developed in sociology. It is too much an affront to our habits of thought.

Structuralism was a departure from the strong theories of the subject of which, in France, postwar existentialism and phenomenology were the dominant cases. In the introduction to *The Raw and the Cooked* Lévi-Strauss says: "By pursuing conditions where systems of truth become mutually convertible and can therefore be simultaneously admissible for several subjects, the ensemble of these conditions acquires the character of an object endowed by a reality proper to itself and independent of any subject."[4] At first reading, structuralism's attack on subjectivist thought seemed conveniently within the limits of modernism. Early structuralism had all the appearances of an objectivist swing against subjectivist extremes. There was, however, much more to the story.

Post-structuralism was born along with, and as part of, structuralism. Derrida, speaking in 1966 at Johns Hopkins to the first major international conference on structuralism (a text I have touched on in chapter 5 above), began with words that recognized the duality and duplicity of structuralism:

> Perhaps something has occurred in the history of the concept of structure that could be called an "event," if this word did not entail a meaning which it is precisely the function of structural — or structuralist — thought to reduce or to suspect. Let us speak of an "event" nevertheless and use quotation marks to serve as a precaution. What would this event be then? Its exterior form would be that of a *rupture* and a redoubling.[5]

The words are opaque. They announce an event that ends events. They claim that the idea of structure had come to a point that would end both structure and event, yet they would remain in quotation marks, redoubled beyond this rupture.

For those not committed to its language and program, post-structuralism seemed (and seems) a stupid play with words. But from within it uses its language seriously, to liberate the play of words and ideas. Derrida announced a shift in Western thought. For this purpose he required the prior existence of structuralism, just as structuralism entailed, in Derrida's view, poststructuralism. The "post" in poststructuralism was a tactical joke, a playfully serious trick. Structure, Derrida went on to say, had served to limit and confine modern thought. "Event" — the concept structuralism sought to eliminate — was the false alternative, the artificial hope for emancipation from this confinement. Event was, after all, the code word of existentialism — and a cognate to other subjectivist ideals — the ideally free subject, consciousness, rational choice, subjectively intended meaning, the essential nature of "Man," and so on.

Structuralism, insofar as it led to poststructuralism, was its own gravedigger. These two awkwardly bound perspectives attacked the formative conviction of modernist thought, that the world could be viewed through the lenses of the subject–object dichotomy. Structuralism, with all its first appearances of objectivism, was the beginning of the end for objectivism and subjectivism. At least this was the claim of Derrida and others who were central to the poststructuralist movement in the late sixties and through the seventies — Foucault, Lacan, Kristeva, Barthes, among others.

But this claim required a still subsequent movement, postmodernism. If October 21, 1966, the date of Derrida's talk to the Johns Hopkins conference, was the beginning of poststructuralism, then with equal daring one might accept Charles Jencks' statement that postmodernism began with the death of modernist architecture at 3:32 p.m., July 15, 1972 — the moment at which the Pruitt-Igoe housing project in St Louis was destroyed.[6] Both dates are of course symbolic, expressing only the unique feature of the departure. Thus, if Derrida's talk identified poststructuralism as the end of the structuring of thought in the human sciences, postmodernism extended that principle to the end of structure in modern culture, beginning with the point at which culture and the built environment intersect, architecture. "The post-modern world heralds the collapse and the unfeasibility of the grand, centralized systems with which one once attempted to explain everything."[7] Pruitt-Igoe, therefore, is a convenient symbol. This massive housing project in St Louis represented modernist architecture's arrogant belief that by building the biggest and best public housing planners and architects could eradicate poverty and human misery. To have recognized, and destroyed, the symbol of that idea was to admit the failure of modernist architecture, and by implication modernity itself. If this is too oblique a symbol, social theorists may take 1979 as the better inaugural date for postmodernism, the year of publication of two frequently cited texts, Jean-François Lyotard's *The Postmodern Condition* and Richard Rorty's *Philosophy and the Mirror of Nature*.

Lyotard began with a statement consistent with Derrida's in 1966. "Our working hypothesis is that the status of knowledge is altered as societies enter what is known as the postindustrial age and cultures enter what is known as the postmodern age."[8] Rorty states that the "therapeutic" aim of his book is "to undermine the reader's confidence . . . in 'knowledge' as something about which there ought to be a 'theory' and which has 'foundations.'"[9] His view is comparable to Lyotard's that the conditions of knowledge have fundamentally changed because in the postmodern era knowledge, most especially "scientific knowledge, is a form of discourse."[10] These assertions built upon ideas that had developed in the preceding two decades. They were, therefore, consistent with Derrida's definition of the poststructuralist event within structuralism: "This was the moment," according to Derrida, "when language invaded the universal problematic, the moment when, in the absence of a center or origin, everything became discourse."[11]

One way or another, everything in the three structuralisms comes back to language, or more accurately, to a specific commitment to the idea that language is necessarily the central consideration in all attempts to know, act, and live. Though there are substantial disagreements within the structuralist line, all three movements — structuralism, poststructuralism, and postmodernism — intend to replace modernist principles of positive knowledge in the sciences, the social sciences, and philosophy with a new approach based on language. This conviction distinguishes this line of thought from others, like Habermas's, that similarly accept the importance of language.[12]

As the movement took each redoubled step, its language became more and more obscure. In the original structuralist phase the writings were difficult but not obscure. Lévi-Strauss's "Structural Study of Myth" and Barthes's "Elements of Semiology," like much of Althusser in this period, were hard to read, but readable. But when poststructuralism emerged full blown in the late 1960s, the writings became more and more resistant to normal reading. One leaves many of these texts with a barely liminal comprehension. One gets something, but what one cannot be sure. Critics frequently complain about this aspect of French social-theoretical writings. It is important, however, to understand that it is intended. The effect is sought as a matter of principle.

I propose, as an example, the first phrase of Derrida's 1966 statement: "*Perhaps something has occurred in the history of the concept of structure.*" The reader senses (though perhaps not consciously) that the first, surprisingly conditional word, "perhaps," serves a tactical purpose. It both brings Derrida's readers in and keeps them at bay. On the one hand, Derrida addressed his remarks to a largely American audience in

Baltimore. The "perhaps" seeks out their relative unfamiliarity with his subject and the French style. It says: I won't quite insist on the following. Yet, on the other hand, what follows is very much an insistence: an event has occurred in the history of the concept structure. Derrida is proclaiming prophetically, insisting. The juxtaposition of the "perhaps" opens a space between his utterance and his readers. He wants the event to proclaim itself. This, we learn a few paragraphs later on, is the space in which language can play out its effects and announce itself. This is why some feel they don't quite understand or can't quite "get" the line of argument.

Derrida's argument is that this event was *"the moment when language invaded the universal problematic, . . . the moment when . . . [a] . . . everything became discourse . . . [b] . . . a system in which the central signified . . . [c] . . . is never absolutely present outside a system of differences."*[13] The three ellipses (marked [a], [b], [c]) mark places where Derrida imposes significant qualifications. When the material is excluded, as above, the argument is relatively neat. But in each of these places Derrida's actual text presents material that strains the reading by introducing qualifications which make a philosophical statement, namely:

[a] *"in the absence of a center or origin,"*
[b] *"provided we can agree on this word [discourse] — that is to say,"*
[c] *"the original signifier."*

Each qualifying phrase contradicts a reader's attempt to understand the event Derrida announces as a positive, factual moment in history. The first, [a], and the third, [c], introduce philosophical claims that cannot be proven, and each is so sweeping as to be beyond argument. The absent center, for example, refers to the assumption that prior to poststructuralism all traditional thought, including modernism, relied on a restrictive, transcendent principle. This, of course, is less a point of fact than of interpretation. Even as a point of interpretation it would have been hard to argue convincingly in 1966 that this was the essential nature of modernist thought. It is hard enough to argue the point today. The second qualification, [b], *"provided we can agree"* on the meaning of the term *"discourse,"* is both an acknowledgment of the strangeness of his idea to his readers and an expression of his now famous principle of deconstruction that we must use familiar language to express the totally unfamiliar.

The overall effect of the passage is to subject the reader to an insistence triply qualified, presented in the guise of an argument. It is not an argument that one can "follow" along a direct line of clear and distinct logical understanding. It is not a statement open to logical or empirical verification, but an invitation to enter a different, postmodern (that is, in 1966, poststructural) language within which one finds that everything is language. The argument which is not an argument is found only in a series of juxtaposed, different elements — conditional "perhaps" proclamation, structuralism/end of structuralism, poststructuralism/continuity of structuralism, argument/insistence. One wants to ask, what does Derrida mean? To which he would reply, if he were to reply at all: I am playing, seriously. "Play is the disruption of presence," he says near the end of the text.[14] All attempts to be clear are based on the philosophical presumption that meaning and reality can be present to consciousness. To "make clear" is to reflect or, in Rorty's term, to mirror nature. These are attempts to get around language which exists, so to speak, on its own terms.

Poststructuralism and postmodernism, though in different degrees and ways, each seek to destroy the ideal of pure, meaningful communication between subjects as a corollary to the disruption of the metaphysical distinction between subjects and objects. This is the way in which language invades the universal problematic. Language is assumed to be that one social thing that, when it is made the center of things, disrupts everything, including the possibility of a center of things. Language looks to the future. Thus Derrida ends this essay with a hesitant, fearful anticipation of a liberating birth, cloaked in a language one understands, barely:

> I employ these words, I admit, with a glance toward operations of child-birth — but also a glance toward those who, in a society from which I do not exclude myself, turn their eyes away when faced by the as yet unnameable which is proclaiming itself and which can do so whenever a birth is in the offing, only under species of a non-species, in the formless, mute, infant, and terrifying form of monstrosity.[15]

Any attempt to develop a poststructuralist, or postmodernist, sociology entails a willingness to face this monstrosity of language. According to such a perspective, when language is taken seriously for what it is, the social world is seen in a particular way. It is no longer possible to view the world as internally and necessarily coherent. To take language seriously, as the structuralisms do in their manner of writing as in their philosophy, is to decenter the world, to eviscerate it of grand organizing principles (God, natural law, truth, beauty, subjectivity, Man, etc.) that mask the most fundamental truth of human life, differences. Those who have followed developments in postmodernist feminist theory and literary theory realize that this conviction is filled with political intent.

> Aware that women writers inevitably engage a literary history and system of conventions shaped primarily by men, feminist critics now often strive to

elucidate the acts of revision, appropriation and subversion that constitute a female text.[16]

> Scores of people are killed every day in the name of differences ascribed only to race. This slaughter demands the gesture in which the contributors to this volume are collectively engaged: to deconstruct, if you will, the ideas of difference inscribed in the trope of race, to explicate discourse itself in order to reveal the hidden relations of power and knowledge inherent in popular and academic usages of "race."[17]

Modernism is taken as the centered, hierarchical, Europeanized, dominant world against which the principle of difference is thrust to assert the realities of those whose daily lives are marked by the experience of difference — women, nonwhites, working class, the third world.

The question for sociology is what is it about language that permits such a long excursion from Lévi-Strauss's rediscovery of linguistics in the fifties to today's politics of difference? And what are the prospects in this for sociology?

Against philosophies of the Center (modernism in particular), poststructuralism introduced an intellectual politics based on the now famous concept of decentering. It is not always understood that decentering is less a philosophy, or a rival concept to those of modernism, than a practice. This is, in part, the point of poststructuralism's unsettling approach to writing.

From one point of view, decentering is a reasonably precise philosophical concept conveying Derrida's and Foucault's original attacks on centered philosophies, most especially phenomenology's extreme subjectivist philosophy of consciousness. This is the sense most accurately associated with the postmodernist rejection of Enlightenment theories of knowledge. From another point of view, decentering suggests a broad political opposition to all traditional and modern social forms, philosophy included, in which structures serve to inhibit social freedom. It is advisable, therefore, to think of poststructuralism and postmodernism as first and foremost forms of knowledge derived from a political practice. This attitude conveys not only poststructuralism's attempt to overcome philosophy for political purposes but also its claim that discourse and writing must be taken as the subject-matter and the means of intellectual work.

Such an interpretation of decentering makes a heavy demand on sociologists accustomed to viewing politics as something totally other than science, or, at most, that to which sociologists contribute expertise.

Poststructuralism claims that intellectual work is political, and it does so with reference to concepts most sociologists would consider anything but political — text and discourse.

Roland Barthes defines the Text as "that *social* space that leaves no language safe or untouched, that allows no enunciative subject to hold the position of judge, teacher, analyst, confessor, or decoder. The theory of the Text can only coincide with the activity of writing."[18] This statement is linked to the claim that decentering is an ongoing intellectual practice deriving from the theoretical decision to interpret the Text in relation to other texts, rather than in relation to its author. For Barthes this involves the distinction between the work and the Text:

> The work is concrete, occupying a portion of book-space (in a library, for example); the Text, on the other hand, is a methodological field. . . . This opposition recalls the distinction proposed by Lacan between "reality" and the "real"; the one is displayed, the other demonstrated. In the same way, the work can be seen in bookstores, in card catalogues, and on course lists, while the Text reveals itself, articulates itself according to and against certain rules. While the work is held in the hand, the text is held in language.[19]

The work, therefore, is seen as the unit of modernist writing in which writing is a transitive activity — the production of literary objects by subjects, authors. Thus, the privileging of the Text over the work is another instance of the philosophical side of decentering, here the rejection of the purportedly modernist belief that the social world is inhabited by self-conscious subjects who project meaning into their works. It is a rejection of subjectivism as a cryptometaphysics.

This move replaces the original modernist couplet — *subject* (author)/*object* (work) — with something else which itself has the appearance of a couplet — *practices* (writing)/(intertextual) *field*. But the relationship of text to its intertextual field is active, creative, and practical. Practices/field has the form but not the substance of a conceptual dichotomy. It looks the same but is different — postdichotomous. Texts are products of intransitive writing, they are outside the subject–object dichotomy. "The Text cannot be thought of as a defined object."[20] It is, as noted, a methodological field, while the work is a concrete object. Texts are, therefore, play in a forever open and open-ended field which they produce and by which they are produced, and in which they must be interpreted.

The important thing to keep in mind is that poststructuralists view this reorientation as a general social-theoretical move. Though they remain close to the language of text and discourse, poststructuralists situate their views with respect to a theory of society. The critique of the subject-author is an instance of opposition to all forms of social domination. Much of Foucault's writing on various topics, from *The Order of Things* to *The History of Sexuality*, is in opposition to dominations represented by the engendered, Europeanized humanism which, in another context, is characterized by the term partriarchy.[21] The link between a general social theory and the problem of the author is apparent in Foucault's "What Is an Author?":

> We are accustomed . . . to saying that the author is a general creator of a work in which he deposits with infinite wealth and generosity, an inexhaustible world of significations. We are used to thinking that the author is so different from other men, and so transcendent with regard to all languages, that as soon as he speaks meanings begin to proliferate. . . . The truth is quite contrary . . . the author does not precede the works, he is a certain fundamental principle by which, in our culture, one limits, excludes, and chooses. . . . The author is the ideological figure by which one marks the manner in which we fear the proliferation of meanings.[22]

In this respect, post-structuralism is a social theory articulated within concrete studies of literary, historical, and philosophical questions.

Poststructuralism is very much a product of the political and social events leading to and ensuing from May 1968 in Paris. Foucault's sexual politics, Lacan's engendering of psychoanalysis, Kristeva and Irigaray's feminist theories, Derrida's politics of difference, Deleuze and Guattari's schizoanalytic politics all are rooted, one way or another, in the late-sixties revolutionary politics that challenged the world-centered ambitions of postwar Gaullism. If, at that same moment, left intellectuals in the United States sought a coherent New Left alternative to both Old Left Marxism and Johnson–Humphrey liberalism, French intellectuals searched for an alternative that rejected traditional communist and socialist party politics and was post-Marxist without being anti-Marxist. In the one joint programmatic statement of the poststructuralist movement, when Foucault, Barthes, Derrida, Sollers, and Kristeva allowed and caused their separate projects to be joined in an edition of *Tel Quel* titled "Théorie d'ensemble" (published not incidentally in the early autumn of 1968), these politics were quite explicit. The introduction stated that their joint project was, in part, "to articulate a politics logically bound to a dynamically non-representative writing, that is to say: analysis of the confusion created by this position, explication of their social and economic character, construction of the relations of this writing with historical materialism and dialectical materialism."[23] It would be a stretch to consider this a social theory in the usual sense, but that theory is there.

In more sociological terms, the implication of this attitude toward writing as an intellectual practice is that action is oriented to an open field of play that lacks inherent, limiting rules. Rules become resources in Giddens's sense; limits are social arbitraries serving only to define the possibilities of transgression in Foucault's sense; the field defines the conditions and terms of practices in Bourdieu's sense. The structured field is viewed as open, that is, characterized by differences, absence, play. Hence the various descriptive terms one associates with this line of thought: discursive formation (Foucault), intertextuality (Barthes), *la langue* (Saussure), *champ* (Bourdieu). To these sometimes implicit visions of a field of play are juxtaposed the correlative notions that describe intransitive actions: practices, writing, speaking, habitus.[24]

On first examination, this would appear to be an interesting theoretical model in the form: *Think of social action as intransitive practices in a dynamically open field of play*. But would not be a sufficient interpretation of poststructuralist thinking. Models, in its view, are modernist attempts to mirror the social world. Models depend on the assumption that the social (or natural) world can be represented, that is, "presented again" in the language of knowledge. Poststructuralism, implicitly, and postmodernism, explicitly, reject the Enlightenment ideas that knowledge is an autonomous and constituting feature of social life. There are no poststructuralist models. "Let us wage a war on totality; let us be witnesses to the unpresentable; let us activate the differences and save the honor of the name."[25] Postmodernist knowledge, such as it is, is the consequence, not a representation, of action in a field of play.

Therefore, what is at stake in a possible postmodern sociology is a willingness to move sociology away from its historic role as a discipline, a social science, a type of knowledge, and toward a more politically self-conscious practice that is neither traditionally Marxist nor liberal. Postmodern knowledge entails a postmodern politics. Like the strange space Derrida sought to open and use in the first words of "Structure, Sign, and Play," a poststructuralist sociology would have to be willing to tolerate the idea of working in a confusing, different social space that is neither epistemological nor political, but both yet neither — a very different idea of knowledge.

The generic name for knowledge that is (nothing but) language is discourse. Discourse expresses, and is, the inherently transgressive quality of poststructuralist intellectual politics, as one can see in Hayden White's definition:

> A discourse moves "to and fro" between received encodations of experience and the clutter of phenomena which refuses incorporation into conventionalized notions of "reality," "truth," or "possibility." . . . Discourse, in a word, is quintessentially a *mediative* enterprise. As such it is both interpretive and preinterpretive; it is always *about* the nature of interpretation itself as it is *about* the subject matter which is the manifest occasion of its own elaboration.[26]

A postmodern social theory, whether avowedly sociological or not, is discursive in this sense of transgressing the subject-matter it interprets by constantly reflecting on the necessity and nature of interpretation itself.

Of course, there are problems with a proposal to make discourse both the subject-matter and the medium of sociological analysis. A discursive sociology would require an uprooting of deeply ingrained convictions — belief in the subject–object dichotomy and the other classical dualities; loyalty to the ideal of sociology as a well-founded, scientific source of knowledge; expectations that good work will produce identifiably worthwhile political and intellectual outcomes.

But the far more serious problem with a discursive sociology in the poststructuralist or postmodern tradition is that posed by taking discourse as an object of study. It is one thing to accept a discursive, transgressive method as the condition of sociological practice, another to deal with evident dilemmas in the discursive analysis of discourse. Sociologists and other intellectual practitioners can be discursive in the sense of appropriating the attitude of constant, as White puts it, to-ing and fro-ing with the real world. Social theory as reflective, intransitive action is thinkable even if objectionable to some. But what are the limits of discourse as an "object" of study? This question demonstrates the severity of the challenges posed by poststructuralism. One must bracket even the term "object." But what do the brackets mean? Does a discursive social theory mean there are no "objects," that is to say, no contents to intellectual practices? Is such a practice forever doomed to a world of talk about talk itself, of the interpretation of interpretation, of a program without performances? The problem is acute when one considers the question, Is there, in the "real" world, nondiscursive social action? It is one thing for a discursive intellectual work to treat other discursive materials of the same sort. This is what the poststructuralists mean by intertextuality in the strictest sense of the concept.

The success of poststructuralism in literary studies may rely considerably on the fact that, in this area, other texts are the proper subject-matter. The most compelling successes, in my opinion, of applied poststructuralism have been among feminist, third world, and Afro-American critics who uncover the discursive power of hitherto silent, oppressed women, black, or third-world writers. In a case like Henry Louis Gates' analysis of the confluence between the African Esu-Elegbara and the Afro-American signifying monkey figures in two separated but historically bound cultural systems, the analyst is applying a discursive method to texts that are found to be surprisingly discursive themselves.[27] Both figures served to contain and express the doubled cultural experience of those who are simultaneously in some fractured way both African and American. The figures are discursive in that they mediate the divided social reality of people for whom colonial oppression and slavery was the decisive social attribute. This discovery of the discursive and political consciousness of so-called nonliterate or otherwise excluded people is parallel to similar discoveries of the study of oppressed women, the working class, and other victims of colonial domination, and this litera-ture — of which E. P. Thompson's *The Making of the English Working Class* is a locus classicus — is familiar and assimilable to even normal soci-ological thought.

The greater difficulty concerns the hint strong within poststructuralist thought that everything social is discourse. Are there no events in the "real" world that lack this transgressive, mediative quality? This, of course, is a very familiar question, arrived at by a different route. What are we to make of the irregular silence of oppressed people? Is their silence merely a latent discursivity, covered by false consciousness? It is one thing to say that certain slave narratives are discursive, and another to suggest that all which is said by, or inscribed on behalf of, slaves is discursive, and still another, by extension, to suggest that slavery is nothing but discourse. This is the question that separates a prospective sociological postmodernism from poststructuralist literary criticism. Sociologists should have little difficulty accepting the idea that there are hidden or underlying variables behind surface appearances. But they will have trouble with the suggestion that those variables are exclusively dis-cursive. Is there nothing in the "real" world but texts and discursive talk? Literary theorists and others, including social historians, can plau-sibly study nothing but texts. Can sociologists? Or, better put, what does it mean to propose that sociology be the discursive study of discursive texts?

In a different guise this is the familiar problem of the presumption of a necessary difference between theory and concrete empirical data. Most sociologists could, if pressed, consider the proposition that theory is the discursive property of any sociological work. This would amount to little more than granting that in theory, whatever else we do, we state and describe both a statement about the "real" world and the rules by which we arrive at that interpretation. Usually, however, even in a radical version of this conviction, sociologists hold to the existence of a "real" world outside of the discursive sway of theory. The world's "reality" is taken, normally, as the source of concrete empirical data. This conviction, we can now see, would be treated with great skepticism by poststructuralism and postmodernism. The idea of a free-standing reality as the source of empirical data partakes of the modernist distinction between the knowing subject and the world of objects, and relies on a belief in attainable knowledge as the arbiter of that distinction. We might grant, therefore, that postmodernism would have this particular philosophical attitude toward the division of theory and data. But, can we grant that sociology can get along without free-standing data, that is, without data from the world as the resource of theory? Viewed through the lens of a postmodern critique, we can see that the question need not be posed so narrowly. We can agree that data are necessary to even a postmodern sociology and *still* accept the proposition that those data are neither necessarily of an order different from theory nor nondiscursive.

This line of questioning requires a reconsideration of the status of our concept of reality; clearly postmodernism would abandon the notion altogether. But it seems possible, even if only for tactical purposes, that one can avoid the threats of such a course. Here is where the poststructuralist ideas of discourse and textuality offer considerable leverage even with their terrible philosophical troubles.

A poststructuralist or postmodernist approach to the concept of "reality" would be pragmatic. What do we intend by it? And can we get around it in order to enhance our ability to know and discuss? Can, therefore, the theory of Texts, including discursive texts, get us around the problems sociology, and other sciences, usually solve with reference to ideas like "empirical reality"?

The prospect of such an alternative depends on the plausibility of four assumptions already presented, explicitly or implicitly:

1   that theory is an inherently discursive activity;
2   that the empirical reality in relation to which theoretical texts are discursive is without exception textual;
3   that empirical texts depend on this relationship to theoretical texts for their intellectual or scientific value; and
4   that in certain, if not all, cases a discursive interpretation yields more, not less, adequate understanding.

Assumption 1 was stipulated in the above discussion. Assumptions 2 and 3 require further discussion. Assumption 4 is best considered with reference to a case study.

Theoretical statements mediate the "reality" contained in empirical texts — answers to questionnaires, performed rituals and observed behaviours (usually inscribed on film or tape or in notebooks), letters, corporate reports, transcripts, interviews, archives, census tracts. It is far from clear that there are any data "purer" (that is, "more real") than these. And none of these is anything but textual in the two senses post-structuralism employs. First, they are literally inscribed on one medium or another and are never used for analysis without being thus written. Secondly, they are useful for knowledge only to the extent that they exist in an intertextual field — with other empirical texts of the same sort, with other empirical texts of a different kind, and, most of all, with the theoretical texts out of which sense is made of them. It hardly need be said that raw data, in whatever form, are useless until they are situated with respect to theoretical statements. Theoretical statements, regardless of the "school" or methodological style in which they are expressed (scientific, humanistic, qualitative, ethnographic, etc.), are never made without a relationship to empirical data or an empirical reference, however abstract. Parsons' most abstract theory of the AGIL paradigm requires a great number of assumptions about the reality of the social world, such as a willingness to believe that societies are patterned, that culture is an effective control over society, that societies need integrative mechanisms like laws. None of these beliefs, however arguable, is held without reference to a wealth of empirical references. These references when held by a reader are necessary to the sense of Parsons' theory. They arise from the many empirical texts — ranging from survey results to everyday life conversations and everything in between — that inform a reader's ability to read. Similarly, such texts are also written, whether consciously or not, as an intervention in the field of existing texts sociologists variously consider germane to their work. It is not at all clear why one needs the idea of an empirical foundation existing beyond such an intertextual field.

Of the four assumptions, 4 is the sternest test of the prospects of a postmodern sociology. In the end, it is hardly worth the while to try something with so many inherent difficulties if there are no anticipated advantages over what we have now. So, then, what are the advantages? A question I propose to answer with reference to a case of undeniable, but still uncertain, reality.

Important as it is to American, and global, history the reality of the war in Vietnam is far from certain. For the majority of those who attempt to interpret it, their most vivid impressions come not from direct experience but from a strange conglomeration of texts — the memorial on the Mall in Washington, films, firsthand accounts of speakers, friends, or relatives, novels, Neil Sheehan's *New Yorker* articles and prize-winning book, college and high school courses, rhetorical allusions by politicians, archives, microfilm and microfiche, and so on. Is it an accident that the most searing film account, if not the roulette scene in *The Deer Hunter*, is *Apocalypse Now*, a montage of craziness and dream-like irreality in which the viewer is made to feel that nothing real was there? Was Vietnam after all nothing more than a repetition of a classic Conradian narrative — a crazed voyage through an exotic jungle in search of an unattainable insane kingdom in the heart of darkness? One wants to argue that this is a fiction and that the reality is still there. Reviews of each serious Vietnam film center on the question: Did this one, *Platoon* perhaps, finally capture the reality of the war?

It is possible that the search for the reality of social things is the true Conradian search. Where would one look for the reality of Vietnam? Are recollections of veterans or POWs more real than *Apocalypse Now*? Are the *Pentagon Papers*? Are Neil Sheehan's articles? Are Stanley Karnow's history and PBS documentary? Is that finer reality still buried in an archive somewhere? And cannot these questions be asked of most complex social-historical events?

In pursuit of a postmodern sociology, what can then be said about the empirical reality of a series of events like the war in Vietnam? I propose that we ignore, for the moment, our sociological thirst for reality, and consider it simply and straightforwardly as though it were, for all intents and purposes, a monstrous but plausibly discursive text. In this respect we should have to entertain the proposition that the war itself was discursive, a global inscription in which the United States sought to mediate its own sense of the irreality of world history.[28]

In the years following the World War II, the United States quickly encountered an intolerable set of contradictions. On the one hand, the United States emerged from the world war as the greatest military and industrial power in history. On the other hand, as early as 1947, the year of George Kennan's famous long telegram enunciating the policy of containment, the Soviet Union was taken seriously, as well it should have been, as a rival power. The United States suffered the contradiction of being the supreme world power, but one of two supreme powers, hence not supreme. The McCarthy blight, in the early fifties, was a flawed attempt to mediate this contradiction by turning inward with the unreal insistence that anyone and everyone could be communist, and cause of America's loss of world potency. In 1954 Joseph McCarthy was censured by the United States Senate. In the same year Dienbienphu fell. In 1955 Eisenhower approved direct military aid to the Saigon government, thus beginning the US presence in Southeast Asia.

Was that presence, and the war that ensued, an attempt to resolve, discursively, the contradiction that McCarthyism failed to resolve? The answer lies in an analysis of the specific texts which articulate the theory that governed American war policy.

The decisive event that led directly to war was President Lyndon Johnson's decision in the first few days of February 1965 to escalate the bombing in North Vietnam. The previous summer, Johnson and his advisers invented an incident in the Gulf of Tonkin as cause to push through Congress the resolution that gave him virtually unchecked authority to engage in war. His defeat of Barry Goldwater in the November 1964 election added substantially to the mandate he claimed both for foreign policy leadership and the pursuit of his plans of a Great Society at home. In 1965 Johnson submitted 63 pieces of social legislation, a domestic program that exceeded even Roosevelt's for its ambition and commitment to America's disadvantaged. Few, if any, American presidents possessed so extensive a social vision. Yet that vision is easily forgotten because it was dreamt along with a view of America's world position that led to Vietnam.

On February 5, 1965, the Vietcong attacked an American installation at Pleiku, killing nine, and wounding a hundred American advisers. Johnson responded immediately by authorizing "Operation Flaming Dart," air raids against the North carefully selected because Soviet Prime Minister Aleksi Kosygin was then visiting Hanoi. The question before Johnson was, will the air strikes be expanded and the American engagement enlarged?

At the same time, on February 6 and 7, Johnson's adviser McGeorge Bundy, en route home from Vietnam, completed the draft of a memorandum that confirmed an earlier (January 27) report that the situation in Vietnam was deteriorating. Bundy's February 7 memorandum coined the ironic and highly discursive phrase, "sustained reprisal." This evidently duplicitous phrase came to justify and be the name for Johnson's evolving war policy. The memorandum argued that a policy of reprisals against the North would eventually "improve the situation in the South" by demonstrating to Hanoi the military resolve of the United States. The policy decision came quickly. On February 24, 1965, Johnson ordered Operation Rolling Thunder, sustained air raids on the North which by year's end totaled 55,000 sorties.

Like George Kennan's famous long telegram twenty years earlier that invented the equally discursive concept of containment, Bundy's sustained reprisal memorandum defined Johnson's fatal policy. By December 1965, 200,000 troops had replaced the 20,000 or so advisers in Vietnam at the beginning of the year. And by 1968 Johnson's presidency and his Great Society program would be in ruins, and the direction of American foreign and domestic policies would be, it now seems, irreversibly altered.

Bundy's February 7 memorandum did not cause the war. Texts don't cause anything in the usual sense. They are practices in an intertextual field. Their significance relies on their relationship to that field. It is easy to see both the discursive nature of the Bundy text and its crucial place in an intertextual field that included Johnson's own statements, the preceding generation's dilemma over America's contradictory world position, and subsequent interpretations of the war itself.

As Godfrey Hodgson points out,[29] Bundy's phrase, sustained reprisal, is a subtly double-sided notion that suits a former dean of Harvard College. Operation Rolling Thunder and all that went with it was surely "sustained" but in the dramatic escalation that followed the very meaning of "reprisal" was subverted. The supposed reprisal for Pleiku (and more remotely the nonexistent Tonkin incident) became initiative. The restraint suggested by the term reprisal was confounded by the reality of devastation that came to pass. Though the Pentagon wanted even more, the reality of over 500,000 troops and countless air sorties in the north and south altered, as we now know, the map of Southeast Asia, just as it altered the terrain of American political and moral conscience. In some very specific sense, "sustained reprisal" literally rewrote the reality of American life as it rewrote the geopolitical fate of Indochina.

Again, one must resist the temptation to say that Bundy's memo caused all this. It was not a cause, but a crucial discursive text that provided the theory which encouraged American desires to have it all — to be supreme abroad, while being a Great Society at home. The text's meaning is lodged in this more complex field, and its discursive value was that it both revealed and masked (to-ed and fro-ed so to speak) the reality of the policy's appeal to the best and brightest who advised Johnson and to Johnson himself. Johnson's famous complex about his Harvardian advisers did not prevent him from sharing their theory. He could not himself utter the language of a Harvard dean, but he could understand it. His own public statement announcing Flaming Dart used quite a different, and richer, metaphor: "We have kept our guns over the mantel and our shells in the cupboard for a long time. . . . I can't ask our American soldiers out there to fight with one hand tied behind their backs."[30] This Alamo metaphor from Johnson's Texas frontier background conveyed the same meaning as did "sustained reprisal." It lacked only the (to him) noxious qualities of a more Harvardian abstraction. He saw himself, as Doris Kearns' biography shows, as a tough, virile man of peace, defending America against an aggressor. "Rolling Thunder," to Johnson, was an act of peace, an instance of what William Gibson rightly calls doublethink.[31] But as discourse it has the same attributes as "sustained reprisal" — a play with words that plays with reality, simultaneously constituting and deconstituting the reality of the words and the world. And both figures of speech take their place alongside the war's most famous expression of doublethink, "We had to destroy the village in order to save it."

Doublethink is the discursive form required when there is no plausible reality on the ground to support the actions in the air of a contradictory theory of the world. This is not to say that nothing happened on the ground of Vietnam, that no one died. It does say, however, that we have no interpretive access to that reality, in large part because those who lived and died in the jungles did so because of the real irreality of a series of highly theoretical texts. The war was whatever reality it was because of a theoretical field in which sustained reprisal and Johnson's Alamo figure stood side by side, without prejudice to all the contradictions they contained.

This intertextual field in which the war in Vietnam was constituted stretches along several axes — horizontally across the differences of language between Johnson and Bundy, and vertically from their gross theory of the world to the irreality experienced by men and women on the ground. Bundy's abstract theory was not of a different order from the accounts of combatants. Hundreds of first-hand accounts by veterans describe the bizarre incongruence between hours spent when nothing happened, a fleeting and often unseen enemy, and eerie nothingness punctuated by death — of buddies, of the enemy, of people who looked like but were not enemy, of old women and children, and eventually of fragged soldiers. Foot soldiers lost all sense of the reality of normal distinctions — between war and just walking around, between enemy and ally, between combatant and civilian. "We knew," said Specialist Fourth Class Charles Strong, "where the North Vietnamese were, but we knew that if we got into it, they would probably have wiped a big portion of the company out. We were really dropped there to find the North Vietnamese, and here we was hiding from them. Running because we was hungry. We were so far up in the hills that the place was so thick you didn't have to pull guard at night."[32] This collapse of reality on the ground is perfectly well explained by the irreality of the theoretical policy that invoked the war. Some might think this destroys the material reality of jungles, death, and Vietnam. But does it? Is it not certain that our men would never find the enemy, or recognize them when they found them, when the war itself had little to do with anything real? After all, Bundy and Johnson could have learned from Dienbienphu that this was to be a war with enemies that could not be found. They ignored this lesson because they were creating another, textual reality having more to do with the Alamo and postwar fear of communism than anything actually on the ground in Vietnam.

From Hamburger Hill to Johnson's situation room the reality of Vietnam was created, then breached, then recreated in countless texts. What after all truly went on there? Where was there? And what is the meaningful distinction among the realities written in journals of American and Vietcong combatants, Johnson's memoirs, Bundy's memorandum, the Pentagon Papers, *Apocalypse Now*, the heartwrenching V-shaped memorial on the Mall, deaths which rewrote family histories, defoliation which rewrote the ecology of Southeast Asia, a military failure that rewrote the political geography of Vietnam? How could there be a study, including a sociological study, of Vietnam based on anything but these texts? Nothing, else is out there, not now, and in an eerie sense not then.

It is certainly not by chance that one of the earliest successful works of postmodern sociology is about Vietnam. William Gibson's *The Perfect War* argues that war in Vietnam was an extensive elaboration of the codes contained in late liberal technocracy of which the Johnson administration was the epiphany. He demonstrates, to take one example, that the bombing around which the war was built was nothing more than an elaborate code for communications with Hanoi. The message was: "We want peace. We are resolved. You stop and we will too." Yet the message had no receiver to whom it made sense. In fact, the air raids on Hanoi's oil storage facilities were based on a certifiable denial of reality. The manifest purpose of these bombings was, Gibson shows, to communicate American resolve by destroying the bulk of Hanoi's oil reserves supporting infiltration of the South. By July 1965, when sorties reached more than 10,000 a month, almost 70 percent of the North's oil reserves had, in fact, been destroyed. Yet the actual daily need for petroleum fuel in the North was an amount that could be carried in 15 pickup trucks. The 30 percent reserve not destroyed was more than enough. This reality was knowable by the simplest of intelligence reports. But the bombing continued, directed in part by Secretary of Defense Robert McNamara who, as a younger man, had directed a study demonstrating that allied bombing missions in World War II had similarly little effect on the course of that war. What did the bombings mean? Their sense had nothing at all to do with an external reality. They were the necessary utterance dictated by a theoretical war policy code.

Gibson ends his book with a statement in which he means every word in a strict poststructuralist, even postmodern, sense. He says, referring to the irrelevance of a distinction between his sociological text on the war and the fated experiences of men and women who lived the war's irreality: "In this *corpus* men and women live and die; the stories of their lives and their deaths have their truths beyond in*corp*oration in any theoretical arguments."[33] In a world where reality is constituted in and by means of texts, everything is theoretical in some sense, because everything is discursive and, in situations where this is the case, what other reality is there?

What then are the prospects for a postmodern sociology? One answer might be found in the fact that in 46 years between 1936 and 1982, the *American Sociological Review* published 2,559 articles, of which a scant 5 percent concerned political and social issues of any kind.[34] This does not speak well for social science's grasp of reality.

Quite possibly a postmodern sociology would do better, however high the stakes. It would not be difficult to do as well.

Part III

Prospects

7

Identities After the Imperium

The world is emerging from a great silence, from a silence so cold that the voices we hear today disturb the stupor to which we have grown accustomed.

Though many are available, one example of these perturbations is provided by Ryszard Kapuściński's account of Russia emerging from the grip of Soviet Union. Kapuściński's *Imperium* is a book about people across that vast, ill-defined land learning to speak against the habit of silence. He tells, for example, of a long wait for a delayed flight, in a remote airport in the extreme Russian north:

> I look around at my neighbors.
>
> They stare fixedly straight ahead. Just like that: staring fixedly straight ahead. One could see no impatience in their expressions. No anxiety, agitation, anger. More important, they asked about nothing; they asked no one about anything. But perhaps they weren't asking because they already knew?
>
> I asked one of them if he knew when we would be taking off. If you suddenly ask someone a question here, you must wait patiently. For you can see in the face of the one queried that it is only under the influence of this stimulus (the question) that he seems to awaken, comes to life, and starts the laborious journey from some other planet to earth. And this requires time. Then an expression of slight and even amused surprise crosses his face — what's this moron asking for?
>
> The person to whom the question is addressed is absolutely right to consider his interrogator a moron. For his entire experience teaches him that no advantage accrues from asking questions, that no matter what, a man will learn — questions or not — only as much as they will tell him (or, rather, won't tell him), and that, on the contrary, the asking of questions is very dangerous and can cause a man to bring a great misfortune down upon his head.
>
> It is true that a bit of time has elapsed since the epoch of Stalinism, but its memory is alive, and the lessons, traditions, and habits of that period

remain, are fixed in consciousness, and will long influence people's behavior. How many of them (or their families, acquaintances, and so on) went to the camps because during a meeting, or even in a private conversation, they asked about this or that? . . . How many lost their jobs? How many lost their lives?[1]

It would be wrong to pretend that this blanket of silence now slowly lifting was laid heavily only by the Soviet Imperium. Imperial designs, whatever their means and intentions, entail the enforcement of a silence. The colonized — whether natives of our lands like those in the United States confined to reservations of economic deprivation, or those similarly marginalized in Europe's former colonies — must learn over time to awaken themselves to a world in which questions and talk are, at least, relatively free of risk. Changes of large, even if well-mannered, proportions, like revolutions of all kinds, including the dream of them, are first and foremost about the breaking of long-established silences.

We now live in a time characterized as much by the slow decline of the American imperium that grew out of the ruins of the British, the French, the Dutch, among others — as by the sudden fall of the Soviet Union's vast imperial order. If, as it is said, there is a new world order, it is at best the nervous order of talk about, and denunciation of, the multiple voices of complaint, which, because of their hitherto long silence, had been thought not actually to be those of any truly existing others.

The academic debate with respect to these disturbing political rebellions, like its counterpart in the better number of civil societies the world over, is about the insistent noise that follows a long silence. The politics called "identity politics" are the politics of nothing other than the struggle to acquire a social place amid the disorderly business that presents itself upon the fall of one or another outpost of the Western Imperium. Hence the political noise attendant on struggles — for ethnic rights in the former Soviet Union, for racial and economic justice in the United States and Africa, for freedom from social punishment against the fact of one's gender or the secrets of one's sex. And more.

Following therefrom, the most urgent, and ubiquitous, question of our day is this one: What are we — whichever we, we might be — to say about these terrifying ethnic, racial, and sexual voices that disturb the silence to which the world had grown accustomed? If we are to consider the social basis and political implication of identities such as these, we must do so historically, as best we can. It hardly need be said that it is impossible to write a history of one's own time without writing pseudo-history.[2] Yet, when the history of one's own time imposes itself as it does today, it would be wrong not to try, however false the outcome.

To that end, I seek here to argue one (and only one) of the lines of such a necessary, if dangerous, history of the present moment, for which I offer the following proposition: *Identity, including identity politics and its expressions in the new social movements, is today a social fact arising from the collapse of the Western Imperium and the subsequent collapse of its well-exercised theory of world culture.*

In all that is said on identities and the new social movements there is everywhere lurking a mistaken assumption — one that corrupts much of what is said on both sides. In one of its more popular versions, this is the mistake of dismissing those struggling to speak, at long last, against the Imperium as preoccupied with themselves — that is, with an inward, private interest in defining or discovering their own selfhoods. From the political Left, this insult takes the form of accusing identity politics and the new social movements of abandoning the classic, Left insistence on a totalizing critique of the totalizing effects of the capitalist political-economy; from the Right the mistake takes the form of demonizing those who work for rights in the name of their race, gender, or sex — as though it were they who are responsible for tearing apart the civilizational values that were thought to have unified all Western people and to have created thereby the only, truly human, world culture.

In the social and human sciences, the mistake to which I refer is more predictably sober, but just as mistaken, when it takes the form of conducting the analysis of *identity* as though it were, or ever could be, more psychological than a social, even political, concept. If the popular versions of the mistake are made because of the threat the new voices pose to the declining order, the scientific form of the error may be caused by a more high-minded reason. It is true that the earliest social-scientific discussions of identity arose in the late nineteenth century out of the lingering effects of an essentially Hegelian concern with self-identity and identarian thought. Surely one of the more famous attempts to work a way out of these dilemmas was the influential formulation in 1890 by William James of the four functional attributes of the self, in respect to which one of the most troubling was none other than "personal identity" (James's expression). Most of the classic self-theories followed James in this by trying to find a way by which the multiple demands of the social self could be reconciled in some inner core of stable selfhood. In James's famous words, if "I have as many selves as there are persons who recognize me," then how can *my* self also recognize *it*self as "the same today as it was yesterday"? Henceforth, and for a long time after, identity was considered, as George Herbert Mead put it, largely the work of the "I," or ego, seeking somehow to rope the "Me," or social self, back in from its many social digressions.[3]

This observation on the early origins of the concept of personal identity is pertinent background to my main point, a connection that can be made with reference to the historical origins of the events that marked the first successful attempts to lift the imperial West's veil of silence. It was not until the 1950s and 1960s, among social scientists of various persuasions, that identity fell under a more robust sociological fate. In the social criticism of that era, a prevailing concern was the decline of the modern inner-directed self and the emergence of a more socially conformist one (as David Riesman put it), or the emergence of an "identity crisis" particularly among the rebellious young in modern societies (as Erik Erikson put it), or the need to reinsert the personal into the political (as C. Wright Mills and, in a different but similar way, Jean-Paul Sartre were then saying — as were political rebels on both sides of the Atlantic).[4] It is not that these new formulations of identity broke with nineteenth-century culture but that they began a process of recognition whereby, thereafter, it had to be thought that personal identity, far from being the instrument by which the self sustains its individuality, is more a product of how the unsustainable individual adjusts herself to the demands of social life.

I do not for a minute believe that those aligned with the identity politics of the new social movements have normally taken time to consult the social scientists. But I do believe that this slight, but significant, shift in social-scientific opinion in the late 1950s and early 1960s was directly demanded by changes in the world that were already well under way at the time. It was, I think, no accident that in this and other areas social thought began to reconsider the power and salience of the social even in relation to the social psychology of the individual — and to do so at the very time the millions subjected to colonial rule were struggling against the Western Imperium — a struggle based in considerable degree upon their desire to redefine the conditions of their subjecthood. This is to say that what took place in the relatively safe closets of academic social science in that era was nothing more than a faint echo of the politically potent social psychologies of the classic sources of decolonization theory. For one example, from Frantz Fanon's 1952 *Black Skins, White Masks*:

> The crippled veteran of the Pacific war says to my brother, "Resign yourself to your color the way I got used to my stump; we're both victims."
>
> Nevertheless with all my strength I refuse to accept that amputation. I feel in myself a soul as immense as the world, truly a soul as deep as the deepest of rivers, my chest has the power to expand without limit. I am a master and I am advised to adopt the humility of the cripple. Yesterday, awakening to the world, I saw the sky turn upon itself utterly and wholly.

I wanted to rise, but the disemboweled silence fell back upon me, its wings paralyzed. Without responsibility, straddling Nothingness and Infinity. I began to weep.[5]

Today one must read Fanon, as well as Aimé Césaire, C. L. R. James, Albert Memmi, Malcolm X, the young Stokely Carmichael, and others of the original theorists of decolonization. One must read them, especially today, if one wishes to understand just why even social science began, at an earlier time, to refer the personal to the social and political; and why, years later, we are faced with the noisy voices that require us to consider the ironic, but hard to refute, assertions — that the personal is political, — that in our time, identity is above all else a category arising from a specific series of *political* events: that, whatever else it is, identity cannot be made sense of as a category of the self alone, or psychology, not even of a social psychology.

The historical reason (even it it is a false one) for this assertion is that it seems obvious, if not perfectly obvious, that the world which for a long time has been thought of as "modern," is experiencing a crisis of grave and global proportions. The long-ruling colonial system of cores extracting resource and wealth from the peripheries is no longer effectively administered from a coherent, unassailable Center. Those, including the United States at the moment, who attempt to be that Center hold their power but for the times of acute troubles, after which they must relent to negotiated accords with jealous partners in order to resist the protests of those who, being hungry and angry, turn more to family and tribes, even to faith — ignoring, or otherwise perturbing, the national powers. There were imperial orders before this one — Greek, Roman, Holy Roman, Ottoman, and others. But this one, now declining, was different for the very reach of its global purposes.

What distinguishes the world claims of modern, Western nation-state cultures is that they alone actually succeeded in establishing a global system of economic control and political administration. Of all the aspirants to world dominance, only the modern West exercised sufficient imperial power to enforce the reach of its culture more or less ubiquitously in all the geographical corners of world space. In fact, it is possible to say that today we use the term "world" in reference to the political geography of the physical earth *because* the modernist culture of the West succeeded so brutally well in imposing its culture on the global space. To the extent that individuals or groups anywhere in the world are willing to consider themselves identified members of the sphere of universal human interests (thus, of the order of human things as such) they will sooner or later be forced to refer to the presumptive claims of the modern West. They may refer to Euro-American culture only to attack its arrogance or demonstrate its limits, but refer they must. This is the sense in which "world" is defined by the political aspirations of a series of colonizing Western societies.[6]

It is surely not by coincidence that the debates over the meaning of social identity are most viciously engaged at the very time when changes in world politics have provoked a related but no less urgent debate. The two entail each other. As the world changes according to indecipherable laws, identity itself becomes every bit as unstable a social thing as the suddenly decentered world economic system. Once an established world system begins to decompose, social instability seems to move with chaotic effect from the smallest to the greatest parts. It is obvious that the destabilizing of the modern world is associated with a curious, but undeniable, energizing of identity as the topic of widespread political interest.

Social identity most fundamentally involves a claim to rights in a social space. In the abstract, a "social identity" is the distinctive collection of social attributes a social environment makes available to an individual. This is distinct from the individual's "ego identity" by which he or she appropriates, or seeks to alter, the social identity made available, a point Erving Goffman may have been the first to make in 1963 in *Stigma*.[7] Though social space may or may not have actual physical correlates, it is clear that individuals, across their many differences of selfhood and ego attributions, live every bit as much in the imaginary but durable space whereby the wider social world offers them normal or deviant moral careers, superior or inferior statuses, permitted or forbidden courses of action, and the like. Social space is, to be sure, the moral geography that Goffman diagnosed so well. Who we are — or, if the moral landscape allows it, who we chose to be — is always, unrelentingly a determination made in order to locate oneself in social space; or, in the cases of those assigned the inferior social locations, it is, under certain conditions of freedom, the struggle to define a location where before none had existed or, if it existed, its moral value was so socially corrupt as to make the occupation of it evidence of personal unworthiness for decent membership in the whole. When the silent begin to speak, they utter the words that begin to create the discursively initiated and organized, but politically and economically powerful, social space from which the imposition of silence was intended to exclude them.

Identity politics are, thus, about the inhabiting of social territories which had previously been closed to those lacking proper official identification. When individuals appropriate a national, racial, ethnic, religious, or sexual identity, they are claiming these as places — always, of course, in relation to some aspect (or aspects) of the world. The world created principally by modernist culture never was reducible to its physical co-ordinates. It was, in effect, the sometimes innocent, other times fully cognizant, work of those who, believing in themselves most sincerely, defined the world as the ideal, progressive possibility of the universal Man. That his racial, sexual, and gender peculiarities were left unglossed in the vocabulary of liberal humanism does not mean that he, so to speak, or at least some of his own, did not realize that the others who served the universal purposes of his glorious culture were not ever about to remain ultimately quiet. They saw too much of what he did in the night shadows. They were too often the subject of his whims, as they were always, necessarily, the providers of the backs and thighs upon and through which moved the most unspeakable violations of the idealization of work as God's means to human worth.

The act of self-identification is, therefore, a personal act requiring, in some instances, political courage and, in most instances, complicated moral judgments that cannot be reversed. When one chooses to pass out from under the silence, under which she suffered or in which he colluded, an individual comes into social being — that is, she or he enters anew into a social space, either for the first time without official permission; or, as many times before but now with an alert regard for the tenuousness of what might have once been an utterly naive ignorance of the noise of identity politics in the prior silence.

Identity politics are, thus, the politics of moral geography and, as in all delicate environments, when the weather changes for some, sooner or later it changes for all who inhabit the territory. It is, therefore, not by coincidence that some of the most important writers associated with identity politics are attempting to recover, and thus to recreate, lost social spaces, as did the first generation of postcolonial writers in the 1950s. Gloria Anzaldúa recreates in her writings a "home" for those whose land was taken from them when the US annexed Texas from Mexico in 1848. This lost space, *Atzlán*, is at once mythical and real. Trinh T. Minh-ha is similarly writing a postcolonial, feminist literature that seeks to recreate the space of exiled, émigré Vietnamese who were displaced to the United States and other parts of the world by the war in Vietnam. Likewise, most postcolonial writers, including most obviously Homi Bhabha and Gayatri Chakravorty Spivak, are recreating the subaltern spaces that, in the colonial situation, were the hidden-from-view social spaces in which identities were erased and resistances were organized in silence.[8] These identity politics — feminist, ethnic and racial, sexual, as well as post-colonial — are mostly about reinventing social spaces that were destroyed by colonial rule and the other indulgences of the Western Imperium. The protests against them are very often the after-the-fact reflexes of the humanistic good fellows who, having naively invited the freedom to speak, suddenly realize that the breaking of the silence entails their own loss of once assured, socially fortunate places.

This is why today the question of identity is, and must be, a question of the status of the actual world culture the West imposed on the globe over the last half-millennium. So long as the Western doctrine of the universality of its world culture held a plausible legitimacy, it was possible (at least in principle) for persons to think of their social identity as a general property of their "human nature." One of the most important social transformations in the present world, such as it is, has been the erosion of confidence of those who formerly considered their world position secure in this way. This was the world position of those in the dominant classes in Europe and North America; that is: mostly male, almost entirely white, educated, economically comfortable, presumptively heterosexual elites. These were the inventors and purveyors of the idea of world culture as an idea that was for them a "self-evident" truth of "all men." The current decline of the Imperium threatens the Western belief in a world culture in which all persons, in all social places, are thought to share a common core identity. In other words, it threatens the foundational conviction of Western values, that is: its belief in universal humanity, which is fundamentally an idealization of the world itself as a stable place in which all human creatures might find some common cultural ground. This was, in short, the culture of a sometimes cruel, othertimes gentle, silence.

In this sense, identity politics exist wherever peoples struggle to retain (even if silently) their own identified worlds against the intrusions of colonizers or other imperial forces. Accordingly, we are all postcolonials, and postcolonial identity is always, to some extent, a result of the necessity of coming to political *and* cultural terms with the prior colonial *and* colonizing experience. Even those of us who have enjoyed as if by right the privileges of birth or family are caught, pathetically, in the struggle for a social space. We who are thus set apart, having formerly set ourselves above, watch with fear, anger, or anxious understanding the others — those peoples who, having suffered the indignity of a dominant culture's imposition of its culture on them, break the silence: feminists, ethnic rebels, gays and lesbians — and, occasionally students, intellectuals, and workers. Identity politics, even when not called by this name, is a near universal possibility whenever an imperium, having succeeded for a while, even a long while, loses its grip on the silence in which it once thrived.

Elsewhere in his book, Ryszard Kapuściński says what could well be said of the world itself:

> It is a fascinating moment, fraught with promise, when this spirit of the times, dozing pitifully and apathetically, like a huge wet bird on a branch, suddenly and without clear reason (or at any rate without a reason allowing of an entirely rational explanation) unexpectedly takes off in bold and joyful flight. We all hear the *shush* of this flight. It stirs our imagination and gives us energy: we begin to act.[9]

8

Representations of the Sociologist: Getting Over the Science Crisis

Sociology is suffering an unprecedented crisis of self-doubt, needlessly.

Even more acutely than before, many sociologists are outspoken in their criticisms of the field to which, in principle, they are devoted and from which they derive both livelihood and professional indentity. We worry and complain. This collective agony may in fact be one of the few shared experiences by which professional sociologists tenuously hold themselves together amid proliferating differences. This is not a new state of affairs. But a previous confidence that it could (or should) be overcome is now weaker. Once it was customary to cover the embarrassment of these differences by reference to sociology as a discrete perspective yielding diverse perceptions. Today even this largely rhetorical move scarcely serves its purpose. Consensus dissolves not simply from internal disagreement, but equally from the readiness of many sociologists to identify with intellectual movements well-organized outside our field of which feminism, cultural studies, and socio-economics are salient instances. More and more, sociologists find professional sociology beside the point of their primary concerns in life and work. Hence the agony of self-doubt.

I undertake the discussion of five quite disparate works,[1] including one modern classic, in order to advance the idea that the self-doubt which gives rise to the agony (or the disaffiliation) is needless at best, destructive at worst. I believe we doubt ourselves because we have mistaken sociology for something it can only partly be and, in any case, something it has tried to be only in the short time of the last three or so generations of sociologists, the time of the dominance of American academic sociology.

There could be no better illustration of my idea than "What's Wrong With Sociology?"[2] Organized and edited by Stephen Cole, a sociologist of science, it is not surprising that the contributors to this special issue of

Sociological Forum are in evident, though not complete, agreement that the cause of the crisis is our failure as a science. Cole opens the symposium with an editorial assertion few would dispute: "Today there is a sense among many American sociologists that all is not well with their discipline." Then, he proceeds immediately to the cause with only slight acknowledgment that it might be less well-received: "Many of us believe that, both organizationally and intellectually, sociology is not making the kind of progress we would like." Cole's own contribution to the symposium, "Why Sociology Doesn't Make Progress Like the Natural Sciences," is a thoughtful discussion of the problems confronting sociology's desire to be a good science.

Randall Collins's essay in "What's Wrong With Sociology," "Why the Social Sciences Won't Become High-Consensus, Rapid-Discovery Science," extends Cole's line of argument to social science as such while basing it on compelling historical evidence. James Davis's "What's Wrong With Sociology?" argues similarly: "Terror of substance and worship of theory are inhibiting consensus," he says in conclusion. James Rule's "Dilemmas of Theoretical Progress" pursues this concern from a hgher metatheoretical vantage. In fact, with only two exceptions, all the contributors to this special issue argue along much the same line. What's wrong with sociology is that it lacks consensus and other qualities of a real science.

Seymour Martin Lipset's carefully documented "The State of American Sociology" attributes "the parlous state of sociology — the changes that have produced serious divisiveness" — to the field's "vulnerability to politicization." In his analysis of the field over the last several generations Lipset argues that the "politics of sociology in the 1960s" (when he and other liberal voices were criticized from *their* left) was the moment of first definite decline into sociology's current mess. This point is obliquely supported in "The Transformation of the American Sociological Association" by Ida Harper Simpson and Richard L. Simpson, who observe that the political pressures from the Sixties generation in sociology were absorbed into the official structure of the American Sociological Association (ASA). This, they believe, forced the ASA out of its historic role as a nurturer of "disciplinary interests" to become a more activist and fractious organization. The continuing proliferation of interest sections, which serve as many members' first line of contact with official sociology, is one sign of what Simpson and Simpson see as an organizational loss. For a number of years, various powers-that-were in the ASA did, in fact, attempt to limit section growth, as though one could stuff the genie back in the bottle.

Among the nine authors contributing to "What's Wrong With

Sociology?" only two dissent from the prevailing opinion. (This number almost surely would have been greater had not all the contributors been male and otherwise identified with the field's traditional mainstream.) For nearly a quarter century, Arthur Stinchcombe has offered his smartly rendered occasional disquisitions on the nature of our field. Who can forget the one in which he observed (no doubt correctly) that it takes at the most six weeks to become an expert in any of the major sub-specialties in the field? In "Disintegrated Disciplines and the Future" Stinchcombe offers still another sardonic commentary on the field. This time he concludes that our disintegrated state is the "optimum state of affairs" in respect at least to teaching.[3] Otherwise there is "nothing to be done but suffer from the fact that deans are not going to like us" and that we will continue to "fight with each other." Stinchcombe's point is that this disintegrated state, though troubling, is at least natural to local customs. I like the sober good sense of this, as I do Harvey Molotch's recommendation in "Going Out" that we need above all else to be less preoccupied with ourselves. Molotch wants us to learn from others in our discipline with whom we disagree and from those in other disciplines, to write for readers outside our narrow disciplinary circles, and not to fear revealing ourselves for what we are. He does not fear the politicization to which Lipset objects.

Molotch's thinking appeals to me the most (marginally more than Stinchcombe's) because of its greater willingness not to take sociology so seriously. Yet, even these two nonconforming voices among the nine contributors are surprisingly well within the confines of normal sociology. They too, like the others, think of sociology as an entity of its own kind, one that deserves a defense and requires a place among the coherent knowledges of man, if not among the sciences. It is this assumption that requires further examination, even when it is treated lightly as Molotch does.

I certainly do not believe that sociology, however it is organized, is of no importance; nor that our field is in any way least among the knowledges, formal and informal, of the human condition. Nor do I mean to suggest that we should not take ourselves seriously. Rather, the questions to ask are: *Serious with respect to what? And what is the mode of seriousness proper to whatever we consider ourselves to be?* These ultimately are questions of our self-understanding. What people think they are, or ought to be, when measured against actual conditions of existence, largely determines how they feel about themselves. In short, sociologists may doubt themselves because they aspire to be what they may never have been capable of being, nor should have been.

The idea that sociology was meant to be a science of any kind (much less a high-consensus, formal, and progressively cumulative one) is relatively new. In fact, this idea owes its currency to the history of American sociology in the several generations immediately following World War II through roughly the Vietnam War years — a period of not much more than 25 years, 1945–70. To be sure, the idea did not begin then. One finds intimations of it in Weber and the early Chicago sociologists, but they were opposed by friends, colleagues, or rivals who cared little about the making of an academic science. Simmel, Spencer, Jane Addams, W. E. B. Du Bois, Charlotte Perkins Gilman come to mind. Even Durkheim, the *locus classicus* of scientific sociology, had a much richer organizational and intellectual agenda than legend allows. True, he had a formal program for scientific sociology. But that academic program was always mixed up with, and pursued for the sake of, an equally ambitious moral and political agenda. Few of those classic figures objected to the politicization of disciplinary sociology for the simple reason that institutional sociology, as we know it today, did not then exist. Neither Weber nor even Durkheim established such a sociology. An institutionalized academic sociology did not take off in France, for one, until well into the 1960s and then largely under the influence of the already waning American model of scientific sociology. Much the same is true in other national sociologies worldwide. The ideal of sociology as a high-consensus, progressive science was convenient to actual historical conditions mostly in America for a quarter century or so. Outside the United States (in Europe especially), those who sought to build the ideal succeeded less well and, as in America, only during the time of postwar social change in which national political elites thought a scientific sociology might provide knowledge sufficient to the making of the good society they would lead. Thus, in the US an inherently leftish sociology enjoyed its greatest institutional success in the 1950s under an inherently conservative Republican administration. Likewise, in France sociology enjoyed its golden years under the Gaullists and declined under the Socialists. Funding for sciences, including social sciences, is governed by the first rule of political support and popular success, What have you done for me lately?

This, I believe, is where our problem lies. Sociologists who believe the ideal of a scientific sociology are more inclined to think of themselves as offering the society just exactly what they suppose it wants and needs — a rigorous science of that society, one productive of knowledge that would support the society's goal of social progress or, if not this, a government's desire at least to contain the spread of social failure. Such a sociology is at the whim of its sponsors. In time like the two decades just after World

War II when rapid economic expansion based on a sufficient surplus of natural and capital resources encouraged the dream of social progress, an enterprise like sociology may be widely perceived as having something good and necessary to give, and will be rewarded. In those days, sociology was. But now the affluence is long gone. The problem is that many of us still believe received illusions about *what* we were. Those short-lived worldly successes were corrupting distractions from what I believe sociology is and should be.

Like any organized gathering of social creatures, sociologists invent and respect their own collective representations of themselves. This is the insight of the other Durkheim of *Elementary Forms*, in which he argued that our modern belief in knowledge (including scientific knowledge) was in fact a collective representation of prior and primitive social arrangements. Hence it follows that sociologists reared and nurtured in a science respecting culture will understand their own sociological selves in some strong regard for this collective representation. All the contributors to "What's Wrong With Sociology?" and most of those who bemoan the field's failure to be a good science can be safely supposed to have been brought up, professionally speaking, under the mighty influence of this collective representation. Few of us active today have escaped it, though (as Lipset observes) those of us who came into the field after 1970 or so are appreciably less faithful to it. Whatever sociologists feel is right or wrong with themselves as sociologists is a function of what they feel the field ought to be, which feeling grows through regular exposure to the collective representations of the field taught us in due affection by our elders. If our elders thought sociology ought to be a science, we will be inclined to think likewise and thus to agonize over our failures when there is a diminished demand for the goods of social science. Having been thus instructed, we cast the blame for a false failure entirely on ourselves. Hence the agony.

There is nothing particularly wrong with sociology that can't be cured. We need, first of all, to work through the collective representations that so exaggerate our limited capacity to be a real science, and thus come back to sociology as it was and was intended by its founders to be.

To this end there are a number of possible guides. One I highly recommend is Said's *Representations of the Intellectual*.[4] Professionally, Said, an esteemed literary critic, is University Professor at Columbia University. He thus occupies a position of prestige in a field that invites contrast and comparison to our own. In many ways, the academic study of literature is to the 1970s and 1980s what sociology was to the 1950s and 1960s. They today, like we then, are the best, most intellectually demanding game in town. In some respects, literary theorists of culture have not just succeeded us, they have replaced us. Today one can learn a good deal of passable sociology from the books and articles of writers who care little and know less about formal sociology itself. Though his appreciation of sociology is an exception, Professor Said is otherwise a prime example of these literary sociologists *extra ecclesium*. At least two of his books, *Orientalism* and *Culture and Imperialism*, are, in my opinion, among the finest works of cultural sociology of our time.[5] He has ventured outside his own disciplinary preserve in these and other instances because he is frankly not afraid to be an amateur. On the contrary, Said considers amateurism when "fueled by care and affection"[6] a much-needed antidote to the dulling effect of narrow specialization within the academic profession.

Representations of the Intellectual is the slightly revised transcript of Said's 1993 Reith Lectures broadcast by the BBC. The book, though brief, is a satisfyingly comprehensive review of the role of the intellectual in the modern era. The title plays on two of the senses of *representation* in our culture. On the one hand, Said offers deft portraits of the ways in which the intellectual has been represented in modern culture in such literary works as Flaubert's *Sentimental Education* and James Joyce's *Ulysses*. These literary works are, however, juxtaposed to the more expository literature of social thinkers like Jean-Paul Sartre, C. L. R. James, Aimé Césaire, and Antonio Gramsci who, in addition to writing about the intellectual, were among the most powerful intellectual figures of our century. These discussions are charmingly nuanced. Said considers conservatives like Julien Benda alongside the more familiar left intellectuals and is anything but reluctant to attack heroes of the left like Michel Foucault.

On the other hand, Said examines the political and moral sense of an intellectual's representative function. He develops his own theory of the intellectual as one who bears a distinctive moral responsibility to represent the unrepresented and unrepresentable in society.

> I want to insist that the intellectual is an individual with a specific public role in society that cannot be reduced simply to being a faceless professional, a competent member of a class just going about her/his business. The central fact for me is, I think, that the intellectual is an individual endowed with a faculty for representing, embodying, articulating a message, a view, an attitude, philosophy or opinion to, as well as for, a public.[7]

Said draws with admirable humility on his own experiences as a part-time participant in Palestinian politics and representative of the Palestinian position in the Western media. Though to many his politics are controversial, Professor Said is, in my opinion, one of a very few who is able to conduct a scholarly life while at the same time acting prominently on his political judgments.

Sociologists will not necessarily find the passage just quoted original. In fact, among the sources of Said's theory of the intellectual are both C. Wright Mills and Alvin Gouldner. This is most evident in the particulars of the theory which might more accurately be described as a call to arms. Said urges today's intellectuals (of whom we academics are among the most important) to resist the temptations of professionalism, to risk an honest and caring amateurism in order to seek the truth not just in other fields or opposing positions but to locate ourselves in the ordinary world where our precious qualifications are of lesser moment. Following Frantz Fanon and Césaire, he considers the work of the intellectual "the invention of new souls",[8] and, after Theodor Adorno's famous skepticism, Said recommends that "the whole is always untrue."[9] Most poignantly his own experience as a native Palestinian living in the New York City (an experience comparable to Adorno's in California far from German high culture, and C. L. R. James's in London just as far from his colonized Trinidad) is behind his view of the intellectual as a "permanent exile." From this he generalizes:

> Even if one is not an actual immigrant or expatriate, it is still possible to think as one, to imagine and investigate in spite of barriers, and always to move away from the centralizing authorities toward the margins, where you see things that are usually lost on minds that have never traveled beyond the conventional and the comfortable.[10]

An intellectual should be more like Marco Polo, less like Robinson Crusoe — always moving, never quite settling in. It has been said that the only important piece of personal property Said owns is a grand piano.

Why recommend Said, especially when the spirit of what he says is already well within sociological memory? The answer is in the question. We know all this. But we have lost the taste for it, and perhaps the courage to live with it. Sociology began as (and for most of its history was) the academic world's Marco Polo. But, in the past several generations, we have become, more even than Robinson Crusoe, a people accustomed to settled accommodations in the university. Though he lived well, not even Durkheim enjoyed the institutional benefits and blessings offered today to new assistant professors. And Weber was not able to suffer the university which, had he kept his post, might have learned to distrust him. These great men were, in their own ways, permanent exiles in their intellectual lands. So were Marx, Simmel, Du Bois, Gilman, many of the early Chicago sociologists, Mannheim, as well as Mills, Goffman, and Gouldner.

It is far past time when we can ask ourselves, and those who count on us, to pull up all our professional stakes, or put at risk the securities we continue to enjoy even in a harsh world. But, we can ask as Said has done, what exactly are we meant to do and be? Or, as he puts it, "I am asking *the* basic question for the intellectual: how does one speak the truth? What truth? To whom and where?"[11] Sociologies that judge the truth of sociology solely by the standards of institutionalized science will be less inclined to ask such questions, if to ask them at all. They are not, it should be said, questions simply of "going out" to the world with our truth (as Molotch suggests), but more a matter of opening ourselves to the question of truth itself.

To be sure, this is not a question sociologists are accustomed to asking. Insofar as we routinely inquire into the nature of truth we do so through the mediation of technical concerns for the validity of our data. This long, and honorable, tradition of rigorous empirical inquiry into the uncertainties of social life is, indeed, professional sociology's most enduring contribution to the human sciences. But, it may also have distracted our attention from the considerable controversy that lies behind Said's skepticism toward broad encompassing truth-claims.

Put simply, the question today is: Whose truth? The current wave of truth skepticism owes a great deal to Michel Foucault's rehabilitation of Nietzsche's classic confrontations with Western culture's will to Truth. Those who have read Foucault will recognize the importance of Nietzsche in his famous (if a bit perverse) 1969 book, *Archaeology of Knowledge*.[12] Here Foucault's now familiar (but poorly understood) ideas on the embeddedness of knowledge in power relations were first sketched in terrifying abstractions. One of the less widely recognized expressions of Foucault's version of the "Whose truth?" question is his influential critique of the classic ideal of the general intellectual. In a now famous 1977 interview, "Truth and Power," Foucault proposed that we can no longer think of the intellectual as the bearer of the essential truths of Western civilization. The intellectual's task, rather, is the concrete labor of exposing the multiple truths that appear in differential and local corners of the culture, truths that are hidden from view so long as the intellectual pursues the ideal of a general and universal Truth. Foucault's "Truth and Power" ended with the words: "The political question is not error, illusion, alienated consciousness, or ideology. It is truth itself."[13] Clearly, this is also a highly condensed criticism of the dominant theories of intellectuals and social knowledge: Marx's, Gramsci's, Mannheim's, and sociology's. The idea of the general intellectual requires a suspension of doubt with respect to the universal possibility of Truth itself. This attitude is in the background of theories like Said's on intellectuals.

The "Whose truth?" question is, today, asked by many others whose relation to Foucault is as indefinite as is their relation to professional sociology.

One such writer is Jerry Gafio Watts, a political and social theorist by training, and professor of American Studies at Trinity College in Connecticut by occupation. Watts' *Heroism and the Black Intellectual* is the first of a projected multi-volume project that, upon completion, will surely be a theory of Afro-American cultural life with which all rivals must contend.[14] *Heroism*, being the project's first volume, quite rightly concentrates on Ralph Ellison whose *Invisible Man* is widely considered one of (perhaps even *the*) most important novels of African-American experience.

There area number of good reasons to consider Ellison as the beginning point of a project like Watts'. The most striking, however, is Ellison's distinctive (and, to some, contrary) attitude toward politics: "When writers write about politics, usually they are wrong. The novel at its best demands a sort of complexity of vision which politics doesn't like."[15] Ellison, thus, rejected the notion that Afro-American art can, or ought, to be explicitly political. By extension, this is the view that the intellectual's duty entails enduring and complex truths which are beyond the passing concerns of politics.

Ralph Ellison's working theory of the intellectual might, at first, seem to be a classic expression of the very ideal of the general intellectual that Said, Foucault, and many others reject. It would be were it not for the fact that Ellison wrote from the concrete circumstance of Afro-American history and culture. He wrote, that is, as a man for whom the first question of truth was unavoidably, Whose truth? This not so subtle, but easy for some to overlook, difference in point of view can reopen the drowsing eyes of those who might consider Said's "question of truth" idea too far beyond the customary interests of empirical sociology.

Jerry Watts, like Said, locates his theory of intellectuals in appreciative relation to the great sociologists of intellectuals,[16] and he considers this book an "attempt at a sociology of intellectuals."[17] But the book's greater value for sociologists is, I think, in the way it exposes the more ordinary life (thus, less theoretically abstract) dilemmas of the question of truth. Situating himself clearly in the tradition of social theorists of colonial life like Frantz Fanon and Albert Memmi, Watts bases his theory of the black intellectual on the "victim status syndrome [as] a primary component of twentieth-century Afro-American ethnic identity":

> The victims are actually torn between hatred and envy of the victimizer. In desiring to be like the victimizer, the victims internalize values that are antithetical to their freedom, for in effect, they valorize the victimizer for denying their own freedom. In this sense, the victims are torn between their hatred and envy of the victimizer. The state of being torn is one in which the victims simultaneously adhere to their own values (the desire to be free and the values that support that desire) and the victimizer's values (the desire to deny freedom and the values that rationalize this domination).[18]

In short, among the implications that can be drawn from such a view is that the *general* truth of the *concrete* situation of the black intellectual is one in which the general truths defined by the victimi*zing* culture *always* have concretely different meanings for those whom they victimize.

Hence the "victim syndrome" necessarily puts the Afro-American intellectual in a vastly more complex situation than that of anyone not forced to think and write from such a social position. Watts concludes his interpretation of Ellison with reference to the title theme:

> Though heroic in artistic intention, the Ellison resolution to this Afro-American intellectual agon is humanistically disturbing. Victimized people are not the material upon which claims for equality and humanity are secured. Only those individuals capable of turning the victimization into art can secure for a people their historical significance. Art endures. Politics is transitory. People only live and then die.[19]

In an after-thought[20] Watts seems, in the end, to hold important reservations about Ellison's position. Just the same, Watts offers a compelling alternate view of Foucault's concrete intellectual, as of Said's exile. Though he does not develop the idea in this book, one assumes that Watts' theory of the victim status syndrome could have reference to intellectuals who represent still other victim histories than the African-American. Watts thus makes an important contribution to the wider theoretical discussion of the social role, and condition, of the intellectual.

A book like *Heroism and the Black Intellectual* introduces sociologists to a nuanced theory of artistic and intellectual work against which we might profitably compare sociology's own traditions and habits. It is not that so white-dominated a field as ours could, or should, presume to borrow, without reflection, from the historic experiences of those Ellison sought and Watts seeks to represent. Rather, a thoughtful reading of such a book puts into sharp relief just how far we are from asking the "Whose truth?" question and, thus, just why in actual fact sociologists have long been wary of public intellectuals who dare to speak sociological truths without proper credentials.

In fact, sociologists have grown so far away from representing themselves as intellectuals that we have, during the short history of the scientific ideal, actually viciously attacked those who have tried. This is a major theme in the story told by Daniel Horowitz in *Vance Packard and American Social Criticism.*[21]

In the late 1950s and early 1960s three of Vance Packard's many popular books were runaway bestsellers.[22] Each was a work of popular sociology. *Hidden Persuaders* (1957), an exposé of advertising culture, was the most successful. It topped the bestseller lists for more than a year, and sold well for years. By the mid-1970s at least 3 million copies were in print. Packard's *Status Seekers* (1959), his contribution to the then current social criticism of consumption based conformism, and *Waste Makers* (1960), a book credited with stimulating the consumer revolt against corporate waste (p. 149), did somewhat less well. But, by any standard, they too were wildly popular books. One or another of Packard's three books led bestseller lists for four years. His influence was enormous. Corporate America reacted with defensive outrage to books that fueled popular social criticisms among readers who were not likely to have read even C. Wright Mills' *White Collar* much less the more profession-respecting sociologies of that day. Packard's books were closer in style and popular reception to Rachel Carson's *Silent Spring* (1962), Betty Friedan's *The Feminine Mystique* (1963), and Ralph Nader's *Unsafe At Any Speed* (1965) — three of the most popular, and influential, among many works of social criticism in the early 1960s.

Vance Packard was more or less self-consciously a sociologist. As an undergraduate at Penn State in the 1930s, Packard had studied sociology with Willard Waller. Horowitz suggests that Waller was a mentor whose influence was fundamental and enduring.[23] Just the same, Horowitz carefully distinguishes the quality of Packard's studies from those of more professional sociological social critics of the time like David Riesman and Mills. Packard is not an unacknowledged sociological great like W. E. B. Du Bois or Charlotte Perkins Gilman. In the days of his literary success, Packard was what he was: a journalist turned freelance writer. He had his sociological and political passions. But above all else he devoted himself to the writing of popular non-fiction. Still, Packard was a sociologically informed social critic who for thousands upon thousands was the only even remotely sociological writer they read. And, he made an important difference. Many Americans learned to think more critically about their social world because of him.

Vance Packard and American Social Criticism is a trustworthy account of Packard's life and work. Very much to Packard's credit, Horowitz's access to Packard's private papers was granted without condition or interference. Though Horowitz worked reasonably closely with his subject, who still lives in New Canaan, Connecticut, he does not refrain from assessing Packard in honest and realistically critical terms. The book provides details of Packard's life and work that may exceed the interests of the average sociologist, but Horowitz's story of this extra-sociological social critic is well worth our reading. We should at least take to heart Horowitz's account of professional sociology's embarrassingly aggressive attacks on Packard's most popular works.[24]

"If the business community took issue with Packard's work, sociologists unleashed a barrage of criticism, especially of the *Status Seekers*." Although the number of formal sociological reviews of Packard's three blockbuster books was not great, those that did appear are notable for their hostility. The sources and titles of several are particularly telling: Lewis Coser, "Kitsch Sociology," in *Partisan Review*; Seymour M. Lipset, "The Conservatism of Vance Packard," in *Commentary*; and by the editors of *Trans-Action* (in 1965), "Is Vance Packard Really Necessary?" Daniel Horowitz comments:

> Especially revealing is the fact that many of the strongest attacks on Packard came not from Parsons, Merton, or Lazarsfeld, but from Coser, Lipset, and the editors of *Trans-Action*. These scholars were to the left of the mainstream and were themselves striving to make contributions as both public intellectuals and specialized professionals.[25]

With a good eye for nuance, Horowitz (an historian at Smith College) shrewdly diagnoses the situation of sociology in the 1960s and 1970s. Those already well established at the time, like Coser and Lipset, were inclined to defend the scientific prerogatives of professional sociology. Horowitz observes (p. 192) that Lipset also was among those who attacked C. Wright Mills for his own violations of the rules of the "sociological fraternity."

In those grand days of the scientific ideal in sociology, Packard, Mills, and other writers with wide readership were seen as threats to the field, irrelevant trivializers. Too much popular success was, then as now, sure sign of scientific inadequacy. Those were the days of the purported end of ideology, when professional sociologists believed that their work was sufficient unto its own scientific purposes. But that idea was already in doubt when Packard was most popular. The doubt would spread.

1995 marked the 25th anniversary of Alvin W. Gouldner's *The Coming Crisis of Western Sociology*, which was the first of a series of books Gouldner wrote in the 1970s.[26] *Coming Crisis* (1970), *The Dialectic of Ideology and Technology* (1979), *The Future of Intellectuals* (1980), and *Against Fragmentation* (posthumous, 1982) constitute what is surely the most ambitious and thorough reconsideration of the intellectual ever attempted by a single author. Gouldner's distinctive view of the sociologist as an intellectual outlaw, or ridge rider, anticipated Said's figure of the intellectual as exile by a quarter-century. In Gouldner's case, left-Hegelian Marxisms were an acknowledged source of the outlaw spirit he described, and embodied. In fact, *Coming Crisis* was a sort of coming out of the Marxism Gouldner, and thousands of others, had suppressed during their coming of intellectual age in the most intense era of American anti-communism in the 1950s.

Coming Crisis was a phenomenon that is said to have inspired the very generation of new sociologists which Lipset and others hold accountable for sociology's decline from its moment of high disciplinary success. It is true that Gouldner, student and life-long friend of Merton, loved sociology. "Loved" may not be the word that comes to mind among those who knew Gouldner personally. He was a difficult man whose passions very often got the best of him. Though he did very much good, he also caused damage and pain among some who crossed his path. But this was the man's nature. *Coming Crisis*, with its emphasis on the necessity that the sociologist take "himself" (his word) seriously, was in part a tender admission of his own personal excesses and failures. "Men must accept their . . . experience of the world. If they find they are distant from the requirement of their culture and role, they should at least face up to, if not accept, the difference."[27] Gouldner's reference to the personal was an important aspect of his idea of reflexive sociology, as it was of his Marxism.

For Gouldner, the sociologist was indeed an outlaw. The best sociology was a third force between the professionalizing sociological scientism he hated, and the no less objectionable cruelties of the more Stalinist Marxisms. This ambition partly explains why *Coming Crisis* is such a monster of a book. It roams mercilessly, but eloquently, over topics few, then, would have thought to consider in one volume — the role of emotion and sentiment in sociology, utilitarian culture, the moralistics of Talcott Parsons, the Welfare State, the new theoretical movements, the disaffections of the young, and the limits of academic sociology, among many other subjects. Its concluding section is a kind of manifesto for reflexive sociology. Though it is not nearly so well known as C. Wright Mills' famous passages on the sociological imagination, Gouldner's concluding essay is evidently more personal, and more subtle.

"Reflexive sociology," said Gouldner,[28] "rests upon an awareness of a fundamental paradox: namely, that *those who supply the greatest resources for the institutional development of sociology are precisely those who most distort its quest for knowledge.*" He meant precisely for the sociologist to be an outlaw to the orthodoxies one is taught, and he believed this to be the truest nature of sociology. This rebellious, passionate ideal was one that offered welcome, if not comfort, to the many young people who, in the early 1970s, turned to sociology after a decade of political activism. *Coming Crisis*, like many books of this sort, was not particularly well read, or at least not studied. It was more a manifesto, read occasionally by those who sought permission of a special kind: "If books like this are sociology, then I can be a sociologist."

Gouldner, had he lived, might not be a hero today. Nor would Mills.[29] Both of them would have had to undergo very considerable changes of character for anyone with the least feminist, or multicultural, sensibility to tolerate them. It is not clear either was capable of such a change, though both might have lived longer at greater peace had they been. Gouldner was often a warm and generous person, but he had a dark side that also defined his sociology. Like Mills, he was not conventionally socialized into the discipline he cared for. Notwithstanding Robert K. Merton's enduring regard for and influence on him, some part of Gouldner was always at odds, always in exile. This unruliness was an important part of what made Gouldner, and Mills, modern classic figures of a deviant kind.

Among the reasons *Coming Crisis* can be profitably read today is that is was one of the few books to predict sociology's present crisis. In 1970 Gouldner was convinced that both academic sociology and state socialisms, with their homologous naiveties as to the virtues of formal programs, would collapse. So, he suggested, would the welfare states that nurtured each in different ways. Gouldner was also one of the first to predict the further proliferation of smaller sociologies of which Goffman, Garfinkel, and Homans were his examples. For those who did not live through it, it may be hard to imagine that in 1970 younger sociologists, however much they were persuaded by Gouldner's moral ideal, had little reason to trust his dire warnings. These were the grand days of experimentation. A paradigm a day! Sociology felt much like a better-organized Woodstock. But, in fact, Gouldner's warnings came to pass. I write just as political forces in the US and across Western Europe have set about to dismantle as much as they can of what remains of the Welfare State. At the very same time sociologists everywhere are wondering, What's wrong with sociology?

What we think we ought to be will determine how, or if, we answer that question in a way that will encourage new generations of sociologists. To suggest that the scientific ideal is a limited one is not, however, to reject it out of hand. It had, and has, a place in the history, and future, of our field. Where it fails is as the sole standard by which to judge ourselves. It is too late for sociology to be other than it has become, too late even to wrench ourselves out of this ill-fitting institutional place we have among the social sciences. But is is not too late to reconsider our way of thinking about ourselves.

If not outlaws, perhaps permanent exiles. At least intellectuals who, whatever their science, inquire differently of ourselves and our task. Not: "What's wrong with sociology?" But: "How does one speak the truth? What truth? To whom and where?"

9

The New Sociologies in the Social Unconscious

Whatever one believes about today's world and its structures, whether they are modern still or postmodern, it would be hard to deny that we live in a stormy sociological time. It is virtually impossible to step even into the more sheltered of public places without good sociological galoshes. The public domain is awash with controversies — political, ethical, economic, racial, sexual, and more.

Not long ago members of the small country church my wife and I attend very nearly came to blows over whether or not, and then for how long, an AIDS awareness poster printed at the Bishop's expense would be displayed in the parish hall. At our family Thanksgiving weekend the same year a relative (newly acquired through remarriage) came forth with a polished but still crude remark about Caribbean "natives" that nearly sent some of us home early. Occasions such as these are always fraught with possibilities for abrupt departures. Ask any parent of a sophomore home from college. Squabbles are common. But, what is different about the general situation today is the extent to which the bickering arises less out of personal jealousies and more from the underground of civil disorder which seeps into the foundations of voluntary associations and families. Churches and like groups endure and the Thanksgiving pies are usually served in negotiated peace, but the events remind just how readily even people of superficially like mind see the world differently and come into it with their own peculiar ideas which are, in effect, rival sociologies of the world.

At the end of the day, sociologies are what people think and say about the world. Sociologies such as these intrude even upon the most simple, if sacred, of daily gatherings, just as they burst upon anyone who still has heart enough to tune in to talk radio. This too may always have been true, at least in the last century or two, when the progressive effects of modernization have brought more and more people into the public sphere in order to stake their claims to the goods they require or desire.

All sociologies rely of necessity on the controversies of their times, which is why, no doubt, academic sociology did not come into its present institutional form before the late nineteenth century when, in Europe and the United States, the clash of public and private turmoils could no longer be silenced, not even in gentle company. Before these conditions of civil vitality and strife obtained, there was insufficient public need of the subject to move the masses to pay the price of its institutional life. Conversely, this may be why the academic practice of sociology has tended to fall into a stupor when the public company is too confused by world affairs to know what it might want to say — as between the two world wars in this century; or when, as in the 1950s, those in cultural authority successfully impose a standardized version of the common dream. To be sure, even in such times there are rival sociologies, even among the academics. But the public influence of rebels diminishes in proportion to the confusions or false accords that dull the collective social imagination. What has transpired in sociology over the years has transpired, it seems to me, in direct relation to the popular demand for workable sociologies. Though the academic sociologies are not always accessible, or of interest, to those who attend little churches or family gatherings, what the sociologists do is always, and necessarily, dependent upon and energized by the popular stomach.

Even if the ubiquity of sociologies of all and frequently perverse kinds is a normal condition of modern societies, as it seems to be, it is surely true that in these latter days of the modern order, sociologies are ever more abrasively necessary to the conduct of out-of-doors public life. As a consequence, we live today in a time when there are numerous new sociologies. To some the more visible epiphanies of these sociologies are the feminist, queer, race-based, ethnic, and other identity politics which, considered collectively, openly resist the social traditions and many of the institutions under which they, or theirs, have suffered. These are the ones most often, if vaguely, considered to be postmodernish freaks and frogs. But, no less loud in the night air are the voices calling out in defense of one or another tradition of the older order. And to these, again, is added a third: a good and prominent number of those who are intent upon imagining entirely new sociologies suitable for the building of some future society. Though we hear of these sociologies through the elites who bring them to public notice, even the most passing attention to talk on the radios, in the bars, down the streets confirm the fear that what we hear on the radio and TV talk-shows are true seeds of new sociologies, great in number and widely sown. About this circumstance, two important observations can be made.

First, the demand is extraordinarily high for new sociologies able to sustain the work of daily life in the waning years of the current millennium. Many popular sociologies rush to meet demands. What they proclaim is so surprising that the phenomenon can only partly be explained by the well-known fact that the expression of a sociological point of view requires no special permission and very little formal training. The ready ability of the many to formulate a sociology is acted upon more in some times than others. This is one of the more times.

Secondly, these new sociologies make appearances among the intellectual elite (including but not limited to academics) in the same unruly and deviant manifestations by which they intrude upon local gatherings, political rallies, and the higher pitches of the radio dial. Even if one grants, as I would, that the better informed the proponent of a sociological opinion, the more reliable it will be, there is no reason to conclude that what takes place among the elite is all that different from what takes place among its presumably less well-disciplined constituent subjects. When an elite rules, it rules falsely in the name of the people and, even when it rules with an iron fist, it seldom is able to rule out popular resistance. Resistance movements work underground where they usually find collaborators even in the ranks of disciplined elite troops. The active resistance of such revolutionaries creates, sustains, and bothers the troubled unconsciousness of the rulers they would overthrow, and sometimes do. Thus, the turmoil of the times should be occasion less for alarm than hope that today there are new sociologies working in, and against, the cultural elite post- or still-modern societies, and that these new, ever more ubiquitous, sociologies, whether popular or professional, are disturbing the scenery of modernity's once largely unplayed-upon field of dreams.

Resistance is the foremost social problem of late modern, or early post-modern, societies. But resistance to what? To many of both right- and left-wing sympathies, the resistance that matters is to the cherished principles of universal humanity. While conservatives and leftists would define such principles differently, the devout on both sides hold fervently to the idea that unless modernity's vision of a common humanity is reaffirmed, the social whole will collapse — either due to a lack of moral virtue, according to the Right; or, as the Left has it, due to a refusal of the oppressed and their allies to work together for social justice.

The most eloquent statement of the problem is Arthur Schlesinger's comment on the effects of multiculturalism on American society:

> The ethnic revolt against the melting pot has reached the point, in rhetoric at least, though not I think in reality, of a denial of the idea of common culture and a single society. If large numbers of people really accept this,

the republic would be in serious trouble. The question poses itself: how to restore the balance between *unum* and *pluribus*? . . .

The question America confronts as a pluralistic society is how to vindicate cherished cultures and traditions without breaking the bonds of cohesion — common ideals, common political institutions, common language, common culture, common fate — that hold the republic together.[1]

Since the United States has practiced the most radical of experiments with social pluralism, the crisis is more acute here, perhaps, than elsewhere. But, the problem is to be found anywhere in the world where the reawakening of ethnic, racial, sexual or other identity-based loyalties causes members of social groups to withhold allegiance to the idea that they are in the same boat, culturally speaking, with all others living under a state regime. Wherever in the world — Brazil or Sub-Saharan Africa, Central Asia or Central Europe, North America or Western Europe — where there are multicultural strains aggravated by insufficient or declining social welfare resources, there will be real political and cultural wars arising in the space left by tremulous national cultures facing demands they cannot supply. In such times as these resistances to the prevailing order are many and effective. Clearly, the world order is itself a reflection of the cultural troubles of large multicultural states like the American.

Schlesinger is not wrong to worry. Nor are those of the more extreme right-of-center, like Allan Bloom, who a decade ago began the cultural wars with the most bitter denunciation of the moral failure of those he believed to have dominated American culture and education over the last generation or so, since the 1960s. The problem with today's thinking, he said, is moral and philosophical relativism.

The recent education of openness . . . pays no attention to natural rights or the historical origins of our regime, which are now thought to have been essentially flawed and regressive . . . [This relativism] is open to all kinds of men, all kinds of life-styles, all ideologies. There is no enemy other than the man who is not open to everything. But when there are no shared goals or vision of the public good, is the social contract any longer possible?[2]

The pages that followed Bloom's call to worship in *The Closing of the American Mind*, like the countless, unmentionable books that rose to his invocation, may not have been so crisply to the point. If one could ignore Bloom's subsequent, goofey interpretations of the culture and philosophies he attributes to the Sixties Generation, it would be easier to agree that he was right to wonder what becomes of the social contract in a multicultural society. Much the same could be said of many world societies, as of the United States.

Writers like Schlesinger and Bloom are at least to be respected for the honesty with which they trust the traditional values. They object to the rise of feminisms, Afrocentrisms, queer politics, and other forms of resistance to those values. They strive for the high road of commonality and moral absolutes, though often without questioning the extent to which those values have disguised the most terrible of deprivations and oppressions. Not surprisingly, those of the more audible Left are sympathetic precisely to the failure of modern society to serve the needs of the poor and suffering. They complain that the sacrifice of their traditional values will eliminate any hope of a principled common ground upon which might gather those who would fight for a more just society. Todd Gitlin, in his youth one of the leaders of the New Left, is a compelling instance of this attitude. In *The Twilight of Common Dreams*, Gitlin castigates the new identity politics and other forms of multiculturalism for their political short-sightedness.

> Democracy is more than a license to celebrate (and exaggerate) differences. It cannot afford to live in the past — anyone's past. It is a political system of mutual reliance and common moral obligations. Mutuality needs tending. . . . Affirming the virtues of the margins, identity politics has left the centers of power uncontested. No wonder the threatened partisans of "normality" have seized the offensive.[3]

Gitlin's view, in short, is that multiculturalism is a dangerous fad, not a state of affairs, and that identity politics is a frivolous politics, not a requirement of the times. He thus overestimates the power of the political Right, which seemed, within a few months of the publication of his book in 1995, less invincible than in the earlier years of the 1990s when he wrote. Gitlin, like others who are rightly troubled by the current situation, mistakes the short-run of his own political and literary life for the long-run of the changes he is attempting to explain, or resist.

There is something good to be taken from writers like these three, and the wider excitement they represent and inspire. It is true that modern society faces a crisis of social cohesion, that its social contract is ineffective, that democracy lacks the delicate care of mutuality. This being agreed, the question remains: Can the vicious denunciations today's pamphleteers encourage, restore cohesion, contract, and mutuality if the social virtues they desire are in decline for reasons other than a failure of moral or political will? In other words, the question least often addressed by writers like Schlesinger, Bloom, and Gitlin — with all their well-regarded competencies as historian, philosopher, and sociologist — is this: What if the collapse with which they are rightly concerned is a consequence less of the bad behaviors of the few than of a deep disturbance in the system itself? Writers like these are well able to attract readers and listeners willing to pay the price of admission to hear authoritative confirmation of their inner fears. But it is well past time to ask whether traditional pieties of common dreams and social contracts might have been a good but passing moment, the revival of which may require thinking and action far deeper than those nostalgia can inspire.

Schlesinger, Bloom, and Gitlin — the names would not normally be uttered in the same breath. Yet, each represents the best intentions of a formerly vibrant, now uncertain, tradition: the liberal wing of the political Left that still trusts the doctrine of *E pluribus unum*; the righteous center of the cultural Right which abhors the degradations visited by the new voices of the Sixties generation; the cultural heirs of the new political Left who, having left the streets for cultural politics, are frustrated by the failure of all the lefts, including their own, to rekindle the fires of revolt. Each takes the inviting, but poorly-lit, path of assuming that resistances to the traditional pieties of the one American way, of evident social contracts, and common dreams of justice are mere and dangerous whims of the moment and not entailments of world structures. Each, in his own way, represents a variant of the very best American tradition of coveting an ideal past, of measuring the present against what is lost, of practicing nostalgia in the name of local versions of the right, the true, or the just. Each fears the beasts, freaks, and frogs who slither out of the cracks in the old order. They imagine that these postmodern things are the terrible alternative to their nostalgic dreams. They are mistaken.

Strictly speaking, nostalgia is homesickness, a longing for home. No wonder writers in the traditions of Schlesinger, Bloom, and Gitlin hate those who resist their versions of the good and true society. Multiculturalism; poststructuralism; and identity politics of all kinds: feminist, queer, African-American, ethnic, and postcolonial; to say nothing of pop-cultural relativisms like Madonna's displays, hip-hop's noises, and much more — these are resistances to one or another of the cultural and political homes nostalgics feel are broken by the freakish abandonments they think of as postmodernism.

But there is a third attitude among the many disturbed by the present structure of things. Apart from the nostalgics who yearn for home, and the postmodern beasts nostalgics fear, a third way is that of the prophetic visionary. Like the postmodern beasts, today's visionaries are inclined to consider the modern order either at an end, or in need of an overhaul that would in effect make it something other than it had been. Like the nostalgics, but unlike the postmoderns, visionaries still rely on the entrepreneurial rationality of the modern order. The visionaries reject Audre Lorde's famous beastly claim that one cannot rebuild the master's house with the master's tools.[4] Though they refuse nostalgia, they believe a next developmental stage of modern or postmodern social order can be invented by practical reason.

One visionary of note is Michael Lind, author of *Up From Conservatism* and, most notably, of *The Next American Nation: The New Nationalism and the Fourth American Revolution.* As the subtitle of the latter suggests, Lind looks ahead for solutions to the current crisis. Like the more liberal nostalgics, he believes that multiculturalism is morally and socially bankrupt, that it may have played its part, but now must be superceded by a Trans-American Melting Pot in the political form of what he calls liberal nationalism. The United States, in Lind's view, has passed through three distinct social periods: first, the Anglo-American Republic (1789–1861), then, the Euro-American Republic (1875–1957); currently, Multicultural America (from about 1972). But, just as the initial, postcolonial republic of English social customs gave way in the industrial period to a more widely Europeanized society incorporating immigrant workers, and as a multicultural America arose out of the turmoil of the 1960s and the 1965 immigration laws, so now must there be a reconstitution of American cultural, political, and socio-economic order into a Trans-America incorporating social differences by equalizing social and economic access.

In prophesying as he does, Lind refuses to take a stand with either the Left or the Right.

> Multiculturalism is not the wave of the future, but an aftershock of the black-power radicalism of the sixties. Nor is multiculturalism, in the broadest sense, to be blamed entirely on the left. From the beginning, conservatives have been as instrumental as liberals in promoting racial preference politics, for tactical reasons.[5]

Similarly, Lind seeks a fresh start beyond the traditional political categories. Like much of the Left, he encourages a "war on oligarchy," a radical social leveling in which the sharp inequalities of status and income in the occupational structure will be softened such that janitors as well as doctors might become members of the educated middle classes by 2050.[6] At the same time, like many on the Right, he opposes what conservatives call "racial preference quotas" and other social policies the

Right imagines to be the source of multicultural America. Lind's policy alternatives include: strict campaign financing reform that would open elective office even to the poor; a multiparty political system based on proportional representation election laws; and a national Senate that would reduce the disproportionate power of the sparsely populated, rural states. Lind believes that these policies would establish more equal voting power across all social and economic groups in the United States and, thus, eventuate in an effective attack on the oligarchy of privilege and wealth.

But the heart of Lind's social program is the *social market contract*, which again combines policies of the Left and Right to propose a better order. Like the Left, Lind would have government, not the corporations, be the direct provider of necessary social benefits like health care. Like the Right, Lind would increase the number of high-wage jobs by restricting immigration. The heart of his new sociology of American life would be "a post-New Deal social market contract [which] must promote high wages for American workers without bankrupting either employers or the government, or imposing excessive rigidity in the labor market."[7] Evidently, rational prophets like Lind reject nostalgia, but they are far from ready, as many think the beastly postmodernists are, to declare the modernist system dead and gone. Lind's ideas — sometimes bland (campaign financing reform? limit immigration?), sometimes daring (national Senate! social market!) — still trust in the resources of the modern order of things. Above all else, whether it is social or economic, Lind believes there is a market out there in which well-intended actors will rationally work their individual ways toward a progressive good society.

There are other visionaries more radical than Lind, like Jeremy Rifkin, who look to a far-distant but coming future. In *The End of Work: The Decline of the Global Labor Force and the Dawn of the Post-Market Era*, Rifkin puts himself somewhat at risk of being considered a freak (notice the "post-market"). Yet, he is saved from ignominy by the plausibility of his social diagnosis and the upbeat good news of his prophecy. Rifkin predicts that by 2050 (the year Lind would hope janitors will achieve the status of doctors) there will be few income producing jobs as we have known them. Unlike Lind, Rifkin believes the day of the marketplace, whether social or economic, is past. His solution to the absence of job-based income is the social wage — that is: income given for social and civic service. Rifkin's sociology of the new age puts its trust in the third sector, or what more traditional sociologists usually call civil society. He points out, rightly, that this third sector between the corporation and the state controls a considerable economic wealth as measured by total combined assets (more than $500 billion), to say nothing of an enormous volume of human capital (more than 20.5 billion hours of volunteer labor annually).[8] Rifkin imagines that through creative taxation policies the magnitude of the third sector's economic capital can be multiplied, thus generating revenue for the new social wage that will, in turn, provide the majority of citizens of the post-market society with social service vocations.

> Providing a social wage — as an alternative to welfare — for millions of the nation's poor, in return for working in the nonprofit sector, would help not only the recipients but also the communities in which their labor is put to use. Forging new bonds of trust and a sense of shared commitment to the welfare of others and the interests of the neighborhoods in which they serve is what is so desperately needed if we are to rebuild communities and create the foundations for a caring society.[9]

One should no more sneer at this vision that at the good intentions of the nostalgics. Visionaries are nothing if not expansive. Rifkin, for example, is one of the few who, in the same book, is favorably prepared to cite Ronald Reagan and George Bush on the social value of volunteerism and Herbert Marcuse on the devastating effects of technologization. Yet, though more radical, like Lind and other visionaries, Rifkin continues to trust the effective decency of a major sector of the modern world order. He may be right. It would be swell if he were. But most who look out on the world see fewer of the caring civic values than does Rifkin.

It is likely that when the imagination is pressed to the limit a visionary sociology like Rifkin's or Lind's eventually comes back upon itself to the subterranean social space from which all three of these contemporary sociologies arise. William Julius Wilson, for example, is hardly a dreamer, any more than he is a nostalgic. Yet, he and others who face up to world reality provide a chastening illustration of the need for thinking differently, with entirely new attitudes, about the world. Curiously, his 1996 book *When Work Disappears*, begins on a surprisingly nostalgic note, with Wilson recalling the day, not all that long ago, when South Side Chicago was a rival to Harlem as a center of economic and cultural hope for American blacks. Today the South Side, where Wilson has based most of his primary empirical research, is a ghost of its former life. Though Martin Luther King Boulevard, its main thoroughfare, is undergoing a revival that is drawing many middle- and upper-middle-class blacks back into the area, the vast declining reaches of the South Side show the marks of a long economic decline since the better days of the 1950s and before. The area is more commonly known for several of America's most tragic and dangerous public housing projects, where the violence bred of the disappearance of jobs and hope haunts the streets that once were alive with work, commerce, strong communities, and productive lives.

Wilson's way of thinking about the terrible ends to which the global economy has brought neighborhoods like those he studies allows him to remain a visionary without flinching at the facts of poverty and social misery. He describes a situation in which the withdrawal of corporate employers from the major urban centers has left several generations of people not only without work but without the cultural and practical skills necessary even to apply for jobs, much less hold them. For them, social hope is so far from their worldly reality as to be virtually beyond imagining.

Urban centers like these are found across the globe, many ever more desperate than the South Side. They are hardly the places where one can envision a rebirth of civil values and the work ethic without some fundamentally different way of conceiving the world and the social policies intended to heal it. Social dreams that allow either nostalgia for the past or naive cheerleading about the future, to ignore such realities as the disappearance of work will fall flat in places like Chicago's South Side. Wilson might agree with Rifkin about the disappearance of work, even with Lind about the importance of new governmental initiatives, but only after full recognition of the stakes involved in any attempt to rethink the world. Near the end of the book, Wilson describes his approach to social imagination:

> My aim is to galvanize and rally concerned Americans to fight back with the same degree of force and dedication displayed by those who have moved us backward, rather than forward, in combating social inequality. I therefore do not advance proposals that seem acceptable or "realistic" given the current political climate. Rather, I have chosen to talk about what *ought to be done to address the problems of social inequality*, including record levels of joblessness in the inner-city ghetto, that threaten the very fabric of our society.[10]

Social dreams will always be unrealistic to those unwilling to face the facts of human misery. A realism of the sociological imagination is one that remembers what life in the world once was, that faces the sometimes brutal disappearance of that world, then seeks solutions that reach for the ought that may be necessary, even if politically out of fashion.

While most others (including the American President who has called on Wilson for advice) are moving away from governmental initiatives, Wilson proposes his own version of the social contract in which the federal government *must* play a major role in supporting family life among the poor. training men and women for work, and providing dependable access to honorable income. Among the policies he favors is a renewed version of the Works Projection Administration. This neo-WPA approach is among Wilson's proposed solutions not because it is an appealing idea but because it is an idea that may be *required* by the unavoidable realities of a world changed so starkly that pious talk of putting the poor to work is the cruellest sort of foolishness when there are no jobs for the most poor.

Wilson is a visionary who remembers the past as do the nostalgics, and who is willing to dream as do the visionaries, but he is also ready to consider the first fact of the day — that the world is not what it was, and may never be again. Ultimately, Wilson's sociology is ironic in the best, most serious, sense of the term. He is a famously sober, empirical social scientist who is able to set naive realism on its heels precisely because the reality is so grave. This may not be a programmatic postmodernism, but it is not unlike the moral challenge a sensible postmodernism calls for. In any case, it is clearly a brand of sociology that seeks to draw on the instincts the other visionaries, as well as the freaks and nostalgics, only partly embrace.

Nostalgia, freakish irony, and prophetic visions — three seemingly incongruent attitudes toward the current state of world structures. One might abandon all hope were it not for two things that can be said of them all. First, all three agree that there is something terribly wrong with the world. Secondly, each seems to have a decent grasp of some part of the puzzle and its solution. At the risk of appearing too ready to reconcile the impossibly different, I wish to propose where, amid the furor and contradictions, there is at the least a lesson to be learned from them all.

It was not all that long ago when I moved from the house which had been, after divorce, a kind of transitional home for me and my sons. We left it behind when they went on to other things in life and I remarried. When I awoke on moving day, our stuff packed and ready, the place was still the home in which we had lived with pleasure and pain for some good years. But by afternoon, the movers had stripped the joint. Nothing was left but bits of lost change from the transactions of daily life — paper clips and dust balls, topless Bic pens, a bare spot behind the bookcase I had always meant to paint, and nearly four dollars in coins from the sofa alone. As I perfunctorily swept the empty floors, I still had the idea that the past spent there was of such moment that leaving it would leave me partly empty. I cried some in the darkening light, as I absently loaded the last few things into our old Mazda pick-up. Out of town, just when I began to think of our new home and of how Geri and I were going to feed that night, I ran out of gas, miles from anywhere. Several hours later, thanks to strangers on the road, I made it to the home to come. We ordered in pizza, opened a few boxes, unrolled a futon, and slept. A new life in a new place began. Though I pass the old place often, I don't miss it as I thought I would.

Whenever the prevailing structure of things is unpacked, moved, and resettled, beastly things long hidden from memory escape from under sofa cushions or behind an old furnace. People then yearn for the good times gone, try to forget the bad ones, and, as best they can, throw themselves toward the new. I've even heard of some who for one reason or another called-off the movers, unpacked their stuff, and lived-on in the old place. Still, as upon going back to a lost lover, the past is never, thank goodness, quite what it was. Sometimes at least that unreachable spot gets taken care of.

One day, who knows when, some graduate student will figure out whether the last years of the twentieth century were, in fact, a moving day for a good but transitional world of social things. For the time being, the rest of us, notwithstanding our several and varied differences, must, as best we can, settle accounts with what we feel and think about things as they are. Some, usually for reason of their stations in life, are more inclined to fear the changes. It is right for them to long for their pasts. Nostalgia has its place. Others — those who, for whatever reason, are by nature ironic — accept the move for what it is but hang around to get the old place broom clean. Someone must deal with the freakish remnants of habit. Others, having had little real attachment to the old place, have gone ahead with the movers, unpacking the old stuff into new rooms, discovering already that the delicately tattered sofa looks just awful in the fresh light.

Nostalgia, irony, and vision are appropriate, if mutually annoying, vocations for the differing kinds and conditions of men and women. We who chose one over the others suspect (or hate) the remaining two because they give voice to what we do not own within ourselves. When the world changes, some inner aspect in most persons yearns for the home lost. Only those most bitterly injured by its deprivations give up the past with no sense of loss. As improbable as it may seem to the nostalgics, even they cannot help but harbor an ironic taste for the primordial monsters which inhabit the night air when one runs out of gas. Why should all the memories be kind? Most of us realize, even if only in the darkest corners of the soul, that we have witnessed, or experienced, terrible, unmentionable deeds enacted under the covers of family decency. The postmodern interior of most decent people is the part that knows we must not leave before all the stories are told, even the unspeakable ones. It is only the visionary, the prophetic within, that expresses the native, if highly bourgeois, confidence that the new place can be made over to suit a better life. Like prophets called to plan the new before the last haul is made, the visionary in most of us is that part we enjoy until such time as all the boxes are unpacked and the ill-suited sofa dealt with, one way or another. Five years later now, ours still sits there, its shabbiness reminding us of the transitional girlfriend who unloaded it on me, and of the hard reality that even the best new home is usually furnished with junk from the past.

Thus, it is possible to understand the three groups of new sociologies as contestants in a cultural war over troubles widely shared. These sociologies are, in fact, variant epiphanies of the social unconscious that harbors the superficially calm tides of human nature — of a persisting undertow by which desire, disturbance, and dreams allow the future to ebb from the past. These new sociologies, whether nostalgic or beastly or prophetic, arise in times of uncertainty because these are the times that provoke the social unconscious to new heights of imagination. Whenever the world changes, whether by the hands of invading Goths in the fifth century, or by the prophetic rebels and colonizing explorers in the sixteenth, or by something else in other such times, there is urgent need for imagination to draw the past out of its old habits — some dear, some not, all duplicitous. Were we to resist the instinct for imagination at such times, or scoff too haughtily at those who love, or those who make jokes upon, the past, we would be bereft of our dreams without which it is impossible to decide what to save for the new or how to rearrange whatever one brings along.

There is, then, this additional sense in which postmodernism is not what you think. Those writers, artists, actors, and performers who are said to be postmoderns — like those who feel what they do and say is foolish business — are not primarily engaged in thinking; not even when thought, or theory, is what they produce. This remark (call it, perhaps, a thesis) is doubly controversial. For one, it links the freakish, ironic practices of the postmodernisms to the objections of their opponents, thus bringing them both out of the realm of righteous judgment into the common space of all those who, one supposes, must live on in the face of changes they cannot understand. For another, the thesis draws the controversy out of theoretical debate into feeling — into, that is, the shared emotion of those who recognize the change and recognize that it is of such global proportions as to give permission for public display of feelings normally withheld.

As a consequence, the social imagination thus required cannot remain within the normalizing constraints of knowledge, whether pure or practical, and certainly not within formal academic knowledges — not even the theories so notoriously associated with the postmodernisms and their dismissals. Theories, where they have become the form of expression for the permitted feelings, are the result, not the cause, of the new sociologies. Homesickness, fear of bugs and beasts, defiant visions of the unknowably new give force to an array of palpable effects caused by subterranean shifts among the structural plates of world as we knew it for this half-millennium or so.

When professional sociologists declare that *sociological imagination* is the answer, they do not always consider the question. C. Wright Mills, the inventor of the phrase, meant for the sociological imagination to inspire a more rigorous attention to the analysis of large, prohibiting social structures, which attentions were intended to encourage individuals better to understand the extent to which their personal troubles in the world may in fact be public issues not by their own failure but of the world itself. Mills' version of the idea was, simply, a call to information through which the isolated individual in mass society could begin to think about the world. An uncle of the New Left already when he wrote his famous essay in 1959, Mills and those who followed his lead believed, then with good enough reason, that a true sociology of the world could be had and that the having of it would, through direct political action, ease the suffering of the weaker classes of men and women. Their actions, working collectively with actions of others worldwide, including those dismantling the colonial system in Africa, Asia, and the Caribbean, led to the events now defined, simply, as "the Sixties." Much was accomplished among the failures of those cultural and political experiments in the 1960s. Not least has been the grudging acknowledgment of the enduring power of aboriginal forces then unleashed.

Many will agree that the cultural politics inciting today's new sociologies have dealt a devastating blow to knowledge. But what does this mean? It does not mean, to be sure, that knowledge is beside the point. Many of the nostalgics are right to rebuke the antinomian comedians who seem to believe that wisdom is a good joke. But what must still be reckoned is that, in and of itself, technical knowledge, no matter how rigorously composed, is insufficient to the times. These times are about feelings that run before and beyond what the mind can bring forth or the hand put to words. The sociological imagination deserves to be taken with deeper, analytic seriousness than it has been. Trust in knowledge is a good thing and there is no reason one may not so trust even while believing that truth is never free of power's distortions. But what is needed today is a sociological imagination that conforms to the reality of worldly things, and this is where the trouble tightens. To define reality as if it were a sphere of things awaiting their proper names only defers the regress of analytic difficulty. Social reality refers, as we have seen, to a troubling world of uncertain human relations in respect to which the truth of the things is there to hit one's head upon only after their practical meaning is agreed upon. Often, as in the case of the terrible, worldwide inequality of social opportunities, the practical meaning is readily available, though even this sort of social pavement is questioned by the clever yearners for privilege who still insist that the poor are the cause of their poverty. In other cases, as in most of the social policies used or proposed for the easing of social disadvantages, there is virtually no assurance of agreement as to real causes and effects.

To speak of the imagination in relation to social reality requires a more honest attention to the imagination than most have been willing to allow. By its nature the imagination is always a mental bastard — proudly but illegitimately fathered by what the visionary would just as soon forget, longingly mothered by the necessity of inventing a better past than present troubles permit. A social imagination sufficient to possible, actual, or even suspected changes in world structures can never arise solely from available factual information. Knowledge is insufficient to the social imagination by the very definition of the present situation. When social things are changing, actually or possibly, then the most fundamental reality of such conditions is that reality itself is open to discussion. This is why, as I have tried to remind, the linguistic turn came when it did as harbinger of the unsettlements already evident in the decolonizing movements altering the arrangements of the modern order. Heirs of the colonizers in America and Europe, preoccupied with their own, selfish Cold War, largely ignored the longer term effects of the loss of the usual cultural methods for maintaining their once unchallenged position in the world order.

What is one to do, after the Imperium, when the American Century is dragged along in the wake of a millennium? These are strange times. If there is any one factual statement that can be made of all living creatures these days, it is that none of us, not even descendants of those prehistoric cockroaches, has ever lived in such a time.

Just the same, if memory serves, the last three millennia in the West ended better than this one. At the end of the previous one, for example, people had not quite yet gotten over the Dark Ages. But things were coming along, the Moors were saving Aristotle's ideas and the Holy Roman Church had thrown its sacred cloak over the territory that would become Europe. The millennium before actually ended well. The Romans were coming into their own — building aqueducts and roads, sending armies to far corners, crucifying provincial nuisances, and all else that goes with keeping a good empire. The one before that was, like the present one, unlikely to inspire confidence. Still, in the cradle of civilization, though the Babylonions were losing their grip, David was king in Palestine, and the Greeks were beginning to migrate. Promising things then lay ahead.

Today, such prophecies as there are describe the day early in the next millennium when there will be no jobs, when all the social welfare programs will be bankrupt, when social conflicts will be all the more severe, when the poor are abandoned. Still, there is some reason not to suppose that the mere turning of a thousandth year is grounds for despair. Nor, to be sure, ought the end of so regional an Imperium as the Soviet one depress the higher hopes. And, certainly, the ending of a single century is no cause at all for gloom, as we know from the last fin-de-siècle which turned on a confident note.

Endings do brace the soul, if only because they are so infrequent. The present ones, coming all at once, are, however, decidedly more than a wake-up dip in a mountain pond. This because there is reliable, if not conclusive, reason to suppose that something more than time is passing on its way. When an Imperium like the Modern one (as distinct from the Soviet one) gives up its hold, time and space fall clumsily into an unexpected embrace. This is why some sociologists use the hyphenated expression "time-space" to describe the weird reality in which televisual media import other times and spaces into the mundane here and now of cluttered bedrooms in rented apartments.[11] To what extent the despair today might be cured as we grow more accustomed to this still-screaming electronic brat, no one can say. But the reason one might pause before making a full commitment to the likes of e-mail is that such mediations unquestionably corrupt the user's normal sense of time's relation to space. Their whining inducements to the instant reply, like the charm of a freshly suckled baby, create the false impression of human conversation across global space. Messages sent from nowhere by persons one has never met, or not seen in a long while, and may never see again, may well, in quickening the stomach, harden the heart. This too is yet to be revealed.

The modern world was built on the progressive conquest of global space which, over the time of its settlement, became bedrock of the modernist illusion that historical time was moving ahead toward some indefinite but well-advertised improvement upon present circumstances. The foundation of modern culture was, therefore, the illusion that time marched across self-renewing, never-ending space. Time was measured, allowing space its limitless horizon. Modernity, thus, reversed the logic of common sense well understood by the poor who, above all others, know that time must be the more open-ended of the two. Otherwise, there is no escaping the guarded spaces in which they are confined. Modernity is the class culture of the near or actual middle classes who, having moved to the suburbs, convince themselves that the quarter-acre lots they inhabit for the blink of a mortgage are proof positive of the world's goodness and of their own worthiness. In such a world, there is no reason to ponder the past, much less the past within. To do so is to deny reason itself. Reason, truth, and knowledge are, under such arrangements, the assurances that so long as there is space enough, the metronome will yield its monotonous power only before the evidence of good deeds attenuated over the moral time of human being. By this reckoning, reason is the idealized means whereby the merciless march of calendrical time is redeemed by the facts of progress.

What was progress in the modern age? At first, it was the conquest of Brazil and the Congo, then of the plains of Argentina and the Dakotas, then of the ores and fossil fuels that joined railroads and highways, then of the stellar skies through which men flew only to burn each other at war. Ultimately, for the middle classes, reason was the move to the suburbs, or to the receding countryside, there to await the coming of Pizza Hut, the Gap, Radio Shack, and Barnes & Noble. But the day is coming and now is when one can order pizza, jeans, pagers, and cook books without stirring from the worn comforts of home. That will be the day when time, encountering the stupid resistance of real space, curves back upon itself, breaking the seal of self-confidence, opening the cracks for beasts and other things.

The social unconscious, like the psychic one, is the space of dreams that cannot, and need not, be proven. Just a century ago in 1900, when Freud published *The Interpretation of Dreams*, the modern age was confronted with its first rigorous theory of unconscious life. Ever since, people have been attempting to explain away the unconscious. Freud's own theory was clean and compelling. He gave evidence from his clinical study of the dreams of his patients that the regular occurrence during sleep of these wild stories we tell ourselves is the private work of resolving the painful desire for that which is denied us in conscious life. Dream-work is the work in which the ego — the self of the selves, as William James put it — allows the psyche to express its deepest wishes in forms sufficiently distorted that the dreamer gains the double benefit of having tasted the desired, but forbidden, fruit while still obeying the normal rules of the social garden.

Are social dreams any different? Are they not the shared stories whereby well-meaning, civic minded men and women wish, in the case of modernity, for a better life than the one they are permitted to have? Modernism was the dream of a future good life held in time's distant space. Like all dreams, this one served to censor the worst impulses stored in the social unconscious. Only the most pious of the politicians and preachers could claim that everything we moderns did over the centuries was entirely to the good. Even they usually pronounce against the sins of the past. But the sins of the past are never past. They are with us, living up the road, on the next block, downtown, even in our memories of those terrible things we saw as children when our mothers thought we were asleep.

Postmodernism is, in fact, the phantasmagoria of a prior, freakish world. Those who fear the beasts are not wrong. Their nostalgia for a kinder home than they have wells from the same unthinking place of insensate feeling that authors principled dreams of a better world. The freaks and beasts are signs of a bad dream in which the social ego has failed to restrain these deeper realities.

Though it has excited many theories, postmodernism cannot be thought through. Whatever the truth of the world's future, these unthinkable ironies are the intrusions of the social unconscious — the unbearable evidences of nasty deeds done in the name of good. They are the frogs that might become the princes of some other good world, if only we could kiss them.

Notes

1 Beasts, Frogs, Freaks, and Other Postmodern Things

1   Many of the facts supporting these trends are summarized in: The Worldwatch Institute, *Vital Signs 1996* (W. W. Norton, 1996). See also *The Human Development Report* (Oxford University Press, 1996). As for jobs, see Jeremy Rifkin, *The End of Work* (G. P. Putnam's Sons, 1996). For a particularly bleak, if controversial, narrative account of the world situation, see Robert D. Kaplan, *The Ends of the Earth* (Random House, 1995). Among other sources, see James Garbarino et al., *Children in Danger* (Jossey-Bass, 1992); William Julius Wilson, *When Work Disappears* (Alfred Knopf, 1996).

2   Anthony Giddens, *Politics, Sociology and Social Theory* (Stanford University Press, 1995), p. 10.

3   N. J. Demerath III, "Postmortemism For Postmodernism," *Contemporary Sociology* 25 (Jan., 1996), p. 27.

4   Steven Seidman, "Postmodern Anxiety: The Politics of Epistemology," *Sociological Theory* 9:2 (1991), pp. 180–90. "PoMo Phobia" appeared in a University of Georgia Press ad in *The New York Review of Books* (July 11, 1996), p. 49.

5   Todd Gitlin, "Hip-Deep in Postmodernism," *The New York Review of Books* (Nov. 7, 1988).

6   Andrew Ross, quoted in *The New York Times* (May 18, 1996), p. 25.

7   Katha Pollitt, "Pomolotov Cocktail," *The Nation* (June 10, 1996), p. 9.

8   Fish, "Professor Sokal's Bad Joke," *The New York Times* (May 21, 1996), p. A23.

9   The magazine did invite the *Social Text* response in its subsequent issue as part of an eleven-page forum, "Mystery Science Theatre: Sokal vs. *Social Text*, Part Two," *Linguafranca* 6 (July/Aug. 1996): 54–66.

10 "Hot Type," *The Chronicle of Higher Education* (May 31, 1996), p. A10.

11 Sokal, "A Physicist Experiments with Cultural Studies," *Linguafranca* (May/June 1996), p. 62.

12 Ibid., p. 64.

13 Ibid., p. 62.
14 Steven Weinberg, "Sokal's Hoax," *The New York Review of Books* (Aug. 8, 1996), p. 12. Weinberg, it should be said, generally approves of Sokal's hoax.
15 Daniel J. Kevles, "The Assault on David Baltimore," *The New Yorker* (May 27, 1996), pp. 94–109.
16 For editorial comments on the controversy and the court decision, see "A Judgement Fit for Prime Time," *Nature* 381 (June 27, 1996) and "Imanishi-Kari Ruling Slams ORI [Office of Research Integrity]," *Science* 272 (June 28, 1996).
17 Survey cited in Robert S. McElvaine, *What's Left* (Adams Media Corporation, 1996), p. vi.
18 Janet Browne, *Voyaging: Charles Darwin* (Knopf, 1995), p. 542. Many of the details of the Darwin section, especially concerning *Vestiges*, are from this book.
19 Ibid., pp. 542–3.

2   Postmodernism Is Not What You Think

1 Marshall McLuhan, *Understanding Media* (McGraw-Hill, 1964).
2 "The Disneyland imaginary is neither true nor false. It is a determined set up to rejuvenate in reverse the fiction of the real." Baudrillard, "Simulacra and Simulation," in Mark Poster, ed., *Jean Baudrillard: Selected Writings* (Stanford University Press, 1988), p. 172.
3 Though she would not put things as I have, most of the following section is influenced by the thinking and writing of Patricia Clough. Most of her writing on television is in recent as yet unpublished essays. But her line of argument is outlined in *End(s) of Ethnography* (Sage, 1989).
4 For examples, see Jean-François Lyotard, *The Postmodern Condition* (University of Minnesota Press, 1984/1979); Richard Rorty, *Contingency, Irony, and Solidarity* (Cambridge University Press, 1989).
5 It is too easy to forget that Max Weber wrote his famous and persuasive book, *The Protestant Ethic and the Spirit of Capitalism*, nearly three centuries after the events the causes of which the book examined. It takes about that long to really see historical change. Even then one could not prove his point.
6 Fredric Jameson, *Postmodernism, or, The Cultural Logic of Late Capitalism* (Duke University Press, 1991); and David Harvey, *The Condition of Postmodernity* (Blackwell, 1989).
7 For the principal example see Immanuel Wallerstein, *The Modern World System, Vol. I* (Academic Press, 1974).
8 "Core state" is from Wallerstein, *The Modern World System, Vol. I*, for example.
9 See Todd Gitlin, *The Whole World is Watching* (University of California Press, 1980).

10 Guy Debord, *Society as Spectacle* (Black and Red Press, 1984), paras 1 & 2.

11 Baudrillard, *Cool Memories* (Verso, 1990), p. 147.

12 Lyotard, *The Postmodern Condition*, p. 82.

13 Theodor Adorno, *Negative Dialectics* (Seabury Press, 1973), p. 366.

14 Theodor Adorno, "The Culture Industry Reconsidered," in Stephen Bonner and Douglas Kellner, eds, *Critical Theory and Society: A Reader* (Routledge, 1989), p. 128.

15 Jürgen Habermas, *The Philosophical Discourse of Modernity* (MIT Press, 1987), p. 343.

16 Among sociologists, the most important radical modernists are Anthony Giddens and Pierre Bourdieu. For a discussion see Charles Lemert, *Sociology After the Crisis* (HarperCollins, 1995), chapter 7.

17 See Linda Nicholson, *Feminism/Postmodernism* (Routledge, 1990) and Patricia Clough, *Feminist Thought* (Blackwell, 1994).

18 Though I cannot go into it here (more in later chapters), this idea also involves an extraordinarily technical argument about the effect of phonetic and semantic differences in the functioning of language, for which the classic source is Ferdinand de Saussure, *Course in General Linguistics* (McGraw-Hill, 1959/1911).

19 Lacan, *Ecrits* (W. W. Norton, 1977), p. 5.

20 Louis Althusser, *Lenin and Philosophy*, trans. Ben Brewster (Monthly Review Press, 1971), pp. 127–88.

3 An Impossible Glossary of Social Reality

1 *The Compact Edition of the Oxford English Dictionary* (Oxford University Press, 1971), "G," p. 231.

2 Ibid., "D," p. 331.

3 *The Autobiography of Malcolm X, As Told to Alex Haley* (Ballantine Books, 1964), pp. 172–4.

4 Robert D. Kaplan, *The Ends of the Earth* (Random House, 1996).

4 The Political Reality of the Linguistic Turn

1 Some examples: Most famously, see David Harvey, *The Condition of Postmodernity* (Blackwell, 1989), p. 350. Harvey's bestselling academic introduction to postmodern culture ends up in a pathetic Marxist and modernist lament of postmodernism's nihilistic, relativistic, and narcissistic properties. These are also at issue, though more appreciatively discussed, in the well-known feminist criticism of Foucault in which he is taken as the straw man of postmodernism who by allowing power to be everywhere is thought to have eliminated the prospect of emancipatory power. See, for examples, Nancy Hartsock, "Foucault on Power," in Linda Nicholson, ed., *Feminism/Postmodernism* (Routledge, 1990), ch. 7; and Nancy Fraser, *Unruly Practices* (University of Minnesota Press, 1989), especially part I.

Similarly on this theme, though less systematically thought through, see Anthony Giddens, *The Consequences of Modernity* (Stanford University Press, 1990), especially pp. 137–50. One of the more surprising misunderstandings of the "comic" and its relation to irony in postmodernism is Jeffrey Alexander, *Fin de Siècle Social Theory* (Verso, 1995), pp. 23–9. For "pseudo-history," see Craig Calhoun, *Critical Social Theory* (Blackwell, 1995), ch. 4. Todd Gitlin uses "obsessive" in reference to the emphasis on differences common to postmodern movements like multiculturalism; see Gitlin, *Twilight of Common Dreams* (Henry Holt, 1995), p. 236.

2   Peter Blau, "Structural Effects," *American Sociological Review* 25 (1960): 178–93, and *Exchange and Power in Social Life* (John Wiley, 1964). Harrison White, *An Anatomy of Kinship* (Prentice-Hall, 1963).

3   Emile Durkheim, *Elementary Forms of the Religious Life* (Free Press, 1965), p. 29.

4   Roland Barthes, *The Semiotic Challenge* (Hill and Wang, 1988), p. 308.

5   Barthes, *Mythologies* (Seuil, 1957) and *Le degré zéro de l'écriture* (Seuil, 1953).

6   Derrida, "Structure, Sign, and Play in the Discourse of the Human Sciences," in Richard Macksey and Eugenio Donato, eds, *The Structuralist Controversy* (Johns Hopkins University Press, 1971). Derrida first made the remark in 1966, about which more in chapters 5 and 6.

7   Barthes, *The Semiotic Challenge*, p. 5.

8   Ibid., pp. 5–6.

9   See, more recently, A. J. Greimas, *The Social Sciences: A Semiotic View* (University of Minnesota Press, 1990).

10   Umberto Eco, *A Theory of Semiotics* (Indiana University Press, 1976).

11   Barthes, *Semiotic Challenge*, p. 7.

12   Ibid., p. 8.

13   Richard Rorty, *Contingency, Irony, and Solidarity* (Cambridge University Press, 1989), p. 60.

14   Robert Kaplan, *The Ends of the Earth* (Random House, 1996).

5   Letters From Brazil: Structuralism's Zero Signifier

1   Though some of Henry Louis Gates's writings might be considered in a post-modern spirit in the sense that he seeks to rewrite and rethink the canon of Western literature by introducing a canon supplement of African-American literature, he has never been, in the least, self-consciously postmodern or poststructuralist, or anything of the sort.

2   In his 1960 introductory lecture to the Collège de France, Lévi-Strauss acknowledges his debt to Durkheim and Mauss. See Lévi-Strauss, *The Scope of Anthropology* (Jonathan Cape, 1967). For a discussion see Charles Lemert, "The Canonical Limits of Durkheim's First Classic," *Sociological Forum* 9 (1994): 87–92.

3   Lévi-Strauss, *The Savage Mind* (University of Chicago Press, 1966), ch. 9.

4   Durkheim and Mauss, *Primitive Classifications* (University of Chicago Press, 1967), pp. 55–62.

5   Sontag, "Anthropologist as Hero," in *Claude Lévi-Strauss: Anthropologist As Hero* (MIT Press, 1970), p. 186.

6   Lévi-Strauss, *Tristes Tropiques* (Atheneum, 1974), p. 393.

7   See chapter 7 for a discussion of the furor over and implications of identity politics, the current expression of what began a generation ago as personal politics.

8   Derrida, "Structure, Sign, and Play in the Discourse of the Human Sciences," is discussed in greater detail in chapter 6. It is reasonably considered the manifesto of the poststructuralist movement inasmuch as it was the most sensational of the talks given at 1966 conference on structuralism at Johns Hopkins University. See Richard Macksey and Eugenio Donato, eds, *The Structuralist Controversy* (Johns Hopkins University Press, 1971).

9   Lévi-Strauss, *Elementary Structures of Kinship* (Beacon Press, 1969), pp. 24–5. Emphasis added.

10 Lévi-Strauss, "Structural Analysis in Linguistics and in Anthropology," was originally a 1945 journal article before it was republished in his *Structural Anthropology* (Basic Books, 1963).

11 "Structural Analysis in Linguistics," pp. 32–3.

12 Ibid., p. 35. Later emphasis added.

13 *Structural Anthropology*, p. 94.

14 Ibid., p. 89.

15 Jakobson is present without citation in the fact that the famous analysis of the Oedipal and Zuni myths in "The Structural Study of Myth" (in *Structural Anthropology*) depends on diachronic as much as synchronic analysis.

16 Derrida's "Structure, Sign, and Play" lecture was an intervention in a conference on structuralism. Its poststructuralist declaration was based on a famous, close reading of Lévi-Strauss.

    Derrida's one explicit mention of the zero signifier is, again, to Lévi-Strauss's appeal to Jakobson's zero phoneme, in 1950, in a note in his "Introduction à l'oeuvre de Marcel Mauss" (in Mauss, *Sociologie et Anthropologie* (Presses universitaires de France, 1950)). It is not incidental, I think, that the issue appears in Lévi-Strauss in a discussion of a famous Durkheimian. Saussure, by the way, could only avoid the zero signifier by an explicitly Durkheimian reference to social contract, which he in turn qualified: "But the thing which keeps language from being a simple convention that can be modified at the whim of interest parties is not its social nature; it is rather the action of time combined with the social force" (in *Course in General Linguistics* (McGraw-Hill, 1959), p. 78). Thus, Saussure anticipates what Lévi-Strauss states and Derrida calls attention to: even an escape from historical time (culture) into the nature of language requires the return to time. The zero signifier, itself relatively unarticulated in the theoretical discussion, is that which saves the system from lapses into either nature or culture. In effect, language is the boundary and explanation for signification, including language.

17 Derrida, "Structure, Sign, and Play," p. 247.
18 Ibid., p. 249.

6 The Uses of French Structuralisms in Sociology

1 Raymond Boudon, *The Uses of Structuralism* (Heinemann, 1971).
2 Claude Lévi-Strauss, *Structural Anthropology I* (Anchor Books, 1970), especially the famous essay "The Structural Study of Myth." Louis Althusser, *For Marx* (Vintage Books, 1970). Roland Barthes, *Writing Degree Zero and Elements of Semiology* (Beacon Press, 1970).
3 Michel Foucault, *The Archaeology of Knowledge* (Pantheon Books, 1972), pp. 210–11.
4 Lévi-Strauss, "Overture to *Le Cru et le cuit*," in *Structuralism*, ed. Jacques Ehrmann (Anchor Books, 1970), pp. 44–5.
5 Jacques Derrida, "Structure, Sign, and Play in the Discourse of the Human Sciences," in Derrida, *Writing and Difference* (University of Chicago Press, 1978), p. 278. This famous essay first appeared in English in the collection of talks given at the 1966 Johns Hopkins conference on structuralism, in *The Structuralist Controversy*, eds Richard Macksey and Eugenio Donato (Johns Hopkins University Press, 1971).
6 Charles Jencks, *The Language of Post-Modern Architecture* (Rizzoli, 1977), p. 9.
7 Paolo Portoghesi, *After Modern Architecture* (Rizzoli, 1980), p. 106.
8 Jean-François Lyotard, *The Postmodern Condition* (University of Minnesota Press, 1984).
9 Richard Rorty, *Philosophy and the Mirror of Nature* (Princeton University Press, 1979), p. 7.
10 *Postmodern Condition*, p. 3.
11 "Structure, Sign, and Play," p. 280.
12 See Rorty, "Habermas and Lyotard on Postmodernity," in *Habermas and Modernity*, ed. Richard Bernstein (MIT Press, 1985). See also Fredric Jameson's foreword to Lyotard's *Postmodern Condition*.
13 "Structure, Sign, and Play," p. 280.
14 Ibid., p. 292.
15 Ibid., p. 293.
16 Elizabeth Abel, ed., *Writing and Sexual Difference* (University of Chicago Press, 1980), p. 2.
17 Henry Louis Gates, ed., *"Race," Writing and Difference* (University of Chicago Press, 1985), p. 6.
18 Barthes, "From Work to Text," in *Textual Strategies*, ed. Josué V. Harari (Cornell University Press, 1979), p. 81 (emphasis original).
19 Ibid., pp. 74–5.
20 Ibid., p. 74.
21 Foucault's attacks on the logocentric and anthropocentric basis of modernism are explicit, if not as well-known as Derrida's. See Charles

Lemert and Garth Gillan, *Michel Foucault: Social Theory as Transgression* (Columbia University Press, 1979).

22   Foucault, "What Is an Author?" in *Textual Strategies*, ed. Harari, pp. 158–9.

23   *Théorie d'ensemble*, a special issue of *Tel Quel* (Seuil, 1968).

24   For *champ*, see Bourdieu, *Outline of a Theory of Practice* (Cambridge University Press, 1977), among other places. For "structuration," see in particular Giddens, *Constitution of Society* (University of California Press, 1984). For "discursive practices," see especially Foucault, *Archaeology of Knowledge*. For "intertextuality," see Barthes, "From Work to Text," among other places.

25   Lyotard, *Postmodern Condition*, p. 82.

26   Hayden White, *Tropics of Discourse* (Johns Hopkins University Press, 1978), p. 4.

27   Henry Louis Gates, *The Signifying Monkey: A Theory of Afro-American Literary Criticism* (Oxford University Press, 1988).

28   Sources for the following are: Mike Gravel, ed., *The Pentagon Papers*, Vols. I–IV (Beacon Press, 1971); Doris Kearns, *Lyndon Johnson and the American Dream* (Harper and Row, 1976); William Gibson, *The Perfect War* (Atlantic Monthly Press, 1986); and Stanley Karnow, *Vietnam: A History* (Penguin, 1983).

29   Hodgson, *American in Our Time* (Vintage Books, 1976), p. 229.

30   Kearns, *Lyndon Johnson*, p. 261.

31   Gibson, *Perfect War*.

32   Wallace Terry, *Bloods* (Ballantine Books, 1984), p. 55.

33   Gibson, *Perfect War*, p. 476.

34   Russell Jacoby, *The Last Intellectuals* (Basic Books, 1987.

7   Identities After the Imperium

1   Ryszard Kapuściński, *Imperium* (Vintage Books, 1994), pp. 143–4.

2   Craig Calhoun, *Critical Social Theory* (Blackwell, 1995), ch. 4.

3   The lines quoted from James are in *Principles of Psychology*, Vol. I (Harvard University Press, 1981). Quoted here from James, "The Self and Its Selves," in *Social Theory*, ed. Charles Lemert (Westview Press, 1993), pp. 173, 176. I discuss both this idea and others in the present chapter, in "Dark Thoughts About the Self," ch. 3 in *Social Theory and the Politics of Identity*, ed. Craig Calhoun (Blackwell, 1994).

4   David Riesman, *The Lonely Crowd* (Yale University Press, 1950). Erik Erikson, *Childhood and Society* (W. W. Norton, 1950). C. Wright Mills, *The Sociological Imagination* (Oxford University Press, 1959).

5   Fanon, *Black Skin, White Masks* (Grove Press, 1967/1952), p. 140.

6   See Benedict Anderson, *Imagined Communities* (Verso, 1983), still the *locus classicus* for the idea that the "world" came to be as a political and economic reality because of the delicate workings of its cultural imagination.

7   Goffman, *Stigma* (Simon and Schuster, 1963).

8 Gloria Anzaldúa, *Borderlands* (Spinsters/Aunt Lute, 1987). Trinh T. Minh-ha, *Woman, Native, Other* (Indiana University Press, 1989). Homi Bhabha, ed. *Nation and Narration* (Routledge, 1990). Gayatri Spivak, *In Other Worlds* (Metheun, 1987) and, most famously, "Can the Subaltern Speak?" in *Marxism and Interpretation*, eds Cary Nelson and Lawrence Grossberg (University of Illinois Press, 1988), pp. 271–313.

9 Kapuściński, *Imperium, p. 85.*

8 Representations of the Sociologist: Getting Over the Science Crisis

1 This chapter was originally a review essay appearing in June 1996 in *Sociological Forum* (11/2:379–393), which had earlier published (in 1994) a special issue, "What's Wrong With Sociology?" edited by Stephen Cole. Other books discussed here are Edward Said's *Representations of the Intellectual*, Jerry Watts' *Heroism and the Black Intellectual: Ralph Ellison, Politics, and Afro-American Intellectual Life*, and Daniel Horowitz's *Vance Packard and American Social Criticism*. The fifth book discussed is Alvin Gouldner's *The Coming Crisis of Western Sociology*, which was selected for the *Sociological Forum* essay because 1995 (when my review essay was supposed to have been published) was the 25th anniversary of its publication. Further publication details are presented near the beginning of the discussions.

2 Stephen Cole, ed., "What's Wrong with Sociology," *Sociological Forum* 90/2 (June 1994): 129–291.

3 Ibid., p. 290. The quote following is p. 291.

4 Edward W. Said, *Representations of the Intellectual* (Pantheon Books, 1993).

5 Said, *Orientalism* (Pantheon, 1978) and *Culture and Imperialism* (Knopf, 1993).

6 Said, *Representations of the Intellectual*, p. 82

7 Ibid., p. 11.

8 Ibid., p. 41.

9 Ibid., p. 55. Quote following ("permanent exiles") is ibid., p. 56.

10 Ibid., p. 63.

11 Ibid., p. 88.

12 Foucault, *Archaeology of Knowledge* (Pantheon, 1972).

13 Foucault, "Truth and Power," in Charles Lemert, ed., *French Sociology* (Columbia University Press, 1981), p. 307. The interview is reprinted in virtually every comprehensive collection of Foucault's writings.

14 Jerry Gafio Watts, *Heroism and the Black Intellectual: Ralph Ellison, Politics, and Afro-American Intellectual Life* (University of North Carolina Press, 1994).

15 Ibid., p. 49. Watts is quoting Ellison.

16 Ibid., p. 14.

17 Watts to Lemert, personal communication, Feb. 1995.

18 Watts, *Heroism*, pp. 18–19.

19 Ibid., p. 20.

20 Ibid., n. 44, pp. 144–5.

21 Daniel Horowitz, *Vance Packard and American Social Criticism* (University of North Carolina Press, 1994).

22 Ibid., p. 133. The quote later in this paragraph ("corporate waste") is ibid., p. 149.

23 Ibid., pp. 37–40.

24 Ibid., pp. 185–95. The quote immediately following ("Especially revealing . . .") is ibid., p. 185.

25 Ibid., pp. 189–90.

26 Alvin W. Gouldner, *The Coming Crisis of Western Sociology* (Basic Books, 1970).

27 Ibid., p. 505.

28 Ibid., p. 198.

29 My views on Gouldner and Mills are discussed at length in Lemert, *Sociology After the Crisis* (Westview/HarperCollins, 1995), ch. 1.

9   The New Sociologies in the Social Unconscious

1 Arthur Schlesinger, *The Disuniting of America* (Whittle Direct Books, 1991), pp. 79 and 82.

2 Allan Bloom, *The Closing of the American Mind* (Simon and Schuster, 1987), p. 27.

3 Todd Gitlin, *The Twilight of Common Dreams* (Henry Holt, 1995), p. 236.

4 Audre Lorde, "The Master's Tools Will Never Dismantle the Master's House," in *Sister Outsider* (Crossing Press, 1984).

5 Michael Lind, *The Next American Nation* (The Free Press, 1995), p. 13.

6 Ibid., p. 326. Some of the words and all of the ideas summarized in this paragraph of from ch. 8 of *The Next American Nation*.

7 *Ibid., p. 319.*

8 Jeremy Rifkin, *The End of Work* (G. P. Putnam's Sons, 1996), pp. 241–2.

9 Ibid., p. 258.

10 William Julius Wilson, *When Work Disappears* (Alfred Knopf, 1996), p. 209.

11 With respect to rethinking time-space, see, most notably, Anthony Giddens, who has influenced some urban geographers and numerous sociologists; in, for example, *The Constitution of Society* (University of California Press, 1984), ch. 3.

Acknowledgments

This book, like the series to which it belongs, issues by the grace of a long line of Blackwell editors, most of whom have gone on to other pursuits. Peter Dougherty first conceived of and signed the book and the series sometime late in the eighties. Romesh Vaitlingum, charming as always, tolerated it in good spirit. During his three years in the US, and in spite of the fact that in those days our communications were few and uncertain, John Davey was an important editorial presence, reminding me, and so many others, that in a few places brilliant editing is still a presence in the better publishing houses. Simon Prosser's understanding of and enthusiasm for the project helped me at last to realize it was time to write the book which had been agreed to nearly a decade before. I thank all in this lineage for their patience and help, as I do Susan Rabinowitz, Cameron Laux, and Louise Spencely who came upon the project later and helped me in many ways.

The book did not appear of a sudden after all these years. A few parts of chapters 4 and 5, for instance, came to mind in Helsinki in late winter 1988 at a colloquium on politics and semiotics organized by Pertti Ahonen and the Finnish Political Science Association. But a good bit of the thinking that stands behind the whole of Part II began much earlier in the early 1970s, when I was the most fortunate of young academics for having enjoyed the support of excellent colleagues at Southern Illinois University at Carbondale and countless others whom I encountered in a succession of visits to Paris. Of the latter, I thank especially Pierre Bourdieu who generously encouraged several visits to Paris.

On the other hand, in spite of these early beginnings of some of its parts, nearly all of the book is of recent vintage and little of what appeared before is untouched by revision. An earlier version of chapter 2 and the glossary in chapter 3 appeared, as I note in the text, as part of the McGraw-Hill *Primus* collection edited by Craig Calhoun and George Ritzer. As it turned out, I read the manuscripts of Craig's book on critical theory and of George's on postmodernism about the time I was thinking through what I wanted to say on these subjects. Though I disagree with each of them in different ways, those moments of intimacy with their thinking helped me to decide how I would write this book. Craig, who edited the *Primus* essay, provided helpful comments.

An early version of "Identities After the Imperium," chapter 7, was first presented at Seoul National University in June, 1995. This was the occasion of a reunion with Sang-Jin Han, who had been one of the most brilliant of the young scholars I worked with in Carbondale and who is today, quite probably, Korea's leading sociologist and certainly a respected presence world-wide among those concerned to make social theory an instrument of social justice. I wish also, and again, to thank Sang-Jin, Young-Hee Shim, and Hong-Woo Kim for generosities during that visit to Korea that will not be forgotten. The "Identities" essay underwent substantial revision at a colloquium sponsored by Willibrord de Graaf and Robert Maier at the University of Utrecht, the Netherlands, in the fall of 1995; then again for presentation at the faculty seminar of the Public Affairs Center at Wesleyan University. Respondents in all these places helped me in many ways. Chapter 8, "Representations of the Sociologist," was previously printed in *Sociological Forum* in the review section when it was edited by Gary Marx, a friend and colleague of many years, most memorably during my year with him at MIT.

It is a bit eerie to reflect on these debts to people who go back over so many years. I have been playing (to use the proper Derridean term) with this subject for most of my professional life as a sociologist. Not many in my home field have taken to it and its precursors as I and few others have. Of those I mention above, few would ever think to call themselves postmodern, and several would be insulted by such a call. Still they have tolerated me, if not "it," and thereby allowed me easy reference to the world others see differently.

As for the more formal acknowledgments, here following is the list of previous appearances for which permissions were arranged at the time of first publication:

- Versions of chapter 2 and part of chapter 3 first appeared as "Postmodernism and Social Theory," in *Primus*, Craig Calhoun and George Ritzer, eds (McGraw-Hill, 1997).
- An entirely different version of chapter 4 was "The Politics of Semiotics and the Semiotics of Politics," in *Texts, Contexts, Concepts: Studies on Politics and Power in Language*, Sakari Hanninen and Kari Palonen, eds (The Finnish Political Science Association, 1990).
- A small portion of the latter part of chapter 5 was published in

"Political Semiotics and the Zero Signifier in Semiotics," in *Semiotics and Politics*, Pertti Ahonen, ed. (Walter de Gruyer, 1993).

- Most, but not all, of chapter 6 appeared with much the same title in *Frontiers of Social Theory*, George Ritzer, ed. (Columbia University Press, 1990).
- Chapter 8 was previously published with nearly the same title in *Sociological Forum*, vol. 2, no. 2 (June 1996), pp. 379–93.

No one but I is responsible for anything I say and do on these pages. This standard disavowal is especially important when the subject in question is as troubling as the one of this book. In point of fact, even though much of this book has roots in earlier work, and my debts are many and constantly in mind, the book as a whole could not have come into the shape it is in until recent years, and the great bulk of it did not exist until the spring and summer of 1996 when I wrote most of it. That summer no one was around, except Geri who read it all, as she always does. Matt and Noah later read parts of it. Patricia Clough's way of thinking about these themes is an abiding influence, though not so directly during that summer. Sandy Becker checked copy for me. Otherwise, I did it myself, and stand by it.

Index